Brazilian Immigrants
in the United States
Cultural Imperialism and Social Class

A book in the series:

The New Americans: Recent Immigration and American Society

Edited by Steven J. Gold and Rubén G. Rumbaut

Brazilian Immigrants in the United States
Cultural Imperialism and Social Class

Bernadete Beserra
Preface by Michael Kearney

LFB Scholarly Publishing LLC
New York

First published 2003 by LFB Scholarly Publishing LLC
First printing in paperback, 2006

Library of Congress Cataloging-in-Publication Data

Beserra, Bernadete.
 Brazilian immigrants in the United States : cultural imperialism and
social class / Bernadete Beserra ; preface by Michael Kearney.
     p. cm. -- (The new Americans)
 Includes bibliographical references (p.) and index.
 ISBN 1-931202-68-0 (acid-free paper)
 1. Brazilian Americans--California--Los Angeles--Social conditions.
 2. Brazilian Americans--Cultural assimilation--California--Los
Angeles.
 3. Immigrants--California--Los Angeles--Social conditions. 4.
Americanization. 5. Los Angeles (Calif.)--Ethnic relations. 6.
Brazil--Emigration and immigration. 7. United States--Emigration and
immigration. 8. Brazil--Relations--United States. 9. United
States--Relations--Brazil. 10. Imperialism--Social aspects--United
States. I. Title. II. New Americans (LFB Scholarly Publishing LLC)
 F869.L89B68 2003
 979.4'94004698--dc21
                                    2003009020

ISBN 1-931202-68-0 (casebound)
ISBN 1-59332-156-2 (paperback)

Printed on acid-free 250-year-life paper.
Manufactured in the United States of America.

Table of Contents

v

List of Tables

Preface

Recently, research and writing about migration and immigration have become a growth industry. Nowhere has this explosion of research and writing been more prolific than in California, which receives the greatest number and the greatest diversity of newcomers than any other region of North America. And in California, the greater Los Angeles area is the major destination of most immigrants to the state. With well over 100 language communities, the region represents a significant cross-section of the world's nations. Because of its history and geography (California was once part of Mexico), the largest group of migrants and immigrants in California are Mexicans. Indeed, Mexico City is the largest city in Mexico, and by some estimation, Los Angeles has more Mexicans residing in it than Guadalajara, which is the second largest city in Mexico. But there are also 100s of thousands of immigrants and migrants from Central America and other nations in Latin America. Indeed, California is part of greater Latin America. The author of this book, who is Brazilian, was drawn to California as an anthropologist because of a notable absence in this broad and varied spectrum of Latin American migration to the region, namely the relative and absolute low presence of her co-nationals. Indeed, it is remarkable that Brazilians, who are the largest national group in Latin America, are about the least represented, in absolute and relative terms, in Southern California.

One of the most significant contributions of this book is its demonstration of how Brazilians, who migrate to California, reposition themselves within transnational fields as strategies to augment

ix

acquisition of forms of economic, social, and symbolic capital. Central to these strategies is the auto-construction of their identity in the new environment. In dealing with the identity of the migrants, Beserra takes a non-essentialist view, and indeed, shows how the migrants construct distinctive identities, in response to the new conditions in which they find themselves. For, as is obvious, to be a "Brazilian" in Los Angeles is a very different experience and a very different activity than being a "Brazilian" in Brazil. Indeed, the identity of Brazilian migrants in Southern California is shaped in large part by the perceptions of them and the attributions applied to them by other non Lusophone Latino migrants and immigrants, as well as by other immigrants and non-immigrant minority communities, e.g., Asian and Anglo.

This book thus raises and explores intriguing questions about how social and economic conditions in California shape the construction of the identities of the Brazilian migrants. One of the most intriguing of these questions is: Are Brazilian migrants *Latinos*? In other words, do they and do others construct them as *Latinos*? They are, after all, from Latin America. But as Beserra shows, a significant strategy of the Brazilian migrants is to define themselves as *non-Latinos*.

Much theory about transnational migration and identity has been framed in terms of "assimilation," and "acculturation." But such assumptions have recently been called into question by research concerned with how migration and immigration appear to be associated with socioeconomic and cultural differentiation that seems to lead to multi-culturalism and ethnic diversity. While such forms of cultural difference are often rightly celebrated, Beserra's work documents how they are also perniciously used as the targets for neo-racism and other new forms of discrimination against immigrants, and thus promote class new patterns of economic and social inequality in this era of globalization. This line of analysis recasts questions about the effects of transnational flows of commodities, money, and persons on the identities of migrants, immigrants, native residents, and on the cultural and economic hegemony of both receiving and sending nation-states.

To capture the complexity of the Brazilian community in Southern California Professor Beserra designed a sophisticated methodology that samples several of its major sub-communities that do indeed vary considerably, one from another. As such, her research is path-breaking work that is rounding out both our knowledge of Brazilian transnational culture and the complex ethnic and immigrant complexity of Southern California. Professor Beserra came to this research well prepared, first of all by being fluent in various class-level dialectical variants of Brazilian Portuguese and by having a firsthand knowledge of various of it's regional and sociocultural permutations. She is a socially committed intellectual and -- this is quite relevant where ethnographic fieldwork is involved -- one who, by personality and temperament, is well suited to the interpersonal aspects of this kind of research. Indeed, she is a committed teacher and does volunteer work with popular organizations in Brazil. In these and other regards, she is an exceptionally conscientious citizen, as well as a dedicated, creative, and productive intellectual.

In sum, Professor Beserra has designed her research so as contribute to our understanding of this understudied community in Southern California in a way that will also enhance our understanding of Brazilian immigrants elsewhere in the United States and further abroad. This book also makes significant contributions to basic migration theory and research methodology.

Michael Kearney
Dept. of Anthropology, University of California, Riverside

Acknowledgments

This book is a product of the time, patience, love, and intellectual effort of many people, and I hope I am being faithful to the ones who most closely helped me to carry it out. I have to start by thanking those who (as naively as I) accompanied me in this adventure of living a new culture, thus transforming their lives forever: my ex-husband, Sérgio, and Lucas, Raquel and Caio, my children.

For introducing me to different expressions of the Brazilian cordiality and consequently also to different ways of living Brazilian culture in the United States, I thank Gisele, Regina, Celso, Cláudia, Ricardo, Risélia, Marinho, Sílvia, Izilda, and especially Edna, for keeping the party spirit.

Tania Haberkorn, Marcelle Chauvet, Gaby and Wladimir Weltman, José Emídio Guimarães, Liana and Ricardo Alagemovits, Rodney Mello, Marco Pinto and Jatir Delazeri shared their knowledge about Brazilian culture abroad and have been kind and supportive all along.

I am very thankful to all those Brazilians who very kindly received me in their homes for interviews, and also to those with whom I talked many times informally and who offered me so many important insights. Unfortunately, I do not have enough space to thank all those who inspired me in one way or another. Yet it would be unforgivable not to mention Pastors Wagner Kuhn, Claudiner Mockiuti, and David Bravo, who provided continuous support and unique insights, as well as Adair and Déa Souza, José Nobre and Witer Desiqueira who became my friends.

From the Brazilian Women's Group I owe special thanks to Ruth Walsh, with whom I learned a lot. Márcia Argolo and Ivênia Ehling, who have been always kind, warm, and hospitable. Lizette Quarnstrom who inspired me with her cunning insights and made me laugh, and Clarice Abrantes, who made me feel at home with her familiar accent.

Other immigrants who called my attention to and taught me about other possibilities of integration into American society were Maria Talamantes, Alena Zimunkova, Sureika Acharya, Ivan and Nadya Dimitrov.

Paul Gelles, Michael Kearney, David Kronenfeld and Christine Gailey provided both intellectual and emotional support, but I believe that I finished writing this book because I knew that Paul really wanted to read it.

Gene Anderson, Alan Fix, Piya Chatterjee, Sally Ness, and Juan Vincent Palerm helped me during different stages of my study. Adriana Sarramea never let me forget my intellectual roots. Maureen J. Hoskyn and Raimundo Hélio Leite saved me by helping me to arrange and interpret the tables in Chapters Three and Four.

Through Ron Chilcote, Jan Rus, James N. Green and Jean Diaz, I thank all my colleagues at the Latin American Perspectives editorial board whose intellectual stimulation helped me much.

Rosemary Galli, Ruben Oliven, and Karl Monsma read a later version of the manuscript and offered me important comments. Raimundo Hélio Leite, my colleague at the Federal University of Ceará, read the manuscript several times and worked with me on its last version.

I also thank Mariana Ortega and Paulo Simões for the proofreading.

And last but not least, I want to thank CAPES, the Federal University of Ceará and the Department of Anthropology at University of California, Riverside for the financial support.

The Scene and the Study

First Motivations

The Brazilian way of living the United States was one of the most common themes of conversation since my arrival in Riverside, California, for my Ph.D. degree, in the last days of August of 1995. My intellectual and emotional excitement in living my first experience abroad was such that I would talk about my visions and experiences of Brazil and the United States tirelessly. I was always comparing everything, and processing my understanding of the United States through the only possible way: my Brazilian life experience. Whether talking to my fellow Brazilians or my American professors and colleagues the theme was always the same. At home, during dinnertime, my husband, my children and I would also share our findings and laugh at the many "mistakes" we had made throughout the day. Our youngest son, Caio, could not forgive us for bringing him to the United States, a place where everybody speaks "only" English. Indeed, when we came our children did not know any English at all. In Brazil, I had been told that it was not really worth teaching them English before they came because "children learn quickly and easily and it is worth the wait to teach them with the *right* accent." Six months later they were speaking "perfect" English, but these were the longest six months of our lives. Lucas and Raquel, the oldest, fortunately benefited from having Spanish speakers, mostly Mexicans, in their classrooms, but Caio's had only English speakers. For the first couple of weeks he would cry and sleep most of the time.

1

These difficulties of adjusting to life in the United States enhanced my interest in understanding why the world has become what it is today. Or rather, I had never felt so interested in understanding why it was that Portugal did not manage to colonize the whole world. Everything would have been so much easier for us Portuguese speakers. I, who had always believed that my main and sometimes only source of communication was the spoken or written language, felt totally incapable of communicating very basic things. I had to get used to people looking at me as if I were completely unintelligent. Of course, observing Riverside's ways of life through this disadvantageous position led me to romanticize my Brazilian life in a way I had never thought I would need to do before.

These were the particular circumstances of my interest in the theme of foreignness. I would think, talk, and read about foreigners, trying to understand what is different about ways of experiencing foreignness in the United States and elsewhere. The first book I read was Julia Kristeva's *Strangers to Ourselves*. She approaches the theme historically, covering the condition of the foreigner in several historical periods. Starting with Greeks and Barbarians, she explores the Christians and their work of conversion, the Enlightenment, and finally gets to our days of nationalism and neocolonialism. I was not particularly looking for any theoretical appraisal of the subject when I started reading this book. I was simply looking for company. I needed an in-depth dialogue. She provided it. She also provided an incipient understanding of different alternatives of living foreignness. "Civilized people need not be gentle with foreigners. That's it, and if you don't like it why don't you go back where you came from!" (Kristeva, 1991:14). I already knew from my own experience that the treatment given to foreigners depends on who they are. They are not treated equally, and I could observe in my undergraduate years that we, Brazilian Northeastern students, for example, had always been more patient with the broken Portuguese spoken by a Frenchman or an American than by the same broken Portuguese spoken by a Peruvian or an Argentine. When reading Kristeva I realized that we were naively following the colonialist ideologies unaware of our position in the game. When I arrived in Riverside my English was good enough to reach the required score on the Test of English as a Foreign Language

(TOEFL), but not good enough to speak and write.[1] Becoming aware of my language limitation made me feel very frustrated, diminished, and embarrassed. I would certainly have understood this better and taken these feelings easier if I had had a chance to read Henfil's *Diário de um Cucaracha* (*Diary of a Cockroach*) during these times. Henfil, one of the most popular Brazilian cartoonists, explains that he always felt embarrassed in not knowing how to speak English,

> Suddenly, for not speaking English, I'm feeling stupid. I even have to tell myself every once in a while: you know how to draw, make cartoons, you are not stupid! And do you know what I have noticed now and today? That in Brazil we have the same inferiority complex when we hear someone speaking in English. Even in Brazil I felt humiliated when seeing friends of mine speaking English with a foreigner. Totally humiliated. [...] I may become the greatest humorist in the world, but I will be the shittiest of men if I don't learn to speak English or learn how to swim. With swimming I can still get by, I just don't go near a pool. But English is a fiasco. In Brazil, this was already stifling; it already made me into a second-class person. Imagine here. I feel second-class in relation to other men, to other women, to dogs, and to lampposts (1983: 19-20).

Even though I would in general share the same feelings as Henfil, I always noticed that certain people would trigger my embarrassment faster than others. For instance, it was not until classes started that I noticed my language handicap. It was precisely by observing a mixture of disappointment and impatience in my professors and colleagues that I realized that the challenge of passing the TOEFL was just the beginning.

Until verbal communication becomes "normal," silence, observation and conjecture are all that a foreigner has. Starting with language, it is quite easy to discover that what we believed to be natural is in fact cultural and political. Thus, it is easy to know that our way is not the only way. Moreover, our way does not help much in a world that it is not interested in finding out about different ways but only benefits from imposing its own. By then, I could already comprehend why it is so much easier for a foreigner, immigrant, or any other person who changes social position, to understand the layers of the social world, its rules and tricks. Many Brazilians would assert that once you understand the rules everything becomes extremely simple. It is simpler than the Brazilian system, many of them would state. However, until one gets to this point, one has to work very hard. It seems that the only way that a foreigner can find to prove his/her humanity is by acting inhumanly; that is, imposing on themselves the challenge of being much better, much faster, and so forth.

The double challenge of doing our jobs and understanding the new system at the same time requires quite an additional effort. Thus, it is not hard to understand why the experience of a different culture is so radical and provides to all individuals who experience it an analytical ability not acquired otherwise. In this sense, all Brazilians that I talked to had their particular theories about Brazil and the United States, Brazilians in the United States, and Americans in general. Some of them would certainly come out with much better explanations using the data that I have.

By sharing these first stories and impressions, I want to explain that my "fieldwork" started long before I decided to make Brazilian immigration to the greater Los Angeles area the theme of my research.

Several issues stood out in my preliminary conversations with other fellow Brazilians. The main one was the difficulty of living in a country and socializing with people who have no idea of what we are, or what we believe we are. After all, even though they are the fruits of the same enterprise of a global world, Brazil and the United States are the realizations of very different and historically opposed ideologies and ways of life. Whereas the United States was created as an overseas extension of a particular Anglo-Saxon dream, Brazil was created as an extension of Portuguese overseas projects (Morse 2000). Taking into consideration size and history, including the experience of slavery, Brazil is, among other Latin-American countries, the one that most resembles the United States (Hess and DaMatta 1995).[2] However, it is not only because of a historical resemblance that the United States has become one of the most important references for Brazil. As a matter of fact, since the end of the World War II the United States has become a reference for the world, and any comparison between the two countries must take this into consideration. The hegemony of the United States in the American hemisphere, however, precedes by far the period of World War II. Americans must have anticipated their dominion over the continent from when they intuitively started to designate themselves by the same adjective that refers to any citizen of the American continent.[3]

Alceu Amoroso Lima, a Brazilian Catholic philosopher, considers that this "semantic error" says much about the feeling of superiority that the citizens of the United States have in relation to us, who are just as American as they. However, he says,

> it does not seem possible to me, or desirable, to react against the popular use of this term. It is not only the citizens of the United States who use the word American as a synonym for those native to the United States. We all from Latin America do the same. When we speak of an American, what we mean is a citizen of the United States, and not just any child of America. When we want to refer to this person we distinguish him by his nationality: a Mexican, an Argentine, a Brazilian (1955:226-227).

It is hard for a Brazilian, even for one who understands the rules of the global political economy, to deal with the American ignorance about Brazil. It is distressing to understand and accept that even though present in our daily lives as much as the air that we breathe, Americans totally ignore us Brazilians. Therefore it is somewhat depressing getting used to the tiny space that Brazil has in the United States. I still remember how bad I felt when I started going to Brazilian bars, restaurants, and nightclubs in Los Angeles. I always had the feeling that Brazil was being grossly misrepresented. After all, how could such a "big and rich" country like (my) Brazil be reduced to three or four exoticized images? Damned Western history![4]

Naturally there are different ways of dealing with this issue. Some Brazilians assume an air of superiority and try to prove that Americans are ignorant in general and it is truly hard "to understand how they have managed to dominate a world larger and more intelligent than they" (Bahiana 1994:101). Others assume temporarily the position that Americans reserve for us and try to learn more about them from that position. Thus, there are interpretations of the United States as different as Ana Maria Bahiana's *America de A a Z* or Henfil's *Diario de um Cucaracha.* Whereas the first one is an attempt to take revenge on the imperial power by assuming its arrogant attitude, with a little dose of humor, the second one is a more grounded, ironic, and painful but also laughable interpretation of the space that the United States reserves for Brazilians.[5]

Nonetheless, settling in Los Angeles requires from Brazilians much more than relativizing the size and importance of Brazil. It requires, for example, re-learning different ways of dealing with issues of race, class, and religion. In this sense, there is always something to say about American racism versus Brazilian racism; religiosity in the United States and in Brazil; the Latino world in the United States and the complicated inclusion of Brazilians within it, and so forth.

Brazilian Emigration to the United States: Numbers, Profiles and Theories

Only by the end of the 80's did Brazilian newspapers and weekly magazines start presenting their first reports on Brazilian emigration. Until then, Brazilian emigration was an unusual and almost unthinkable occurrence. Rare exceptions included those Brazilians living in other countries against their will, as in the case of those expatriated by the Brazilian military dictatorship, or those who had to live abroad because of their careers, such as Carmen Miranda, for example.[6] Despite having built a tradition as a receiving country and against all expectations created by Brazilian nationalist ideologies Brazilian emigration has increased since the mid-80s.[7] As for now, the Brazilian population abroad, as estimated by the Brazilian Ministry of Foreign Affairs, is about 1.9 million, which represents 1.1 percent of the total Brazilian population (MRE 2001). The largest concentrations are found in the United States (799,000), Paraguay (454,500), and Japan (224,229).

Whereas the Brazilian Ministry of Foreign Affairs estimates the Brazilian population in the United States to be 799,000, the US Census 2000 (Supplementary Survey Summary Tables) estimates it to be 231,270. Thus, the first problem is to understand the difference between these numbers. As we know, census errors are inevitable in general, but they are more likely to occur within new immigrant populations because of questions related to illegality and other reasons for keeping identities hidden (Newell 1988:85-87). Considering, however, that the Brazilian Ministry of Foreign Affairs classifies Brazilian immigrant population in two categories, the documented (404,000) and the non-documented (395,000), and that the turnover rate of the Brazilian population in the United States is high, the disparity between their numbers and those of the US Census seem less significant.[8]

According to the Brazilian Ministry of Foreign Affairs, almost 90 percent of the Brazilian immigrant population in the United States is concentrated on the East Coast in the metropolitan areas of New York (300,000), Miami (200,000) and Boston (150,000) (MRE 2001). Who are these Brazilians and why do they migrate?

Since the US Census does not provide a socioeconomic profile for the Brazilian population in the United States, researchers have built different ones based on their research samples. Margolis (1994:83-88), who developed her research in New York, found that Brazilians who live there are nearly evenly divided between men and women; mostly single (60 percent); fairly young (79 percent of the sample under forty) and with high educational level (46 percent had attended college). Although educated, most of them (around 90 percent) hold typical immigrant jobs.

What Sales (1999:213-218) finds for Brazilians in the metropolitan area of Boston is not very different. Although her sample has more women (60 percent) than men (40 percent), she is aware that this does not necessarily represent the reality of the Brazilian population in the city. As in the case of Margolis for New York, Brazilians in Boston are fairly young (85 percent of the sample are under 30) and are also well educated (47 percent had attended college). However, unlike the Brazilians in New York, their occupation seems to be more varied since there is a larger array of jobs. Only about half of the sample (44.9 percent) holds under-qualified jobs. She also found journalists, teachers, and other salaried white-collar workers.

There are other profiles based on research samples, but all researchers clarify that these profiles do not represent the reality for the Brazilian population in those cities. Yet they give us some idea of how that immigrant population is composed. As a matter of fact, like Martes (1999:59-60) proposes, we should think of several profiles instead of just one. In the case of the profile that I built based on my sample, there are some striking differences with those that the mentioned scholars propose for the Brazilian population on the East Coast. But then, as I will explain in the next section, my sample is very biased, since I mostly interviewed people connected to the two groups where I carried out my fieldwork. Taking all this into consideration, Brazilian immigrant population in the greater Los Angeles area is mostly composed by women (65 percent); married individuals (73 percent); adults in between 30 and 45 years (53 percent), and comes from the most industrialized region in Brazil, the Southeast, mainly from the states of Rio de Janeiro (27 percent) and São Paulo (20 percent).[9] However there is also a considerable flow from the Southern state of Rio Grande do Sul (14 percent), and the Northeastern Bahia (7 percent). The great majority (76 percent) immigrated in the last twenty years, between 1981 and 1999.

Coming from the Brazilian middle-classes, most of them have attended college (52 percent) or have finished high school (32 percent). There is a relative congruency between the educational level of the researched population and the types of job they hold in Los Angeles, and this, as we will see in Chapter Three, mainly because of the time of immigration. For example, considering that most white-collar jobs require college degrees, 52 percent of the 195 surveyed would be expected to hold white-collar jobs. The actual percentage of surveyed holding white-collar jobs is 48, which is just slightly less than expected. Some 32 percent hold blue-collar jobs, 13 percent declared to be housewives and 6 percent are students. Sixty three percent of those who are married have a Brazilian spouse while 30 percent are married to American citizens. The remaining 7 percent are married to Mexican, European, and other South-American immigrants. Most of the Brazilians with whom I conducted in-depth interviews affirmed to have come for reasons other than "making money." Thus, they come to work for Brazilian or American companies, to study, to marry, etc. They either arrive with their families or establish them in Los Angeles, and although going back to Brazil is a dream for many, they struggle to become assimilated into American society.

In the metropolitan area of Los Angeles, the number of Brazilians is estimated at 33,000 (MRE 2001). This community is far smaller than those of New York, Boston, or Miami. However, it shares the characteristics of the larger communities. In Los Angeles, like in the other cities, Brazilians exist as one immigrant group among many in a diverse society where "Latinos," defined broadly, form a major demographic, political, and economic force. In Los Angeles, the Brazilians fill the same unskilled or semi-skilled jobs held by recent immigrants everywhere, but the Brazilian community also includes a middle class, again like in other cities. This middle class consists of Brazilians who have "made it" by founding successful businesses or who have used education and ability to penetrate the professional classes. Finally, in Los Angeles as elsewhere, Brazilians live and socialize through immigrant networks, be they churches in poor neighborhoods or middle-class social clubs. Although smaller than its east coast counterparts, the Brazilian community in Los Angeles (and in California as a whole) has been of unique importance in diffusing Brazilian culture abroad. Riedinger (1997) states that Brazilians have been attracted to Los Angeles because of the recording and, to some extent, movie industries. Through the recording industry and sophisticated marketing, distribution, promotion, and broadcasting services, this community has been able to project the popularity of Brazilian music worldwide. Riedinger (ibid.) proceeds to state that the Brazilian-American community in California is also important for the connections they make with Silicon Valley, since computer technology is also well advanced in Brazil as compared to the rest of Latin America. He also stresses the importance of long-term academic connections: UCLA has a Brazilian Studies Center; Stanford was among the first American universities to offer courses in Brazilian literature; and Stanford and UC Berkeley have had visiting Brazilian scholars and faculty for many decades.

Brazilian immigration has been explained as part of a new pattern of international migration which involves middle-class populations and is connected with the absence of a dynamic job market for skilled workers in their countries.[10] Like in many other countries affected by the restructuring of the global economy in the late 1970s, the succeeding crisis years of the mid-1980s considerably worsened the position of Brazil's middle class, which from that time on started to rely on international migration as an alternative to maintain its class position.[11]

As broadly proposed by Margolis (1994), Goza (1992), Sales
(1999), and Martes (1999), Brazilian immigration is mostly the product
of economic reasons. But economic reasons, when seen from the
perspective of different immigrant trajectories, must not be mistaken by
simple, empty, and straight expressions such as "to make money" and
"improve life." Especially because behind the need for "making
money" and "improving lives" lies a very particular ideology that must
be unveiled in order to allow a deeper understanding of the immigration
process from the perspective of its actors, the immigrants.

I propose to start by broadening the content of the "economic"
category in order to include elements that are not usually clearly
included in it. For this I will be drawing from Bourdieu's concept of
capital, according to which

> capital can present itself in four fundamental guises: as
> *economic* capital, which is immediately and directly
> convertible into money and may be institutionalized in the
> form of property rights; as *cultural* capital *or informational*
> capital, which is convertible on certain conditions, into
> economic capital and may be institutionalized in the forms of
> educational qualifications; and as two other forms of capital
> that are strongly correlated, *social* capital, which consists of
> resources based on connections and group membership, and
> *symbolic* capital, which is the form the different types of
> capital take once they are perceived and recognized as
> legitimate (Bourdieu 1984:7; 1986:243).

I argue that behind "economic reasons" there are all the
possibilities as contemplated by Bourdieu: economic, cultural,
informational, social, and symbolic. It is in this sense that other studies
about Brazilian immigration, Torresan (1994) and Ribeiro (1997a,
1997b), for example, question purely economic explanations. These
studies suggest that Brazilian immigration to Europe and North
America is linked to a new pattern of migration which associates
migration with acquiring forms of "capital" other than economic.
Torresan (ibid: 5) asserts that beyond studying, making money, and
other reasons that Brazilians use to explain their choice to migrate to
London, they also say that they go to reinvent their identities and create

new life opportunities. However, she does not explore what lies behind the Brazilians' necessity of going specifically to London (or cities in the First World in general) to reinvent their identities. I would suggest that in such circumstances "reinventing identities" means changing (or upgrading) identities through the acquisition of symbolic capital, which can be expressed, for example, by the acquisition of the international language, English.

Whether migrating to make money, or to "reinvent identities," immigrants mostly head to places where there is a concentration of capital and power. On the other hand, migrants usually come from places where capitalist development has disrupted prior systems of production and diffused values and positive expectations about "modern" ways of life (Massey et al. 1992:445). Even though they generally aim at spaces of concentration of capital, specific immigrant flows have specific reasons and deserve specific explanations. For instance, despite the existence of several centers of capital, there are special reasons why Algerians mostly migrate to France; the Turks to Germany; Northeastern Brazilians to Rio de Janeiro and São Paulo; and Mexican peasants to California. Likewise, different Brazilian immigrant patterns to the United States ought to be seen as processes with different motivations and outcomes because different flows of immigrants integrate differently according to their destinies. In other words, when variables such as class, nationality, and race are equal, immigrant integration proceeds differently from region to region. Immigrant settlement in New York, for example, is quite different from immigrant settlement in Los Angeles because these cities, centers of economic regions, play specific roles and are developed around different projects. Thus, these cities have attracted different migratory flows and established occupational segmentation based on what is available in each case. In studying ethnic politics in California, Di Leonardo (1984:109) points out, for instance, that Asians and Latinos played in California the same working class role that Italians and Irish played in New York.

Since capitalist development has promoted the dislocation of large numbers of people from "periphery" to "center," or from "backward" to "modern" areas, immigration has been seen as a highly positive phenomenon for the immigrants themselves and for their hometowns because it contributes to modernization at large. Until today the idea that people migrate to "improve their lives" is present not only in the discourse of the immigrants themselves, but also in the scholarship on international and/or regional migration. In general, the same ideology that considers immigration as a positive fact for immigrants and their hometowns considers it a problem for the receiving societies. This shows that the colonialist ranking system operates at different levels, but it operates always towards maintaining cleavages in order to create and justify discrimination and exploitation, both between different classes within a nation and between nations in the global capitalist system.

Many scholars (for example, Kearney 1999; Stolcke 1993; Balibar and Wallerstein 1991) have explored the relation between the academic and political discourse on immigration with other general ideologies that feed and justify capitalist expansion worldwide. However, much remains to be done about the consequences of the American imperial intervention as a factor affecting the theoretical discussion in this specific field of knowledge. In brief, the academic and political discourses on immigration have still to be examined as social, cultural, and political products.[12] Although such an enterprise is beyond the scope of my study, it is my purpose to shed light on this discussion by exploring some connections between the spread of American imperialism in Brazil and Brazilian immigration to Los Angeles.

My idea is to start questioning the innocent assumption that people migrate to "better their lives." I argue that the content of the expression "better their lives" is a very specific one and it has been produced under certain historical circumstances which, in the specific case that I am studying - Brazilian immigration in Los Angeles - are the circumstances and consequences of the spread of American imperialism in Brazil. In other words, "better their lives" means better their lives from the perspective of an American conception of a good life. In this case, a good life is one that allows one to consume the most. Consumerism is not a novelty introduced specifically by the capitalist regime controlled (or protected) by the United States. However, it has been under American control that capitalism has developed this inclination to its largest expressions and consequences.

I propose that Brazilian immigration to the United States be understood in terms of the ways American imperialist ideologies have penetrated Brazilian society. Grounded in American technological development, and in the position that the United States assumed in the international division of labor after World War II, American ideologies diffuse new standards of consumption and new ways of understanding life and happiness across the globe. This is so much the case that the dreams that brought and keep bringing Brazilians to the United States are particularly connected with the impossibility of accomplishing at home the ideals of material and cultural consumption promoted by the United States.

Nonetheless, the United States is much more than just a nation spreading tales of wonder all over the world. More than anything else, the United States is the nation that has achieved control over the process of capitalist development and representation after World War II. In brief, the United States is, at some level, the Capital of the new capitalist empire, or the capital of the global world. This means that the spread of American ideologies and capitalism are, in the age of globalization, the very same thing (Larrain 1994). The American way of life has become the most complete realization of modernization, the core project of the capitalist strategy of development. It is in the name of the "modernization of the world," now also referred to as "globalization," that the United States and other leading nations have promoted disruptions in non-capitalist modes of production and have attempted to standardize life worldwide. It must not be forgotten, however, that the project of modernization of the world is absolutely arbitrary and represents mostly the desires and interests of those who greatly benefit from it (Escobar 1995; Petras 2002; Harris 2002).

In brief, among other reasons, Brazilians migrate to the United States to acquire skills to better survive in a transnational English-speaking world dominated by the United States. Besides filling out spaces in the immigrant job market of such a world, Brazilians as well as other immigrants also perform the important task of convincing the ones they left behind of the importance and necessity of accepting as the best option the life style they have adopted in the country or city to which they migrated. Essentially, they become heralds of capitalist development worldwide, playing, among others, the role of spreaders of capitalist consumerist fashion all over the planet. By divulging only the positive side of their experiences they often go back home and affirm their superiority by reinforcing the myths about the centers from where they are coming. They increase their own value in their home markets simply by having been present in the consecrated centers of national or international power.

Despite being affected by American ideologies in different ways and coming to the United States through different networks, the process of Brazilian immigrants' integration and assimilation into American society ought to be seen as defined a priori by the same ideologies that produce uneven capitalist development worldwide.[13] Balibar & Wallerstein (1991) propose the term neo-racism to refer to the ideology that explains and justifies social differentiation in the era of globalization. Neo-racism is historically connected to immigration in the era of decolonization, and like its biological predecessor, imposes and justifies frontiers between people who now have to share the same space. Unlike the old immigrants (colonizers) who believed themselves to be saving people from paganism to begin with, and then from backwardness, these new immigrants are seen as invaders from whom fellow citizens have to defend their space and culture.[14] Wallerstein (1991:34) explains the dynamics of this racism as follows:

> Racism has always combined claims based on continuity with the past (genetic and/or social) with a present-oriented flexibility in defining the exact boundaries of these reified entities we call races or ethno-national-religious groupings. The flexibility of claiming a link with the boundaries of the past combined with the constant redrawing of these boundaries in the present takes the form of the creation and constant re-creation of racial and/or ethno-national-religious groups or communities. They are always there and always ranked hierarchically, but they are not always exactly the same. Some groups can be mobile in the ranking system; some groups can disappear or combine with others; while still others break apart and new ones are born. But there are always some who are the "niggers." If there are no blacks or too few to play the role, one can invent "white niggers."

This kind of system - racism constant in form and in venom, but somewhat flexible in boundary lines - does three things extremely well. It allows one to expand or contract the numbers available in any particular space-time zone for the lowest paid, least rewarding economic roles, according to current needs. It gives rise to and constantly re-creates social communities that actually socialize children into playing the appropriate roles (although, of course, they also socialize them into forms of resistance). And it provides a non-meritocratic basis to justify inequality [emphasis mine].

Whether "neo" or old, racism, sexism, and ethnocentrism ought to be understood as important components and supporters of the systems of domination in which they are created and maintained. In other words, race, gender, and ethnicity are not independent elements of social stratification but ought to be understood in the context of systems of domination which they endow with meaning (Stolcke 1993:25; Rex and Mason 1986: xii-xiii). All these systems of prejudice and discrimination have two ideological procedures in common: namely to naturalize socially significant differences, and interpret these differences as inequalities (Stolcke 1993:32):

> One characteristic of racism is the naturalization of social and/or cultural differences to justify exclusion and discrimination. In other words, racism is an ideological doctrine which presents systems of social inequality as in the natural order of things. [...] The concrete historical circumstances under which politics become overtly racialized, the social groups which are racially discriminated against and the severity of its consequences, may be distinct. But there is an underlying common element. Racism is always latent in class society and becomes overt at times of socio-economic and political polarization to legitimate socio-economic inequality.

In general terms, the settlement of Brazilians in American society is oriented by the same racist policy that ranks people from the Third World in general, and Latinos in the United States in particular, as inferior. However, the relative positions of immigrants' countries in the

international division of labor, as well as class position of immigrants
in their country of origin, are factors that are differently combined to
determine the place that each immigrant will occupy in American
society.

Discussing the racist policies of classifying immigrants according
to their countries of origin, for example, is one way of assessing the
politics of social class and the exploitation of one class by another in a
historically determined society. The racist policy that generally ranks
people from the Third World as inferior creates a hierarchization that in
principle allows the exploitation of *all* Third World immigrants based
on their differentiated value in comparison with nationals. There are
other ranks, but all of them work to justify the exploitation of those
who hold less "value" by those who hold more (Kearney 2001). It is
from this perspective that I will be "empirically" looking for "classes,"
and interpreting the practical consequences (in terms of integration into
American society) of belonging to different social classes in Brazil.

Such a perspective enables us to explain, for example, why upper
middle-class Brazilians tend to adopt special strategies for repositioning
themselves as members of upper middle-class white society, presenting
themselves as non-black and non-Latino so as to purge themselves of
"negative" capitals. On the other hand, Brazilian immigrants with little
economic capital tend to identify themselves with other "non-white"
groups or to underscore their exotic capitals. This is especially the case
in the context of Los Angeles cultural market demands, which is always
producing new exoticisms and making symbolic values fluctuate.

Doing Fieldwork in Los Angeles

When I started developing my research on Brazilian immigration in Los
Angeles, I understood clearly that explaining Brazilian immigrant
integration into Los Angeles would require much more than simply
understanding the construction of the social profiles of Brazilian
immigrants or understanding immigrant policies at large in California.
Studying integration - meaning acculturation or, in this specific case,
"Americanization" - requires understanding the whole process of
"Americanization," as it has happened to the Brazilian immigrant since
its beginnings in Brazil. It also requires understanding "assimilation" as

an instrument of domination and as a process of social re-location (Bourdieu 1991).

In order to collect the necessary data to portray the patterns of Brazilian immigrant integration into the milieu of Los Angeles, a combination of different methods and techniques was required. Most of these techniques compose what Malinowski (1922) called participant observation. The aim is to decode and ascertain the objective regularity of social groups' practices from their own viewpoint. Through extended interviews and collection of life histories I was able to enter into the consciousness and perception of realities of various social agents. However, as consciousness and perception are not only accessible through oral discourses, I documented "Brazilian" and "Americanized" patterns of education, food, shopping, and entertainment consumption by participating in and observing different activities. I also collected oral histories from each group in order to understand how they have become what they are.

I differed from Malinowski's perspective, by being closer to Bourdieu's (Bourdieu and Wacquant 1992:213-215) idea of participant "objectivation", which demands a critical assessment of the researcher's own position and framework. In other words, I am aware that just by being a Brazilian woman I have been led to experience Brazilianness in Los Angeles in ways totally different from those that would be lived by a non-Brazilian anthropologist, or even by a Brazilian male anthropologist. As I explained earlier, it was my own experience as a foreign student that led me on a search for a better understanding of Brazilian immigration as a broader phenomenon. In this sense I was entirely a member of the group being studied. That is, my family and I experienced most of the problems that other Brazilian immigrants experience in terms of difficulties with language and culture.

My particular circumstances, however, also made me an outsider, as I soon realized when I started doing my fieldwork. I could not believe that by studying my "own kind" I would be constantly surprised, as I have been all along. The first thing that I realized is that Brazil is *larger* than I had always believed it could be, and that the Northeastern experience of Brazil is a very particular one. Thus, several times I listened to Brazilians talking about a Brazil that had absolutely nothing to do with the one I knew. At first I would attribute these differences to different levels of acculturation and so forth. That is, I would interpret those visions as produced by a memory already way too affected by "Americanization." Due to the constant reoccurrence of these situations I decided to go back to Brazilian history, trying to understand the particularities of the historical process in different regions. In order to make sense of Brazilian ways of living in Los Angeles I had to question everything that I was taking for granted simply by being a Brazilian. I had to give up my own version of Brazil or use it only as a reference to understand others.

Despite being a Brazilian and having always clustered around a considerable number of Brazilians, approaching Brazilians in Los Angeles was not an easy task. First of all, my questions as well as anthropology, my area of study, required me to develop my work with "communities" rather than individuals.[15] Brazilians do not comprise a community in the sense that some ethnic neighborhoods in Los Angeles do. Thus, there is no such thing as a geographic space that congregates most Brazilians, but several spaces that congregate small groups. The largest geographic concentration of Brazilians is around Venice Blvd., but I do not think that this concentration amounts to 500 people. Most of the Brazilians that I asked consider Venice a sort of gateway community for a specific group of Brazilian immigrants. They usually say that Venice shelters those Brazilians who are newcomers, artists, or those who have been unable to buy a place elsewhere. An interviewee said that "Venice represents more a lack of option than anything else." Perhaps, Venice represents for Brazilians in Los Angeles something similar (though far reduced) to what 46th street represents for Brazilians in New York. These Brazilians *in transition* who live near Venice are the ones closer to the profile presented by Margolis (1994) based on her research of Brazilians in New York.

My research subject required me to socialize with Brazilian communities whose contours were more clearly cut. But I also wanted "representative" communities, not only of this or that profile of Brazilian immigrants in the United States, but also those that were representative of the Brazilian immigrant world in Los Angeles. In order to make this choice I supposedly had to be acquainted with the several Brazilian immigrant communities in Los Angeles, and only after knowing and evaluating their positions in relation to each other, would I choose the ones I would remain with for my participant observation. As reality does not wait for perfect plans, I ended up developing my work the other way around. That is, I chose my communities before knowing the others well. As I have said, I had already met some Brazilians when I started thinking of which groups I would be studying. Most of the Brazilians I knew were directly or indirectly connected to University of California, Riverside. The two groups that I ended up choosing for the ethnographic work, however, had no direct connections with my Brazilian contacts in Riverside.

I came to know about the Portuguese-speaking Seventh Day Adventist Church in Chino totally by chance. I was in a café, interviewing a Brazilian friend for a preliminary paper on Brazilian immigration, when a young white and slim woman, dressed in a tight, short black skirt approached us by asking, in Portuguese, if we were Brazilians. She had picked up parts of our conversation. I said yes and talked about my research, asking her if she knew other Brazilians. She said, "I think that my aunt, Lúcia, would be very important for your research because she knows more than one hundred Brazilians around here." I had seen from the 1990 US Census tables that some 364 Brazilians lived in the county of Riverside, but at that point I had not met more than two dozen. Thus, I was happily surprised to have finally found a trail to meet a more substantial number of them. I called Lúcia on the following day, February 2, 1997, and after telling her about my research, I heard a long sermon against this new wave of Brazilian immigrants who sell all their belongings in Brazil to try their luck in the United States.[16]

She told me about a friend of hers who had abandoned her job as a High School teacher in Brazil to become a housekeeper here, in Riverside. Finally, she told me about the Portuguese-speaking Adventist church in which she participates. I only met Lúcia and her husband, Omar, in person, eight months after this phone conversation. I went to their house and had a first conversation about their immigrant trajectories. How had they ended up in Riverside? They put me in touch with the pastor of their church and in the following week I had my first conversation with Claudiner Mockiuti, then pastor of the Portuguese-speaking Adventist church of Chino. I told him about my plans of study and my interest in developing my research among them. However, I was not yet sure because I was still screening other Brazilian associations in Los Angeles. Thus we decided that it was not necessary to tell everybody what I was there for until I made up my mind. I would certainly find an appropriate time to introduce my research and myself whenever I decided.

My first visit to the church happened a month later, on November 23, 1997. From that time on and for the following six months, I went to the church almost weekly. My husband and my children accompanied me on my first visit. We arrived when the service was ending and people were getting ready for the monthly potluck. As visitors we had the privilege of being served food first. We sat with Lúcia and Omar.[17] From then on I was always referred to as their friend. Even today, when calling somebody who I have not known long enough to be immediately recognized, I still use their friendship as a reference. But today almost everybody in the church knows about my research, and also knows that my friendship with Lúcia and Omar was established because of it. Even though my husband had accompanied me during my first couple of visits to the church, that did not seem enough for me to be seen as a married woman, perhaps because I do not wear a wedding band.

I asked the members who became my friends about their and other members' impressions concerning the work that I was developing among them. But they either did not give much thought to the case or simply felt uncomfortable about saying anything that could hurt me. However, they did say, for example, that they expected me to focus my attention on those people whose interests or professions were closer to mine. For example, if I am a doctor, professor, or whatever, I should be "hanging out" with my own kind. Thus, they did mention several times that they did not quite understand how I could talk with almost everybody with the same interest and enthusiasm. Even though I did explain that I needed to know as many different trajectories as possible they still considered my ability to switch conversations so easily somewhat strange, as I went from a member of one sex to the other, or an individual of a certain profession to someone with a very different one. Such an ability, however, many times produced suspicions on the part of certain women. I noticed that if I talked to a man without his

wife being present it put other women on their guard. My idea of
interviewing spouses separately did not work. I did not insist on this
because I was aware that this, and also other limitations, were
consequences of my specific position.

Until I started interviewing people, which happened only about six
months after I started my participant observation, everybody had a hard
time understanding what my purpose was. In general I always felt as if I
had time enough to develop relationships at a "normal" pace. I did not
rush to be introduced to all members during the first weeks. I usually
kept talking to the ones to whom I felt more attuned or to the ones who
were friendlier. Despite my slow pace, by the end of my first month of
weekly visits to the church, I had been introduced to most of its
members. I was attending so frequently and participating so actively in
Bible School that by the end of my second month I was invited to
present the missionary letter. These are letters coming from the most
unexpected places in the world narrating stories of conversion.

I decided that before presenting the letter I would introduce myself
and explain about my research. I said that I was a professor at the
Federal University of Ceará, getting my Ph.D. in Anthropology at the
University of California Riverside. My research was about Brazilian
immigration in Los Angeles and I was interested in knowing more
about their experiences because I considered them a very special group,
especially in the sense that they apparently did not relate to the most
common Brazilian stereotypes. For the next few days some people came
to ask questions or to spontaneously tell their stories, but I soon
resumed my position as just one more person in the group. Indeed,
from a certain point onwards, not even I would remember what had led
me there, involved as I got in so many other topics. Always at stake
was the issue of my religion. In this particular, and despite some
temptation, I remained an outsider until the end. I participated in almost
everything without feeling forced or bored. Many times I felt like going
to the church because I enjoyed praying, discussing the Bible, singing,
and meeting people. They would usually notice when I missed a
Saturday, but they were always very understanding about my academic
duties. While I was away writing my qualifying exam I kept in touch
with the ones who had become close friends. They called to check on

me, to invite me to special celebrations, to say they missed me, and so forth. I did that too, several times.

At the end of February of 1999, immediately after I had passed my qualifying exams, I showed up again. I noticed some people whom I had never met before, and also the new pastor, with whom I did not have a chance to talk at greater length about my research. When he was moving into the church I was busy with my exams.

They had introduced a novelty in their potluck. Every month now they were celebrating the birthdays of their members. After announcing the names of the people whose birthdays had taken place in February, Pastor David Bravo said that he would take that chance to congratulate "*our* anthropologist, Bernadete Beserra, for passing her exams." We were all reminded again about my purpose there. There was another fast wave of people asking me questions and joking about me being there to nose around their lives, and so forth.

I discussed my research in detail with several members in Chino. Déa and Adair Souza always brought something new and interesting to my attention. I also received important inputs from conversations with Pastor Claudiner Mockiuti, Pastor David Bravo, and Pastor Wagner Kuhn. The latter suggested interesting titles to include in my bibliography.

With most of the people, however, I talked about everything except my research. When I started "officially" interviewing people, I already knew much about their personal trajectories. For geographical reasons (it was closer to my house), and also for having found in the Adventist church a very friendly environment, I participated in so many events during the first six months of observation that I did not even have time to write about them all. I also took pictures and videotaped several services, potlucks, and special celebrations.[18]

But since I was dividing my fieldwork time between observing the gatherings of Brazilians from the Church in Chino and Brazilians connected with the Brazilian Women's Group, I missed many activities promoted by both groups.

It was also by chance that I found out about the Brazilian Women's Group. One of my advisors, Paul Gelles, had met Marcelle Chauvet, a Brazilian professor at UCR. He mentioned my work to her and learned about the group. We had a meeting and she explained that she had never participated in any of the group monthly reunions, but a friend of hers who is a journalist was a member of the group and certainly could tell me more about it. It was from Liana Alagemovits that I got the president's phone number. It was early November in 1997 when I first contacted the Brazilian Women's Group president. She was still excited and proud about a very successful party that the group had promoted a month earlier in partnership with the City of Hope.[19] She could not help but come back to the same topic over and over. Some five hundred people had attended, and both organizations, the Brazilian Women's Group and the City of Hope, seemed very satisfied with the results of the joint enterprise. In this first conversation she told me that one of the aims of the group is to build a positive image of the Brazilian community in Los Angeles, an image different from that built by "a certain kind of Brazilian" who comes here only to take advantage of Americans. I inquired as to which Brazilians and which advantages, but she mentioned only surfers and started explaining basic differences between American and Brazilian colonization.[20] She had referred to surfers to exemplify one among many other temporary residents and contrast this to her own situation, which is that of a settler. That is, somebody who intends to stay permanently. She said that she is in the United States to help build American society, as many other immigrants have done. She is also here because she believes that living in Brazil is absolutely unthinkable. "I don't understand how people can live there," she told me, mainly referring to the violence in Rio de Janeiro, where she used to live, but also the excessive poverty of Brazilian people.

This conversation allowed me to elaborate some research questions that I doubt I would have thought of otherwise. For instance, if she generally refers to Brazil negatively, why would she bother working for a better image of Brazilians in Los Angeles? Why not forget Brazil and use time for more important missions? In other words, why would she insist on such a problematic connection?

By then I had started locating Brazilian groups, associations, and other Brazilian gatherings in Los Angeles. Before deciding which ones I would choose to work with I wanted to have a general idea of the existent groups. Therefore, I told her that I would go to the next monthly meeting and see if I would stick with them or look for something else. In any case I was very struck by our phone conversation, which had raised many questions that had not occurred to me before. I felt I already had something to investigate. After all, she was the first Brazilian who did not emphasize the positive side of Brazil. It was her assessment of Brazil that helped me to question that of others, my own, and look for explanations to the different possibilities of living Brazilianness in Los Angeles.

My experience with the Brazilian Women's Group was very different from my experience at Chino for several reasons. First, many people from the church live in Riverside and this allowed me to drop by more often for a *cafezinho* or a casual conversation. Second, the turnover rate of the population present in the meetings of the Brazilian Women's Group is always very high. There were several women whom I only met and talked to once. They never showed up again, or if they did I was not there. Little by little I started identifying the most permanent participants and approaching them more regularly. I think that the temporal distance between meetings is another factor that counted to explain the delay I felt in becoming comfortable inside the group. But there were additional factors: most of the members and participants of the group are from Rio de Janeiro and São Paulo, and in the geography of Brazilian internal colonialism, *Cariocas* (born in Rio de Janeiro) and *Paulistas* (born in São Paulo) play the same role that Americans do in international colonialism. Therefore, as a consequence of the discrimination southerners exercise against northeasterners, they are certainly not the individuals with whom northeasterners are most in love. These prejudices blocked my empathy and made me resist to their attempts to approach me by displaying their knowledge about northeasterners. References to my accent or their search to confirm their own ideas about our "primitivism" really bothered me at first. But little by little I started loosening up and finally felt perfectly comfortable, laughing with them at the jokes they have created about us. Of course I still believe that these jokes have a strong racist content, but since we are all aware of it we can laugh about it. I discussed the design of my research with several members, but mainly the ones who were part of the board of directors. They also had a hard time understanding research that did not start with questionnaires and tape-recorded interviews. The president and a few members of the group always knew the purpose of my participation and agreed from the beginning. When I asked for a written authorization, a requirement of the protocol of the University of California system to study human subjects, they wanted to know more about my plans before agreeing. They wanted me to submit to them the model of the questionnaire that I would be using to guide my interviews in case they felt the need to censor questions that they did not consider appropriate. That is when I had to explain that my interviews would not be realized via mail but face to face, and that my research followed a procedure totally different from those based on data obtained through questionnaires answered by anonymous people. In my case, I was supposed to have interacted with a person several times before proposing an interview, since my intent was not to interview everybody but a reasonable variety of cases.

Considering the apparent dispersion of the group and with the aim of understanding the dynamics of the association in circumstances other than the monthly meetings, I proposed that I participate in a couple of meetings of the board of directors. The president did not agree because she said that my presence would disrupt the dynamics of the group and create an artificial environment which would not help much my understanding of the group in general. She also refused to give me their mailing list. She said that just at the time I had become a member they had changed their policy about giving out mailing lists to everybody because some people had complained about receiving junk mail. Although she knew that I only wanted to have the mailing list to locate the members geographically and draw my maps, she made no exception for me. However, when I had already given up on the list, one of the members of the board of directors gave me one because she understood that possessing that list would make my job easier and saw no reason not to help me with such a simple thing. These difficulties made me postpone my decision to do my studies among them. Even after the fourth or fifth meeting I attended I was still unsure whether I would continue with it or not. At this point I had already built some connections with those members with whom I felt more identified, and realized that I was not the only one to feel uneasy about certain attitudes embraced by some members of the group. As a matter of fact, my "pattern of integration" was relatively common. As I understood better the dynamics of the group and found people with whom I felt more comfortable, I started looking forward to going to the monthly meetings and enjoying them.

My idea was to observe the two chosen groups for about six months, and after being acquainted with most of their participants, I would choose some 5 or 6 people from each group based on observable differences of socioeconomic status, physical characteristics, gender, marriages with Brazilians and non-Brazilians, etc. I planned to interact with these people in different settings in order to grasp their different ways of surviving in Los Angeles, but this proved unfeasible. I participated in many scenes of daily life in the cases of the people with whom I became very close, but the aforementioned enterprise proved impossible and otherwise annoying and insolent. Thus I ended up tape-recording in-depth, open-ended interviews with fifteen members of each of the two associations and with ten Brazilians connected to other Brazilian associations and institutions, such as the Brazilian Consulate, the Brazil-California Chamber of Commerce, the Brazilian Sociocultural Committee, the Cultural Gaucho Center, the Brazilian Evangelic Community – Salvation Army, the Hollywood Palladium Carnival, the MILA – Samba School, and the SambaLA – Samba School. I also collected socio-economic data (age, time of immigration, state of birth in Brazil, level of education, type of job before and after immigration, marital status, etc) of 195 people, most of them connected to the two groups being researched. This data was collected through informal conversation that I had with people in their gatherings and, only occasionally, by telephone. The profile on page 8 and all tables in Chapters Three and Four were built based on this data.

In regards to the dynamics of my fieldwork, I thought that by interviewing Brazilians in Los Angeles I would have a good opportunity to disprove general claims about Brazilian hospitality and kindness. Yet what happened was the complete opposite: through my interviews I experienced only different facets of Brazilian hospitality. There was, however, a case that deserves special consideration. I usually interviewed people I had already met a couple of times. I had never before met Jatir and his wife, Irene, but I decided to talk to them because he was then the president of the Cultural Gaucho Center in Los Angeles. I was looking for different ways of expressing Brazilianness and it was quite opportune to find out about a group that carves out

Brazilianness through symbols totally different from the consecrated ones (Beserra 1998). I arrived at their house in Glendale at 7 p.m. after I had been interviewing people since 10 a.m. I had interviewed a Brazilian woman in Hermosa Beach for about 4 hours and headed to Hollywood Hills where I interviewed another Brazilian woman. I was exhausted after spending some eight hours focused on two different histories. I needed time to settle down and take notes, but I did not feel like missing the chance to talk to Jatir and his wife. It was such an exciting conversation that after a few minutes I had come to life again, was asking questions, and sharing my findings and doubts. After some two hours of conversation they invited me for dinner and I said that I would love to but could not because I had to drive back to Hollywood Hills, where I would be sleeping that night to finish the interview I had started that afternoon. If I ate I would be too sleepy to drive back. They said,

- Well then, you just sleep here, *tche*!
- Why would you invite somebody that you've never met before to sleep at your house? – I asked.
- What's the problem?

I was too tired and hungry to argue and promptly accepted their invitation. It was pleasant to see that after so many years in Los Angeles they still kept some of their home customs. But so have most of the Brazilians I interviewed. Many people invited me to sleep over when they learned that I lived in Riverside and sometimes had to drive two hours to get home. But Jatir and Irene surprised me with their invitation after only two hours of conversation.

Another common routine was to be offered food and drinks. In fact, it was not by chance that I gained 10 pounds during my fieldwork. After the first five minutes, 90 percent of all Brazilians I interviewed offered me a *cafezinho*, the other 10 percent offered water, juice, tea or something else. At first I would say, "not right now, thanks." But I found out later that our conversation would flow better if I started saying yes. Otherwise every once in a while they would interrupt the chat to offer me something again. Of course I understand that quite well because I also cannot talk to anybody in my house for more than five minutes without offering him or her something to eat or drink.

Getting around in Los Angeles requires an expertise with maps that I had not developed yet. Until then I had only used maps to dream about places and peoples. I confess that it took me a while until I truly decided to change my ideas concerning maps. It was only after getting lost several times, and truly panicking when this happened at night in absolutely unknown places that I finally decided to become more pragmatic. Usually there was not a single soul available whom I could ask for directions, and whenever I found people who could guide me, they would ask if I had a map. Maps and compasses became my dearest partners on my navigation through Los Angeles' ocean of freeways. My love of Los Angeles followed immediately after I understood the logic of the freeways.

The freeways became my most permanent site during fieldwork. Indeed, I would spend most of my fieldwork time on freeways, either stuck in traffic jams or just taking advantage of my freedom to speed up and enjoy going so quickly from one extreme of the metropolis to the other.

Therefore, the freeways became not only an important space to learn about the ways life flows in Los Angeles, but also became my refuge, my office, my paradise. I had to figure out what to do during hours and hours on the freeways. While driving freely I would just dream, listen to music, and mentally compose poetry or think of new hypotheses for my research. When the traffic was stuck, which happens more often than not, I tape-recorded my observations and even took notes.

Like everybody else I soon learned that in Los Angeles we have to plan our lives around the traffic. Only once did I schedule an interview in Culver City at 9 a.m. Even though I left at 7 a.m. I only got there 2 _ hours later. If I left Riverside around 10 a.m. I would get to the same place around 11:15. In other words, it would take me half the time. A great percentage of the population of Riverside, San Bernardino, and Orange counties work in Los Angeles county. Therefore, all three freeways (91, 60 and 10) are packed going East-West in the morning, and West-East in the afternoon and early evening. So instead of hurrying home after interviewing a person in the afternoon, many times I preferred to check out some Brazilian bar or restaurant. Other times, when I was too tired to keep talking, I headed home and enjoyed confirming Mike Davis' predictions in *The City of Quartz* about the slowness of Los Angeles traffic. Indeed, it is sad and ironic to watch these incredible machines created with a potential to speed up to 150 miles submitting to traffic that flows at about 15m/h. The paradise of the automobile can also become its very nightmare.

The Internet was a very convenient tool to gather information and understand the patterns of socialization in a city as large as Los Angeles. I maintained a systematic communication with several Brazilians through the Internet. I also used the Internet as part of my strategy to reach people that I would not have been able to contact through the networks that I built based on the two groups that I studied more closely.

I planned to share my findings with everybody whom I interviewed in order to give them a chance to question my interpretations and explanations, and also to open up one more way of understanding their perspectives. As part of this desire to share my findings with "my" community and reach people that I would not otherwise, I published two articles about Brazilians and Brazilianness in Los Angeles in *Brazzil*, an international monthly magazine in English that is meant to reach Americans and other English-speaking friends of Brazil as well as Brazilians abroad. I received a few responses from Brazilians, but many from European and American students of Brazilian culture and other non-Brazilians involved with the Brazilian cultural business abroad.

Even though I always kept interested people informed about my general findings, I only had the chance to show them a complete draft of the chapters where I was specifically referring to their associations a few weeks before the oral defense of my Ph.D. dissertation. I asked them to read it quickly, since I did not have much time to write the final version and needed to fulfill my degree requirements. A couple of days after I had emailed them my manuscript I received a phone call from Marta, the former president of the Brazilian Women's Group. She had not liked the way I portrayed her in my study of the group. She felt misrepresented and was very upset about it. I asked her what exactly she did not like and why. At first she answered that she liked nothing in my writing; that everything that I was affirming about the group and its members should be reviewed, especially all that was connected to her. She argued that the quotes that I had taken from her interview were useful only to prove my points and depicted her in a way with which she did not identify. Since this situation was created by my research, I think that it is worth taking a few more lines discussing the ethics or politics of representation. As far as I am concerned Marta did not like my ethnography of the group because I did not follow her guidance throughout the research. Instead of presenting the group according to her view, I was using my anthropological one. I tried to show the dynamics of the group as a whole, the several narratives that are present in it. By doing so, I showed the positive and the negative. Perhaps, as one of the leaders of the group, she did not want to acknowledge the conflicts that are present in her community, which is reasonable, or she simply did not want me to represent at all her community. In any case, I kept the anonymity and used no information that could compromise people personally. What I write about these two groups is what becomes noticeable by participating in them. I am not telling stories that could disclose secrets, which could disrupt people's lives. That is why instead of writing an ethnography full of spicy and forbidden stories, which I could certainly do based on the collected data, I chose to use my fieldwork findings to understand broader questions concerning the ways capitalism has worked to bring Brazilians to the United States, and the ways Brazilians are integrating in the world of Los Angeles.

In any case, I believe and share with Di Leonardo (1994:31) the idea that anthropology is "about engaging in complex emotional interactions with other human beings." Anthropology is about trying out relationships with people who are totally different from us and being able to respect them and their choices, or finding out that people similar to us can also be(come) completely distant and strange. Thus, anthropology consists of learning about others to the extent that I learn about myself and to the extent that I can relate to them. The more I relate the deeper my understanding becomes. The deeper my understanding the less comfortable I feel choosing facts from their private or community lives to support my explanations. What should be brought to light? Whatever the circumstantial reasons for my choices are, I am aware that my explanations represent only one alternative among many.

CHAPTER 1

Ways to Los Angeles: Hollywood, God, and Other Dreams

> Girl I'm going to California, and live life upon the
> waves. I'm going to be an actor in the movies, my
> destiny is to be a star (Lulu Santos, Suddenly California -
> De Repente California)

Why do Brazilians Come to LA?

I always dreamt about the United States. Why? Because everything in Brazil comes from the United States. My father was a fan of the United States. He used to receive imported American shoes. The music was from here, Frank Sinatra. Everything was from here. Everything from here was good. I remember that since I was 10 or 12 years old, when I had my first private English teacher at home, it was she that got me on to this thing about buying dollars. My father used to get a lot of money from Americans who paid in dollars at the store. He sold dollars to Mrs. Margareth. Why did she want currency in dollars? He explained that it was because the dollar is stable, it can be spent in any part of the world, it is recognized. So that's when I had my first economics lesson. I lived through the Second World War, when I was between 10 and 15 years old. When the war ended I was 15 years old.

During the war American influences became very strong...
music, clothes... everything from here was better. Jeans,
tennis shoes, cigarettes, everything! Well, I never again
stopped learning English. And I always believed that one day I
would come here. I got married and had to forget this dream.
But when I got separated after 15 years of marriage, I went
back to dreaming again. I came here for the first time in 1974.
I came to acquaint myself with the work of a Pentecostal
church. I stayed in Orange County. I came again in 1981, and
that's when I met my husband. We married the following year
and I have been here ever since (Elizabeth, age 67, married).

I used to live in Manaus. My father was an Indian (Native-
Brazilian) who worked for those international ships. He died
and was buried at sea. My mom converted to Seventh-Day
Adventism and I met Mrs. Hohmann, she was the Pastor's
wife. I started babysitting their two children and doing all the
domestic work at their home. When they were about to leave
Brazil they convinced me to come with them. She said she
would not survive without my help. I came in 1964, when I
was 19 years old (Léa, age 57, divorced).

I was applying for international schools of Psychology, here
in the States and Europe. I got a fellowship to go to New
York in 1979. I stayed there for 3 or 4 years and came to
California. I got an invitation to coordinate a special program
to prevent and treat cases of violence and abuse related to
poverty and drugs here in Los Angeles (Wellington, age 43,
divorced).

I lived in Caxambu, Minas Gerais, a famous resort for
bourgeois people from Rio de Janeiro and São Paulo. With its
beautiful view, nice weather and excellent food Caxambu
attracts whoever has money to afford it. I used to work for my
uncle who owns the Gloria Hotel. So, I was always in touch
with people from all over the world. We loved Americans
because they would make our work easier. I mean, they did not
care about changing bedclothes everyday and stuff like that.
They would give me those nice mechanical pencils, you know,

just nice little things. Well, one day I saw in the paper that a Brazilian diplomat needed a maid to come with them to the States. I applied for the job and I got it. I've been here for almost 30 years (Lúcia, age 55, married).

I always dreamt of coming and living in the States. I have this uncle who speaks English and never stopped talking about here. I worked for a tourist company in São Paulo and I came here twice as a tourist guide accompanying groups of Brazilians coming to Disneyworld. Then I decided that I should spend more time, so I enrolled for ESL (English as Second Language) classes at UCR (Márcia, age 35, newly married).

I came here through an American friend who later became my husband. I met him in Rio de Janeiro when I owned my Gymnastics and Dance Academy. You know what? I had my apartment, job, money, but I was kind of bored. I needed a break. I decided to come just like that, from one moment to the other. I got a phone call from him and when I told him how I was feeling he invited me to spend some time in Los Angeles. I came in 1989 (Rita, age 42, married).

The quotes above show that with more or less resistance, slowly and by diverse means, the American dream and culture is incorporated into the everyday lives of Brazilians and many of them start dreaming about visiting or living in the United States. I argue that in order to come to the United States a Brazilian has to fulfill two basic conditions: 1) be "touched" (or "taken") by the idea of the American way of life and/or believe that the United States offer ways to accomplish her/his dreams of a "better life," and 2) have the effective conditions to come.

The first condition is produced through direct or indirect contact with American culture and ideologies. Whatever the means, the contact with American culture creates a favorable environment to develop dreams (and needs) of living in the United States or at least being open to such an experience. In other words, coming to the United States requires a certain degree of "Americanization."

By Americanization I mean the process of being acculturated by American society and its ideologies. It implies, as long proposed by

34   *Brazilian Immigrants in the United States*

Beltran (1958) and Ribeiro (1958), a correlation of powers favorable to
those who can afford to acculturate. When understood in the context of
colonialism and imperialism to which it belongs, Americanization
ought to be directly connected to obvious forms of economic and
political power such as multinationals and State Department Cultural
Offices. From this perspective, American ideas and behaviors are not a
matter of choice, but a matter of imposition. They are imposed over
many others - regardless of how interesting these others might be -
because they are an inseparable ingredient of the socioeconomic
transformation that takes place with the expansion of American
imperialism.[21] Naturally, what holds true to any hegemonic ideology
also holds true for the American ideologies that are exported overseas;
i.e., these ideologies are shaped by the interests and world-views of
hegemonic classes or groups. That is, they do not represent the ideas of
all groups that compose American society.

It is essential to understand that Americanization is a complex
process that involves individuals differently in function of several
factors such as geographic region, social class, religion, levels of
education, age, gender and so forth. Thus, there is no reason to expect it
to reach all Brazilians homogeneously, or to produce the same
consequences everywhere. Therefore, when I said earlier that
Americanization occurs at the expense of Brazilianness it is necessary to
understand Brazilianness as a phenomenon that is expressed in different
ways. First, Brazilian history varies from region to region in function
of the ways in which resources were transferred from less to more
"modern" sectors in order to promote "development." Second, different
regions developed different relationships with prior colonial powers and
produced different cultural syntheses. And third, social classes are
differently involved in the process, especially when the fulfillment of
this process requires a certain purchasing power.

As we will see in the next sections of this chapter,
Americanization expresses itself in many ways, and some of them even
stand in paradoxical relationship to the ideology of American
imperialist expansion. In any case, Americanization requires a certain
socio-economic space to be developed, as explained by Roseberry
(1989:113-114):

The growth of a domestic market and the emergence of what Cardoso and Faletto (1979) refer to as the "middle-classes" have had profound social and cultural effects as well, opening space for new expressions of U.S. power. *The growth of a domestic market depended upon the emergence of new social groups living in growing towns and cities* [emphasis mine]. This has meant the growth of a population with a new set of consumption needs and interests. These needs might involve a rejection of anything with the taint of the countryside and backwardness and a celebration of anything considered modern. The urban middle classes might want wheat bread rather than products made from corn meal. [...] Depending on the available technology and the fads of the period, they might want – and need – refrigerators, washing machines, cars, radios, stereos, televisions, VCRs. They want to see films, take trips, shop at supermarkets and malls. In this and other ways, we seem to witness the emergence of a new current that shares certain cultural values that we might regard as "American."

[These] new ways of life and consumption styles open new possibilities for the expression of U.S. power and influence. A few examples will suffice. The demand for modern, elite, or convenience foods creates a dependence on imported foods, which are often provided by U. S. exporters. In urban jobs, many of the opportunities open to the new middle class may be in businesses that are either subsidiaries of U.S. corporations or have extensive commercial dealings with them. Knowledge of English becomes an important job requirement for aspiring managers and secretaries. Television opens many avenues for Americanization in obvious ways, such as the importation of dubbed versions of U.S. dramatic series and comedies or movies, and the broadcast of commercials advertising U.S. products. Here we find a direct linkage between the rise of a social group with urban ways of life and tastes and the proliferation of a domestic market with strong participation by multinationals. The development of technologies makes this connections even more direct. For example, new cable systems and satellite dishes make it possible to produce a much broader variety of programs, such as sports events and dubbed versions of the programs produced by Protestant evangelists in the United States.

Thus, considering that Americanization involves processes as broad as the ones listed above by Roseberry, it is hard to believe that there are many people in Brazil, or in the world, that have not yet come in contact with some elements of American culture.

The second condition Brazilians need to fulfill in order to come to the United States is that of having effective means to do so. In principle one has to have both money and contacts (networks), but at least one of these elements is indispensable. An airplane ticket from São Paulo/Rio de Janeiro to Los Angeles costs around 1,000 dollars, which is equivalent to approximately 18 months of a Brazilian minimal wage (according to the exchange rate in February 21, 2003). This means that, in essence, all Brazilians who come to the United States are able to afford a savings account, which is only possible among Brazilians belonging to the middle and upper classes. Yet the Brazilian middle-classes encompass many definitions and it is reasonable to admit that belonging to the middle class in a small northeastern city is something quite different from belonging to the middle class in the city of São Paulo. In other words, in terms of wages, being middle class in São Paulo requires earning and spending much more than being middle class in, say, Sumé, Paraíba. Also, these classes are affected differently by the phenomenon of Americanization.

When compared among themselves, certain expressions of being middle-class may also be classified as belonging to the lower class. However, belonging to middle class in both big and small cities requires the ability to consume certain goods and services. For example, middle class persons are supposed to own "all-American" domestic facilities, be able to afford a maid, pay for private schools for their children, go to the movies, buy books, and so forth. All these goods and services are priced differently nationwide.

However, there are exceptions. There are some Brazilians who do not belong to the Brazilian middle classes [in any of its expressions], and can still afford to travel to and live in the United States.

As the quotes above suggest, different motives, expectations, and networks bring Brazilians to Los Angeles. This multitude of reasons for immigrating to Los Angeles and the seemingly numberless alternatives of integrating into Los Angeles' social milieu can in fact be grouped into a limited set of alternatives. Such alternatives, as expected, are not the same for all Brazilians. In other words, the chances of concretizing the American dream are not the same for all Brazilian immigrants simply because Brazilian immigrants comprise a very diverse population, socio-economically speaking. As such, Brazilians come to Los Angeles through diverse networks that have been established for many different causes. In other words, the penetration of American imperialism in Brazil has occurred in countless ways and has produced many networks linking the two countries. In my research I identified four main networks through which Brazilians have come to Los Angeles. These networks intersect at some points and overlap in others, but they provide a more nuanced view of Brazilian immigration than the simple explanations of a search for "a better life" or "making money" would provide. These pathways and rationales also echo vectors of capital flows and cultural domination. Let us explore, then, four of these immigration pathways: 1) Hollywood and the Los Angeles arts and media industries; 2) Marriage to Americans; 3) Education, and 4) Church Affiliation. In the next four sections I will briefly describe how these networks have been established and how they work in the sense of promoting Brazilian immigration to Los Angeles.

Lights and Dreams of Hollywood

Carmen Miranda (1909-1955) became known in the United States as the "Brazilian Bombshell" with the funny accent and the tutti-frutti hat. She was the first South American to conquer Hollywood (Davis, 1997:21). It all began when, in February 1939, she was "discovered" by Broadway businessman Lee Schubert as she was performing her dazzling "Bahiana" act in a show at the Casino da Urca in Rio de Janeiro. Schubert offered Miranda a contract to perform on Broadway. Three months later she and her Brazilian band landed in the United States to perform in the Broadway musical review, *The Streets of Paris*. Davis (ibid: 2) says that "not only was Miranda the star of the show, but one of the biggest hits on Broadway. Her success there led to musical

38   *Brazilian Immigrants in the United States*

recording contracts, radio appearances, and offers to appear in Hollywood films."

Carmen Miranda set the norm for a stereotype and a dream, and created an effective media connection between Brazil and the United States. After Carmen Miranda, many other Brazilians came to Hollywood hoping to become movie stars. In 1949, while paying a visit to the United States and visiting Los Angeles, Érico Veríssimo, a Brazilian writer, met two Brazilians in Hollywood. They had come in search of fame and success.

> Brazilians in Hollywood? I met two who for a long while tried careers with the movies. Salvador Yaconelli and M. Banzatto. Both are *paulista*s [from São Paulo]. They're from the time when movies still had no sound. They were brought here by the dream of fame. They encountered tremendous obstacles. What they went through is the subject for a profoundly human novel. They did not allow themselves to be defeated. And if they have not yet seen their names standing out in the cast of any movie, they cannot be considered a failure. Today they have a reasonable financial situation and look to Hollywood without any illusions. Yaconelli is used as a consultant any time a studio makes a movie where the action takes place in Brazil. He was the man who made the poems for *Pinocchio* and it is he who gives English lessons to Carmen Miranda. Banzatto is a quiet, shy, and serious person. He speaks excellent English and recently has been trying to write plotlines for movies. He has an unshakable faith in his own work. (Didn't I say he was a *Paulista*?)
>
> There are also the boys from the Bando da Lua, who accompany Carmen Miranda. They've adapted to life in Hollywood. They've made relationships here. I visited Twentieth Century Fox one day with Oswaldo Evoli. The young man had a friend in every corner. Hello Brazilian! – they shouted – Hello Mr. Samba! And Oswaldo walked from side to side hugging everyone as if he were the owner of the studio. And Carmen Miranda's apartment is a corner of Brazil lost between the green hills of Beverly Hills (Veríssimo, 1949:376-7).

During my research, I met a few Brazilians who migrated to Los Angeles hoping to become movie stars. Maria Medeiros, the aunt of one of my friends, came to Hollywood in the fifties to try her fortune as a movie star. She gave up after many years of trying and became a nurse. Yet it is a mistake to believe that Hollywood is mainly for those, like my friend's aunt, who wanted to be a movie star. Hollywood is for all sorts of people whose dreams are connected to the movie industry: moviemakers, movie stars, musicians, journalists, salesmen, cooks, and maids. Sometimes one comes seeking movie stardom and ends up doing something else connected to the world of cinema, as we have seen in Veríssimo's quote, and sometimes not, as is the case of my friend's aunt. Some Brazilian actors and actresses have tried their luck in Hollywood. Perhaps Sônia Braga is the only one who carved out a more noticeable place by performing in a couple of well-known movies, *O Beijo da Mulher Aranha* [The Kiss of the Spider Woman] for example, and dating Robert Redford for a while. Still, this has not made her widely known to an American audience. In fact, no Brazilian has ever again reached the heights attained by Carmen Miranda.[22]

Within the United States, there is probably no place more instrumental in the worldwide spread of American ideologies than Hollywood. Even though Hollywood has been present in Brazil since the second decade of this century, Carmen Miranda played the role that strengthened the ties between the two countries. Including Latin American stars in the cast of characters was a strategy intended to create some identification between the United States and Latin American countries, so as to further broaden the Latin American market for the American movie industry.

In Chapter Six I will further discuss the reaction of the Brazilian media to the image of Brazil and Brazilians that Carmen Miranda helped to diffuse worldwide. Here, however, I want to give some thought to the role of the middleman that is so important in the expansion of capitalism. By this I mean that the American political-economic project could not have been achieved without the consent and support of Brazilian elites. Sectors of these elites became the effective representatives of American imperialism in Brazil, just as they had been representatives of Portuguese and British interests before. One can see how American interference in Brazilian internal affairs has become stronger during the last fifty years. One can also see how tensions between representatives of so-called internal and external interests were solved mostly to the advantage of the latter.

There are at least two major channels for the expansion of the American economic project in Brazil. One is the partnership with Brazilian entrepreneurial classes and their representatives in the Brazilian State. The other, which can also be called a "partnership," is with intellectuals and artists. In this sense, whether consciously or not, Carmen Miranda was spreading Americanization, and legitimizing it.

What has recently changed, after decades of American cultural and ideological impregnation, and thanks to exceptional advances in transport and communications, is that Brazilians can now play in the United States the many roles played by Brazilians in Brazil. Some international employees of the Hollywood industry are allowed to choose whether they prefer to live in the United States, right at the center of movie production, or in Brazil.

Erik Schulte, for example, worked at Universal Studios in Rio de Janeiro for several years before being offered a position as their representative for Latin America. His job is to sell movies, and to further expand the market for the movie company. As such he does not necessarily have to live in either the United States or Brazil, since he spends most of his time traveling around Latin America. Selling movies is in principle the same as selling any other product. Yet, it creates stronger links between Brazilian and American cultures because it naturalizes the latter to the eyes of Brazilians.

The intellectual performs the complementary work needed to keep the business going. Ever since Los Angeles became part of the London-Paris-New York circuit, the international bourgeoisie has included Los Angeles as a must-see on their international "updating-with-civilization" trips. Brazilians are certainly no exception. Brazilian journalists and artists are here to check out the novelties of Los Angeles, the new "icon of modernity" and, the new center of worldwide production and distribution of fashion and other consumerist ideologies.

Whether consciously or unconsciously, journalists and artists play their role as "agents" of the American imperialist state. They help spread American markets in Brazil further, and many of them are proud of their role because it gives them prestige in the colonized eyes of

Brazilians. No matter how limited their access to the American society they are representing is, they are, at least in Brazilian eyes, closer to the colonizer and his centers of power. Memmi (1991), Fanon (1967), Henfil (1985), and Said (1979; 1994) discuss the colonizer-colonized relationship in general and dedicate some particular thoughts to the role that intellectuals play in the colonial game. On May 7, 1975, while living in New York, Henfil (1985:252) wrote a letter to one of his friends in Brazil saying the following:

> Yesterday I watched a Cuban movie called *Memories of Underdevelopment*. Marvelous. It narrates and explains many things that we, the intellectual bourgeoisie, suffer from. Our boredom when facing our underdevelopment and the anguished longing to be in London, Paris, N.Y., where things are heating up, where there is light. Then comes that terrible suffering; we neither participate in the underdeveloped life of our own country, nor do we manage to enter the happy and frenetic scheme of London-Paris-N.Y.

Despite the honors conferred on them for bringing civilization to the "poor" colonial world, these immigrants are isolated from both worlds and live segregated in Brazilian groups, complaining about both worlds, but mainly snubbing the colonized world left behind. As Memmi proposes (1991:73-74), there is no salvation for the colonized, no matter what social position he or she occupies. He says, "a worker can leave his class and change his status, but within the framework of colonization, nothing can ever save the colonized. He can never move into the privileged clan; even if he should earn more money than they, if he should win all the titles, if he should enormously increase his power."

In any case, and despite the ways the colonizer sees or relates to them, the colonized person who chooses to assimilate and reinforce the politics of colonialism works as a bridge that allows imperialism to work and prosper.

The Exoticization of Brazilian Women and the International Marriage Market

What I call here "the international marriage market" is not the same as the commercial networks created to promote marriage between Western males and Eastern or other "exotic" females. As a matter of fact, these networks are already a consequence of the international division of labor and its racist basis that places people from different nations into different positions of power in the global world. In fact the racist basis of imperialist expansion expresses itself in several aspects of everyday life. For instance, the exoticization of the colonized is mainly a maneuver of the colonizer to keep the colonized in their place. But exoticization works also as a means of commodifying the colonized and their "goods," whatever they may be. Music, dance, and food, for instance, become commodities submitted to the same rules as other products in the capitalist market. And so do people. The masculine cast of the colonizer tends to further exoticize the colonized along gendered lines. Memmi (1991), Fanon (1963; 1967), Sinha (1995), and others have discussed the feminization of colonized men in the depictions of the colonizing powers. Yet the picture for colonized women is more complex. In a global world guided by the values and laws of the dominant countries, the production of images articulates elements other than class, race and sex. Ethnicity and/or nationality are added to this complex formula of oppression. In general, the image of Brazilian women is highly sexualized, yet not in the same terms of both black and white American women (Collins 1990). Elements that underscore their exoticism are added: mystery, wildness, innocence, and submission. Whereas sex, mystery and wildness feed the pornographic industry, innocence and submission are more likely to feed the marriage market.

I propose that Brazilian women have become a commodity in the international pornographic industry and other markets of cultural and sexual exoticism since Hollywood used Carmen Miranda to create and diffuse the myth of Brazilian women's sensuality and grace. In this case, the international marriage market for Brazilian women would have been created more or less at the same time that the leading position of the United States in international politics transformed American men into universally desirable mates, as the dollar became the international currency.

The reason why I propose that the international marriage market for American men is an important network that produces Brazilian immigration to the United States is because 30 percent of the married Brazilians on my research sample are married to Americans. Even though I focused my attention on only two groups, I collected basic information from 195 Brazilians with whom I had a chance to talk while living in the Los Angeles area between 1995 and 2000. Therefore, I collected information regarding the citizenship of the spouses of 174 Brazilians. Out of these 174 married, widowed or divorced Brazilians, 113 are female and 61 are male. This disparity between male and female subjects in my sample does not reflect the proportion for the whole Brazilian population in Los Angeles. It was produced because one of the groups of my sample is a gender-based group (for women only). Despite this, the proportion of Brazilian women married to American men as compared to that of Brazilian men married to American women suggests that the marriage between Brazilian women and American men deserves a special explanation. Out of 174 Brazilians, 110 are or were married to other Brazilians, 52 are or were married to Americans, and 12 are or were married to people of other nationalities. Out of the 52 Brazilians married to Americans, 45 are female and only 7 are male. Therefore, Brazilian men represent only 14 percent of my sample of Brazilians married to Americans.

The quotes below bring about different circumstances in which Brazilian women met their American husbands. Jociclênia was 29 years old when she first met Michael at the Mall in Salvador, in 1987:

> I was at the Mall, looking at things, when suddenly I saw a gringo there. He was a guy about 50, tall, strong, muscular, and had very blond hair and very red skin from all the sun he had taken. "Ah," I thought, "my, this guy must be German." At the time I was doing my third semester of German and was anxious to find someone with whom I could speak in German. He kept looking at me, but continued walking. I thought, I think I need to say hello to that gringo, because he seems rather shy. He got in line to buy coffee, I approached, looked at him and got in line ahead of him. He asked me if I spoke English. I said a little, but then I asked if he spoke German, and it turned out that he was the American child of German parents. So then we began talking, mixing German, English, and Portuguese, because he also had an English/Portuguese dictionary. He asked me to take him to the Carmo Convent and there we began talking about our lives. It was then that he

told me he was there in Bahia looking for a woman to marry. He said that he very much wanted to have a child. He wanted a child who would be a pianist. I too dreamed about leaving Brazil. I thought that it wasn't worthwhile having a child in Brazil because to be born under the weight of a foreign debt like ours is disadvantageous. I knew he had to return to Los Angeles because he had business to care of. I thought he would never show up again. One week later he was back. And he asked me to start preparing my visa. So, we went to Rio de Janeiro and stayed there one week while we waited for the visa. I came here and one month later we were married. Two months later I was pregnant.

Among the Brazilian women that I met and interviewed in Los Angeles there is a considerable number who met their American husbands in circumstances similar to Jociclenia's.

Margarida Anderson, age 74, met her husband when she was working for the American Air Force, in Rio de Janeiro,

I met John on March 9, 1947 and we wrote to each other until I came to the United States on September 7 of 1947. I was 22 and went to work for the Coffee Bureau, for the Brazilian Government. I married in 1948 and went to live in Massachusetts and hated every minute I lived there. There was nobody who spoke Portuguese. I spoke fluent English, but one likes to speak one's own language, right? So I started to teach John and our children Portuguese. We moved to California in 1954 and have been here ever since.

Tania Spencer, age 51, divorced with no children, also came to the United States to marry an American man she had met in Rio de Janeiro.

I came here because I married an American. I lived in Rio and worked for a Brazilian bank that had a lot of contact with American banks, so I knew a lot of Americans who worked in Brazil. At the time I met my ex-husband I wasn't even working at the bank, but for another company. But a friend of mine, an American, who was also a friend of my husband's, invited me to dine out with him. So then it happened what is called here a blind date. That is how we met. He had never lived in Brazil, but he had lived in Mexico many years and spoke Spanish perfectly, and also spoke Portuguese. I met him on February 5th, 1978. He returned there from the United States on February 25th. On April 1st I came to visit him. I liked him a lot, was in love with him and wanted to see him, so then I ended up staying and we decided to marry.

Whether they met their husbands casually, as in the case of the Brazilian woman who met her husband at the Mall, or were introduced through friends or co-workers, most of the Brazilian women married to Americans belong to a Brazilian social class similar to the one their American husbands belong to in the United States. I found some cases of hypergamy in my sample; that is, cases where the Brazilian woman married an American man whose class position is superior to hers.

I tape-recorded many love stories involving Brazilian women and American men. They could simply be seen as casual encounters in a globalized world. But this is not the case, since the chances are different for men of other nationalities.

Josiana, Katia, Telma, Marialva and many other Brazilian women also met their American husbands in Brazil. Whether looking for wives or not, a few American men came back from a trip to Brazil with a native mate by their side. Marialva, divorced and remarried, says "I will never forgive my parents for having let me come to a foreign country in the company of a stranger. Gosh, I was so young and stupid, why would they let me do such a thing?"

It seems that the same myth that feeds the dreams of Brazilians who want to come to the States, the land of opportunity, also feeds American men's dreams in regards to Brazilian women. As a matter of fact, by transforming Carmen Miranda into a movie star, Hollywood simultaneously produced two myths. The first is that Brazilian artists can reach the universe of Hollywood. That is, the boundaries of the Brazilian job market, at least for artists, end in Hollywood. The other myth is that all Brazilian women are like Carmen Miranda: sensual, beautiful, graceful, bubbly, and so forth. The broadcast of the Samba Schools Parade in Rio de Janeiro carried the original Miranda myth even further. The phenomenon that Miranda produced plays an important part in understanding the way racism works to maintain the boundaries

between nations and justify them: only artists and "beautiful" women
are "invited" to come. If, on the one hand, the United States selects
which Brazilians should be welcomed, on the other hand, the Brazilian
market of brides is open to any American, because men of the class that
can travel and stay long enough to develop any kind of relationship
shape the image of "the American man." Consequently, any American
is good enough to compete in the global market for brides. This is
because by simply being an American man one has an extra value added
as consequence of the position the United States has in the international
division of labor. The concept of American men as generally desirable
husbands allows them to have whomever they choose in the broad
international market of potential mates. To marry an American is
perceived as a triumph, since, as Marialva said, some Brazilian parents
do not even concern themselves with investigating their children's
husband's background. Being American or having the chance to go to
the United States speaks for itself: opportunity, success, social
mobility, "a better life," or even the possibility of a "life of leisure."

I would now like to further explore Jociclênia's observation that it
is not advantageous to have a child in Brazil because the Brazilian
international debt is too high. Every Brazilian is born already owing
something. There is no question that providing your child with the
privilege of being born in the United States instead of Brazil means
giving him or her the opportunity to compete more easily in broader
markets. This is a belief that may serve particular individuals from
different social classes, but its overall impact is to bolster a racist
ideology (white master husband/brown servant wife) that feeds
capitalism and patriarchy, and benefits dominant classes nationally and
internationally.

The social production of ethnic, economic, and racial stereotypes
is, as I have pointed out in the Introduction, a structural need of the
capitalist system. There is in fact a hierarchy of exploitation and
discrimination upon which capitalism bases itself in order to survive.
Thus, it is not enough to exploit the working classes of the centers of
power, it is necessary also to create many other cleavages that allow
exploitation to be processed. The colonial enterprise and its
contemporary consequences is certainly one of the most important
sources of profit for the system. That is why it is so indispensable to

create labels and stereotypes that discipline and control exploitation through different channels.

While living in New York in 1975 and learning about the value Brazilians and other Latin Americans had in the American market for symbolic capital, Henfil observed (1985:195): "Despite being a man like any other American, in reality I am not. I am an intruder, a penetrator, a foreigner, an alien, even worse: I'm a Latino. I have eyes, ears, legs and arms like the Americans, but in the lottery of life, I was born in Brazil. My ticket as a person only has validity within a determined space called Brazil."

Thus Jociclênia's opinion is perfectly valid from the perspective of somebody who wants to succeed in the system following its established rules. Even though American women are also prized and have their value increased in the international marriage market, I want to stress that the marriage market works mostly for American men and Brazilian women, not for Brazilian men and American women. As I showed earlier, Brazilian men married to American women represent only 14 percent of the population of Brazilians married to Americans in my sample. Why is that so?

There are several reasons. Behind the exoticization of women there is the idea that whoever they are, these women have a chance to overcome their "primitiveness," "blackness," "Latinoness," or any other "backwardness" by hypergamy, marrying up with men who will preferably fit the colonizer stereotype. There is hardly any ideology that divulges the special value of native grooms in an international marriage market. There is the myth of the Latin lover, but male lovers do not hold the same social space as husbands; they represent desire, but not reproduction, commitment, or financial security. I would not connect the marriages between Brazilian men and American women to this image. It seems that in general the Brazilian men married to American women are not common middle-class Brazilian immigrants. Most are artists, businessmen or other professionals who have achieved exceptional success in their careers. I found a few cases among people connected to the Brazilian music and arts scene in Los Angeles. Outside this world I found two other cases, one was a Brazilian surgeon who has achieved an international reputation, and the other was a surfer who met his wife in Brazil when he was among the best surfers in the country.

The apparent refusal of Brazilian men to compete for American brides is an example of how patriarchy is strengthened in the absence of other grounds for domination. Or rather, patriarchy is stronger in lower classes where the only ground of superiority left for men is over their wives. Walter Guimarães, Brazilian, age 35, and married to a Brazilian woman, suggests,

> First you have to remember that we were raised in a culture that says a woman is submissive. The American woman is not submissive, she is an equal. So the Brazilian man wants to marry a woman who will cook, clean the house, and continue raising children. He marries an American, then she says, "Ah, this won't do." So the Brazilian man doesn't do well with an American because he is macho and the American woman will not accept his machismo. I know at the most two Brazilian men who are married to American women. The Brazilian woman adapts herself because she does everything for the American, then he falls in love, right? Ah, this is the one I want! She washes, cooks, and goes to bed. Another thing that happens is that you won't see many Brazilian men coming here with a high cultural level. You know that the majority of Brazilians who come here come to try out life, to better their lives. As in the case of the Church, the largest part of the people who are there are hard workers, but they are people who didn't study much and who came here to better their lives. This is a class which is very macho, who thinks the woman is submissive. By the measure in which you climb in social class, machismo is decreased. When you get to the top, machismo doesn't exist, everyone is equal. Those who marry American women are those who already have a more elevated cultural level. He accepts the woman going to work, and I love this! This is how I think. I evaluate everything from the cultural level because how you will treat your wife depends on your education. I'm not saying I'm not rough, I know I am rough. But at least I know what is wrong and what is right. It's nice to see the woman as equal to you, that you both are equal, that you bring in the same bread to the house.

Walter proposes that Brazilian men do not marry American women as often as American men marry Brazilian women because Brazilian men are used to unequal relationships that favor them and American women demand equal relationships. But even an equal relationship between a Brazilian man and an American woman in the United States would seem unequal because in principle it favors the American partner. In general, the question of equality is not an issue for Brazilian women who, whether married to American or Brazilian men, have to cope with asymmetrical relationships. The exceptions might be those cases where both partners belong to the middle or upper classes and have college educations, as Walter pointed out. But I would say that the asymmetry works even in those instances.

The United States and the Scientific Imperialism

Beginning with the Second World War, science and technology would be the two main products that the United States would negotiate in the global market. Such products guaranteed its military supremacy and ideologically shaped the unequal exchanges between countries. Such products also justified the sociopolitical classification of countries as developed, developing, or underdeveloped, besides offering to all of them the formula for modernization (Escobar 1995). Modernization signified, in this case, the establishment of technology as a universal value, and the measure of all things as a function of its control.

The establishment of American hegemony over Latin America implied the adoption of those plans of development that the United States designed both for Brazil and for Latin American countries in general. This created a dependency that would extend to all aspects of life, since a plan of development requires the reorganization of society as a whole, and, consequently, the reorganization of its educational system. After World War II, a variety of organizations (Ford and Rockefeller Foundations, AID, World Bank) began to intervene much more directly in the growth and development of Brazilian educational institutions. Despite the resistance of certain sectors of Brazilian society, these foreign institutions came to dominate the formulation of educational policy in Brazil (Sá 1980:34-38).

It must be stated that Brazil operates on a model that benefits mostly the United States and the Brazilian managerial classes. This is a model that would never work properly for the benefit of all social classes in Brazil because it requires profit from unequal exchanges between countries, regions, and classes. In other words, the American educational model works mostly for the United States because of its position in the international division of labor.

I propose that, in principle, Brazilian students come to American universities to learn the required know-how to implement the American economic project in Brazil. The United States benefits from this business in several ways. First, it spreads its economic project. Second, it makes a profit from the sale of knowledge (Ph.D. and Master's degrees, Certificates and so forth). Third, it benefits by absorbing talented students who become overqualified for the Brazilian professional market or simply do not find a job in Brazil after their return since the Brazilian demand is more limited than the American.

In the case of the Brazilian students who are absorbed by the American market, the loss is even greater because in that case Brazil supports the production of technicians for the United States at no cost to the latter. On average, a graduate student costs 200 thousand dollars, and is generally financed by the Brazilian government with money obtained from international loans.

Even though the majority of the Brazilian students who come here to get higher degrees go back to Brazil, I found in my limited universe some cases that demonstrate why exceptions to this rule occur. Besides getting jobs more rewarding than in Brazil, many Brazilians stay because they get married to Americans.

I said above that Brazilian students come to American universities to learn the required know-how to implement the American economic project in Brazil. In other words, they come to help further spread American domination. Yet things do not happen in such an effectively Manichean way, and it is very interesting to observe that, in many cases, what these students learn in the United States gives them even more ground to oppose imperialism. This means that opposition to American domination can come through the same channels that are created to promote and guarantee American domination. Roseberry (1989: 106) calls attention to the cooperative exchange of knowledge between Latin American and American social movements.

As U.S. imperialism generated oppositional currents in Latin America, it also generated them in the United States. This was especially true in relation to the more directly political and military expression of imperialism, the control of Cuba and Puerto Rico, the manipulation of Panama, or the military occupation of Nicaragua, Haiti, and the Dominican Republic. These oppositional currents in the United States were in turn connected with a variety of progressive and socialist movements in the early twentieth century. Latin American and U.S. oppositional currents could enter into direct contact, in part because leaders of Latin American oppositions would go into exile. Though exile might take them to other Latin American countries or Europe, it could also take them to New York, New Orleans, or Los Angeles, where they might go to school, form friendships with progressives, actively participate in and contribute to their movements, and place their own struggles in international (and sometimes internationalist) perspective.

What Roseberry states above is certainly true. But it is also true that the world of social, political, and economic sciences as well as the revolutionary world are generally ruled by the same laws that reign over the capitalist market of unequal exchanges. In other words, in these fields of power Americans also have a clear interest in imposing their hegemony. An example of this is the endless debate between American and Brazilian scholars on who has the key to understand racism in Brazil.[23]

American Religions Go Abroad

The networks established through American expansion in Brazil are countless. The case of the spread of American religions is useful to understand the different levels and competing ideologies of American expansionism. I will now sketch the politics of ramification of Seventh Day Adventism in Brazil, and its relation to Brazilian Seventh Day Adventists who immigrate to the United States.

Maria Alcântara was born in 1923 in Belém, Pará. She was 32 years old when she came to California, in 1954, with her husband and six-year-old daughter. They came because her husband wanted to finish his studies in Theology at La Sierra University, a Seventh-Day Adventist university. He could have finished in São Paulo, where he was studying, but he had been strongly motivated to come to the United States. Pastor Hohmann, an American missionary who became their friend in Brazil, provided concrete support by getting him a job and helping him apply to La Sierra University. Maria Alcântara and her husband came to the United States exactly six decades after the first American Seventh-Day Adventist missionaries had started their missionary work in Brazil during 1894.

The Seventh-Day Adventist missionaries arrived before American industrial companies, which began to establish themselves in Brazil more systematically from 1912 onwards. But they certainly benefited from the incipient American hegemony. For instance, the first Adventist publishing house had been founded in Rio de Janeiro by 1900. Today the Brazilian Adventist publishing house, located in the state of São Paulo, is the third largest in the world. They have grown at such a fast pace that in less than a century the Brazilian Adventist population has become the biggest in the world. Brazil has never been their only target. The Seventh-Day Adventist Church is spread all over the world. Their numbers and their method of growth would make Universal Pictures Corporation direly envious. Their strategies of expansion include much more than Bible Schools and evangelism at large. In other words, they are much more than a church where members attend on Saturdays for the weekly service. A good Adventist is not only concerned about life and death. Pastor Claudiner Mockiuti, a Brazilian Adventist pastor working now in a Hispanic church in Glendale, says that "what makes them different from other Christian churches is their special commitment to proclaim to *all peoples* the word of the Lord [emphasis mine]."

As a matter of fact, they have undertaken their mission so well that membership in the world Church has already passed the 10 million mark.[24] When it was founded in the U.S. in 1863, it had around 3,500 members; today, nine out of ten members live elsewhere, in 205 other countries of the world. Seventh Day Adventists have one of the most extensive centralized Protestant educational systems in the world (5,416 schools, colleges and universities), and one of the most comprehensive networks of health-care providers (159 hospitals, 306 clinics, medical launches and planes, orphanages, and homes for the elderly). The publication and distribution of literature is also a major factor in the growth of the Adventist movement.[25]

To close the circle, Adventists also grow and process their own food all over the world. This produce goes to their schools and hospitals, and is also sold in their stores.

The Brazilian Adventists who have come to Los Angeles do so as part of this broad network and, in general, their survival here depends on the ways this network functions. They come because of studies, work, marriage, and also to try their fortune in the "country of opportunities."

Naomi and Eduardo Fonseca also came to California in 1954. He had been invited to work as an accountant at the Loma Linda Food Company. They were both born into Brazilian Adventist families and studied in Adventist schools, where they met, dated, and married. When they came, both were already college educated and were working in an Adventist College in São Paulo. She taught Education and he worked as an accountant. During their entire life they had been in touch with American pastors and teachers, and had been invited several times to come and spend some time in the United States. Naomi proudly says that they were "formally invited" to come, and that is why they did. As legal residents they motivated a few Brazilian Adventist friends to come, and occasionally got formal invitations for them through their American acquaintances. But not many Brazilians arrived. Between 1950 and 1970 only about 30 Brazilian Adventist families were living in the greater Los Angeles area. These numbers have changed and grown but not in alarming proportions. I estimate that today there are about 100 families of first generation immigrants without including their children, since 95 percent of them have been totally assimilated into American society, and many times do not even speak the Portuguese language.[26]

Sara Cruz came in 1988 with her husband. She was forty-three years old and had just finished law school at a private university in Rio de Janeiro. She was a federal employee working as a secretary for the Brazilian Institute of Geography and Statistics (IBGE). She came because her mother, with whom she lived, had died a few years earlier and her closest sister lived here in California. Her sister had come thirty years earlier to work as a maid in the house of an American Adventist Pastor. Sara told me that this Pastor had been a missionary in Manaus,

Amazonas, the state where she was born and lived until moving to Rio de Janeiro in 1960. Sara's sister worked for the Pastor and his wife while they lived in Manaus. When they came back to the United States they wanted to keep her as a maid. Thus, they applied for her green card and she came in 1958.

Walter Guimarães, age 35, came in 1987. He also had finished law school – receiving a special award for being the youngest student ever to receive the law degree at the Federal University of Goiás. He came to find out more about the market for musical instruments. He owned a store specialized in selling musical instruments in Goiânia, the capital of Goiás, and he was interested in importing musical instruments from the United States. But he explains that his general interest for the United States was mostly developed through his friendship with an American Pastor who stayed in Goiânia for eight years. His missionary time had finished in Brazil and he had to come back to the States. He wanted his Brazilian friend to have an opportunity similar to the one he had had in Brazil. Walter says that he would not have come if it were not for his American friend's moral support. "It was this friendship that made me come, because if I had not had this support I wouldn't have come. I needed that moral support, you know? You're moving to a foreign country, don't know anything, and need some moral support." California was not Walter and his wife Teresa's first destination. They first went to Berrie Springs, Michigan, where his American friend lived.

Diane and Amaury Silva came in 1993, soon after getting married in Curitiba, Paraná. Amaury wanted to open an import/export business, since he had some experience selling goods from Paraguay. Before coming here he had spent a couple of months in Switzerland with a friend, which had motivated him to try his fortune in the United States. In the beginning he wanted to go to Florida because the Brazilian immigrant population there is bigger and there are consequently more networks to explore and rely on. A friend of Amaury told him about another Adventist friend who lived in California and could get him a house and a job. What better start could they wish for? They came right away to California.

João and Sônia Cândido also came in 1992, with two children. They had been closely following the trail of a friend, also from Vitória, Espírito Santo. They had been together in Rondônia, where they traveled to try their luck in a land which, still in expansion, would supposedly have more opportunities for them. Nothing worked the way they expected and they went back to Vitória six years later. Their friend married in Rondônia and soon after came to California because his parents-in-law were living here. His in-laws had been invited by the brother of the mother-in-law, who had come because he used to have an Evangelical musical group and had been invited for a tour in the United States. He and his family got used to being here and ended up staying.

The above cases are enough to observe that the Adventist Church as an institution does not invite or motivate Brazilians or Adventists of any country to come to the United States. They come through their personal relationships. After all, Brazilian Adventists do not choose the United States as their missionary field, though such a trend has recently begun after a more systematic flow of immigrants from Brazil to the United States has occurred. Indeed, the United States is not considered to be a missionary field because it is already a Christian country and is thought to have its religious frontiers already established. From a general perspective all countries have open religious frontiers, since one always can be re-converted. The question is who can convert whom – and who has effective conditions to do so. The general politics of converting other people has historically required the dominant economic position of those nations or regions to which the converters are linked. In fact, in the history of Western civilization, religion and power have always worked together, and religion has been one of the ways of imposing superiority over others.

Seventh-Day Adventism started growing all over the world, and in Brazilian territory specifically, when the United States already occupied a prominent position in the Americas and had started to compete for markets worldwide. With a structure much simpler than other multinational companies, the Adventist church was able to take advantage of their country's prominent position to spread their "word" overseas. Little by little, Adventist American and German pastors and missionaries opened publishing houses in Brazil, as well as churches, schools and hospitals, creating what we can call a truly modern industry of faith. Potential Brazilian Adventists encountered very solid organizations that could operate in their lives in many other ways besides that of teaching the word of the Lord. Adventist missions in

Brazil, as elsewhere, work both as churches interested in evangelizing and as providers of jobs and goods. Most of the Brazilian Adventists that I met here had jobs or careers connected to the missionary needs of the church. For instance, the most common professions among them are Nursing, Medicine, and Education. They usually try as hard as they can to keep their children in their own schools, where they will be educated far from worldly distractions, and where they will find an appropriate mate.

What I have presented here shows that Brazilians who have been born and raised as Adventists have been Brazilians in a very particular way. They are disciplined within the Adventist truth through different vehicles: work, schools, church service. They show how diverse and complex the process of Americanization in Brazil is, and how it has produced many different connections with the United States.

CHAPTER 2

Brazilians in Los Angeles

A Few Words about the Political Economy of Immigrant Integration

The integration of Brazilian immigrants into American society depends not only on what they bring with them, but also on what they find here. In other words, their integration depends on how their class position in Brazilian society will translate here. There are general issues that all Brazilian immigrants have to deal with regardless of their social position here or in Brazil, such as the condition of the colonized. Generally speaking, however, one finds different things according to where one goes. Thus, the reasons why Brazilians come and the networks to which they are connected count as much as the conditions they find here.

Bourdieu (1987:4) argues that connections and group membership (networks) are part of the resources that define class position, which means that different networks bring individuals to different social places and opportunities. A Brazilian who has a working class background, for example, would hardly come to the United States through an upper class network unless such mobility had already been processed in Brazil. For instance, there is the case of menial laborers serving the Brazilian international diplomatic corps. Even though they come through a network that belongs to the dominant class, they have a very specific, inferior position within it. When they decide to stay, they hardly settle within the limits of the network that brought them here. They generally find and get along with other Brazilians who share similar backgrounds, and it is through these new relationships that they learn how to get around Los Angeles. This I will show through an analysis of the integration process of Brazilians connected to the Portuguese-speaking Seventh Day Adventist Church of Chino and the Brazilian Women's Group.

I argue that, in principle, any Brazilian who is "successful" here should be able to be "successful" in Brazil. But before exploring this idea further, I want to clarify that "success" and "successful" are not absolute categories. They do not mean anything in themselves, and there is no general formula that defines "successful." The meaning of these categories varies from one social space to another. Besides success being broadly connected to determined patterns of consumerism, there is nothing defined in regards to what to consume. There is not even a dominant pattern of consumerism connected to a certain definition of success, but several. Indeed, as Bourdieu's notion of *habitus* suggests, different groups create dreams and expectations differently within the ideological boundaries of their possibilities (Bourdieu 1984:63 and 1994:163).

Thus, there are different standards of success for different classes, communities, groups, etc. In this sense, specific contents of success are the result of a combination between what society in general defines as such and what each group or community can afford.

Following this reasoning, Brazilians would not come to the Unites States only because they were not able to materially succeed in Brazil. We have seen in the previous chapter that there is a considerably large array of reasons why Brazilians come to Los Angeles. They come expecting to acquire skills, experiences and/or money which will allow them to socially reposition themselves in position higher than the one they had in Brazilian society before migrating. This means far more than just acquiring money or prestige in general. It means getting closer to the colonizer's stereotype and detaching oneself from the fate of a colonized person. One example is the effort that Brazilian middle class parents make in order to provide their children with the opportunity to live in the United States for at least a few months as exchange or English students.[27] These few months' experience, which aims at learning English and getting more acquainted with the novelties of the civilized world, has become part of the basic education of any child whose parents are concerned about providing them with the skills to survive in a highly competitive market. I have presented some elements in the Introduction that can be used to understand the non-meritocratic basis of this competition and its racist contents. However, it is worthwhile to remember that the contents of such ideological beliefs are not clear and accessible to everyone, and that is why they play such an important role in the maintenance of the status quo. They are essential components of social practices, have a strong impact upon these practices, and guide and justify them at a global level. Despite historical differences from one country to another, imperialist ideologies are spread everywhere, and their tenets are as useful in maintaining the status quo in both the United States and Brazil. In this case, it is essential that Brazilians, or at least the majority of Brazilians, consider any initiation into American culture and society positive and superior.

However, the potential (and effective) value that is added to an individual after spending some time in the United States does not immediately transfer in a superior repositioning in Brazilian society. A Brazilian who comes to the United States will not, no matter how hard he or she tries, become an American in the eyes of Brazilians. They become Americanized Brazilians, which is quite different. And this will not always have the expected results, since there is also a certain rancor for those who sell themselves out to the next colonizer, as I will discuss on Chapter Six. Despite the mentioned resistance, Americanization (meaning the acquisition of technological skills, the language, and so forth) obviously opens doors, increases wages and produces a clear and immediate differentiation in relation to other individuals of the same class, group or community. But this does not operate miracles. Americanization in itself does not promote mobility overnight, and yet, it does add value to individuals and increases their chances of social mobility. It also works as a sign of distinction within the same social class.

What happens when the process is the other way around? When Brazilians come to the United States? First of all, there is no automatic transference of class position. As a matter of fact, when Brazilians come to the United States the opposite immediately occurs: there is a general devaluation. This devaluation occurs despite the social class to which one belongs. Even though different networks enable different insertions, all individuals have to cope with discrimination during their integration. The process of integration requires a general reconstruction of identity based on rules and criteria many times different from the ones prevailing in Brazilian society. A combination of the following factors is at the basis of immigrant integration in the United States: 1) the position of the country of origin in the international division of labor; 2) color and social position of the immigrant in its country of origin; 3) the relative position of each immigrant population in relation to other immigrant populations, and 4) circumstantial needs of the American job market.

The above mentioned factors or criteria are all informed by the imperialist ideologies that propose the naturalization of differences that are at the basis of social inequalities such as race, ethnicity, and gender.

According to such an ideology, Brazil is a peripheral country, politically and economically dependent on the core countries, and mainly the United States. In spite of the geopolitical and cultural particularities of Brazil in South America, Brazilians and other Latin Americans all become Latinos or Hispanics in the United States. According to the general wisdom, Latinos are impoverished immigrants who come from "poor" and "backward" countries to tarnish the United States and strip it of its goods. That is, they prevent the United States from appearing as the wonderful image of itself that is spread in tales all over the world.

Indeed, one of the toughest problems that Brazilians have to cope with in their process of integration is the process of becoming Latinos, in the terms in which this category makes sense in California.[28] Regardless of their social position in Brazilian society and desired or effective position in LA, Brazilians in general do not like to be included in the Latino category. Nevertheless, those immigrants who come from higher social positions in Brazil have better chances to negotiate to their advantage "negative" components of their identities, such as color and nationality. On the other hand, when coming from lower social positions and working in low paid jobs, even color seems to matter little when defining their identities and positions in Los Angeles.

Marta Anderson, age 45, immigrant since 1989, is an example of how Brazilians who come from higher social positions in Brazil may negotiate their *Latinidade* in Los Angeles.

I'm going to speak of what I see at my children's school, because that is the place where I interact with the largest number of people daily. Well, in general, all of them are white, upper-middle class Americans. The first impression that they have [of me] is that I am a Brazilian, a Latina, an immigrant, have an accent, etc... and such. Even being white and having this Anglo look I have...they keep me off... I think [Latino] is sort of devalued... When [European Americans] are going to say something that may involve social and economic status they even take a certain caution because this person is, poor thing, a Latina. They always think that we, Latinos, are poor, that we must have some sort of scholarship because it isn't possible that I, a Latina, could pay 15 thousand dollars a year for an elementary school for my child. It's impressive how they change when they come here to my house... Even so the first question they ask me is if my husband is American, as if to say, "Wow, this *Latina* was very lucky to marry an old rich man." But thank God my husband is young, my age, and he is very Brazilian!

Marta is also an example of how the classification forged by colonizing countries situates people differently based on their birthplace. Even though the position of Brazil in the international division of labor does not prevent Brazilians from re-locating themselves in American society in social spaces that suit their power of purchase, it certainly colors their movements, thus interfering in their integration. All the more when integration means full adjustment into American white society.

Marta's case shows that regardless of their social position in Brazilian society, Brazilians have to deal with the consequences of being identified as Latinos. There is no question, however, that coping with discrimination as an upper middle class individual is quite different from coping with discrimination while being a maid for that same upper middle class family. For instance, Telma Haller, age 46, who, in 1975, migrated to Los Angeles as a maid for employees of the Brazilian Consulate, and currently works as a cook, observes:

> I think that now, after all these years here, I ended up learning to see the people as the Americans see them. I define quickly what they are. The race. It's not that I want to, I don't even like to! Here Americans always want to know if one is black or white. So I also began defining persons. I am even ashamed of saying so, and I don't even think I am racist, but I don't like it when anyone speaks in Spanish with me. Simply because I don't want people to think I'm Mexican, or from Guatemala because they are races that the American denigrate. They are... How can I say it? Latinos are like a lower class for the Americans.

There are clear differences in the ways *Latinidade* is experienced by Marta and Telma. Marta is only connected to Brazil, a Third World country, when she speaks and answers the question "Where are you from?" Otherwise, she has the option of passing for a European immigrant, or, simply, white American. Telma's case is different. She has a job typically held by immigrants, and she is physically closer to the phenotype of the Mexican peasant than to that of the white American. The last sign of distinction left is her language, Portuguese, or her English with a non-Spanish accent. So, whereas Marta is included in the Latino category when she chooses to declare her nationality, Telma is automatically included because of her job and physical appearance. Thus when Telma says that "Latinos are like a lower class for the Americans" she is saying that in her experience of integration in Los Angeles her connection to the Latino label has served to assign her a place with which she does not feel comfortable because of its poor immigrants, cheap labor, and low status connotations.[29] In Marta's case what comes first is the relationship to an economic region: when she says that she is Brazilian, Americans do not necessarily connect her immediately with a social fortune in the United States. She is from a Third World country, which in terms of general status is not good either, but she is not a Latina in the terms that Telma is because of her appearance and place in the job market. She is, instead, a Latin

American. In other words, someone from Latin America who is not necessarily connected to a low status in American society.

Telma's quote also calls attention to the differences between the construction of racial categories in the United States and Brazil. She says that in the United States she learnt to see people as U.S.-born individuals do: one is either black or white and color alone is enough to ascribe a person a place in society. But when she says that she does not like to be taken for a Mexican or Guatemalan she is also saying that the non-white category fits more races than just black, and that being Latino also ascribes to a low ranking place in the American social hierarchy.

Aware of these meanings, Brazilians explain their *Latinidade* in a way that seeks to detach them from this image of Latinos. Telma and other Brazilians that I interviewed rarely stop to wonder why the Latino category has a meaning so different here from the one it has in Brazil. They fall more easily into the racist trap and prefer not to face their own *Latinidade* because they believe that Brazil, and consequently Brazilians, are also superior to other Latinos. They believe that they can benefit from the same racist politics that discriminate against them, and many of them certainly do benefit from the countless hierarchies of power proposed and practiced by the imperialist regime. This confirms that the political position of a nation in the international scenario is relative and that racism works hierarchically, as does exploitation and oppression. In Balibar's (1991:89) words, "in a sense, every modern nation is a product of colonization: it has always been to some degree colonized or colonizing, and sometimes both at the same time." Thus Brazilians see that in terms of economy Brazil is hierarchically inferior to the United States but superior to many other countries, which, broadly and ideologically speaking, make Brazilians feel superior to people from these nations.

So far, I have used the terms Latino and Hispanic as if they were equivalent. They are certainly similar from the perspective of mainstream ideologies, and they were considered as such by most of the Brazilians with whom I talked during my research. However, politically and historically speaking these two terms have different origins and meanings. The Federal Office of Management and Budget created the term "Hispanic" in the 1970s (Hayes-Bautista and Chapa, 1987:64). It is therefore an imposed label which serves both the general politics of ethnic classification and discrimination in the United States, and the political purposes of representatives of this minority.

The term Latino has a different history. Its origins are connected to the rise of the social and political movements in the 1960s. Prior to that time, says Giménez et al. (1992: 3), "The identity labels of 'Negroes,' 'Spanish-Americans,' 'Orientals,' and 'Indians' had generally been imposed by those in control of society's institutions. These movements contributed to the rejection of those labels. 'Black' replaced Negro, 'Chicano' and 'Boricua' replaced Spanish-Americans, 'Asian-American' replaced Oriental, and 'Native American' replaced Indian."

The Chicano movement was a historic first attempt to shape a politics of unification on the basis of a nonwhite identity and culture (Muñoz, 1990). However, with the new wave of immigration from Central and South American countries the term Chicano has been questioned as too restricted to the case of Mexican immigrants and their descendants. Thus, the term "Latino" is an attempt to include all Latin-American immigrants under the same political category. The fact that the term "Latino" has a different history from its "Hispanic" correspondent does not prevent it from being problematic in terms of scope. In other words, despite their original intentions, all these ethnic labels have a double connotation, as Giménez (1992:13) proposes:

> On the one hand, they are presented by minority leaders and educators as the symbols of cultures and identities of which people should be proud. On the other hand, in the context of social science research and mass media discussion of social problems or of census information they identify populations that are disproportionately poor and plagued by all sorts of social problems and deviant/criminal behavior. In the case of Hispanic, the label "upgrades" Chicano, Mexican-American, Puerto-Rican, and, broadly speaking, Latin-American cultures by making them clones of the culture of Spain; it gives them a European veneer that denies both their Native American dimensions and their originality. At the same time, because it is used to identify a stigmatized population, it "downgrades" all these groups, stigmatizing their cultures as the source of the problems faced by a significant proportion of their

members while denying the economic and political causes of those problems.

A similar interpretation holds true for the term "Latino," although the downgrading connotation is the first one to be referred to when the term is mentioned among Brazilians in Los Angeles. Perceiving themselves as different and superior to certain other national groups or ethnicities helps Brazilians insist on carving out a place that supposedly suits them better. In other words, such perception somehow helps them in their process of integration into the world of Los Angeles, as I will show on Chapters Three, Four, and Five. However, it seems that no matter how Brazilians perceive themselves, our American hosts are not interested in understanding details about the ranking of colonization. For them we are all "Hispanics" or "Latinos." Maybe more humorous than other "Hispanics," thanks to Hollywood and Carmen Miranda, but still Hispanics. Perhaps halfway between the colonized and the colonizers, but still seen by the colonizer simply as a colonized inferior.

This is not all, however. Brazilians embody the ideology that discriminates them when trying to differentiate from the "other" Latinos in terms of their attitudes towards the ideas of improvement, progress and so forth. In this sense they also believe themselves to be closer to the colonizers, in terms of mental disposition if not of color. This places them above the "other" Latinos, whom they consider distant in terms of attitude.[30] Telma's interpretation of the differences between Brazilians and Latinos in the United States illustrates this well:

> One thing I see is that when the Brazilian race gets here, out of 10, 8 want to climb up. They go to school, they learn English. And out 10 Latinos [Mexicans], none of them wants anything. They come here and want to live in the same world they were living there. For example, when I studied English I had a lot of friends among the Latinos I found in school (not anymore). I'd go to their homes, and everything was very simple, tacky. They were people who lived only within their little worlds. Being able to afford a slightly better life here, they brought inside their houses those tacky things from their countries. This is my way of seeing things. I know I am

wrong, but I always wanted to grow, and in my opinion I don't think that Latinos want to, they want to live forever in their small worlds. I even think that they could progress if they wanted to. I met girls who crossed the border illegally and went to school and grew. They even went to UCLA and today have degrees and everything. There are people who want it and others who don't.

Though she is aware of the generalized discrimination against Latinos in Los Angeles, Telma continues explaining their actions as if they were only dependent on individual effort. Thus, as Stolcke (1993:33) points out,

> The illusion of equality of opportunity for all could obscure social inequalities to a degree but, by at the same time challenging class inequality, it reinforced the tendency to naturalize social relationships. If the self-determining individual, through persistent social inferiority, seemed to be incapable of making the most of the opportunities society offered to him, this then had to be due to some essential, innate and therefore hereditary deficiency. The person, or better even, his or her biological endowment, rather than the socio-economic order was to be blamed for this.

Americans, Brazilians, and certainly a few "others" who also feel superior to Latinos, blame them. It does not really matter whether the Brazilians' survival in Los Angeles depends or not on Latino networks, Brazilians in general refer to Latinos within the same dominant racist discourse. On the other hand, in situations where access to resources is enhanced, Brazilians do not mind being identified with Latinos, at least partially. For instance, Telma ends up accepting her Latino identity, but before doing so, she makes sure that I understand the differences between Brazilians and other Latinos. In other words, she makes sure that I understand the special way Brazilians fit the Latino stereotype. The fact remains that the integration of Brazilians into American society is oriented by the same racist politics that ranks people from the Third World as inferior in general, and Latinos in the United States in particular. Therefore, in a general manner Brazilians lose "capital" when they are inserted in the Latino category. They observe, as Telma so clearly pointed out, that "Latinos are like a lower class for the Americans."

Despite corroborating the mainstream racist discourse, Brazilians are aware of the limitations of their social mobility in American society. The following quotes exemplify such an understanding.

I don't feel Latina in regard to my manners. Of course I'm Latina, because I'm from Latin America, but I don't have anything from what they here call Latin culture. I have nothing from the Spanish or Mexican culture, but until I explain this to them it takes a long time. So I just say I'm Latina and that's it. To explain that I'm from Brazil and that Brazil was colonized by the Portuguese and such takes too long! But here you have to belong to a group or else you can't achieve anything. I never needed any ethnic groups for anything, but if I want to struggle for something I'm going to have to join the group of Latinos. Here things only work this way. Brazilians here are a very small number, we don't have a presence yet. This is why we have to join with the Latinos who speak Spanish (Nilce, age 47).

I see the relationship between the American and the Hispanic as a relation of disagreement; the American doesn't want to lose his space. For example, when you use a telephone company, or a national aerial company, any company, you have the option of using Spanish. Well, the American doesn't want to lose his space, but he understands that if he wants to sell something he will have to give way for the Spanish speaker because the Spanish speaker wants to buy. But there is still this crazy discrimination against the Latino. Accident... if it is between two Americans they try to verify who was at fault and such, but if it happens between an American and a Latino, it makes no difference if the Latino is or is not at fault, he's to blame. So I see on one side the Anglo defending his space, and I see the struggle of the Hispanic trying to gain space and this happens everywhere. For example, in the church leadership. I notice that for a

Hispanic leader to become the president it is very difficult...before the foreigner they will give the spot to a black man. And they don't want a black man, so we even have this other barrier. I believe that this reality is the same in other businesses. This functions like a pyramid, those on the top don't want to lose their place, and those on the bottom want to get there. What do they do? They put a restraint here so that you can't get there. And what is this restrain? They are the assistants, those who may possibly have an interest in not allowing these others to reach the top because they are also candidates for getting there. In other words, the restraint is the administrative hierarchy. This is normal, they want to guarantee their own space; it's not a defect, it's our human nature (Claudiner Mockiuti, age 48).

What Pastor Mockiuti calls human nature, Wallerstein (1991:34) calls racism, and explains it as having a very clear purpose in a capitalist society: to exploit and justify exploitation based on "natural" differentiation, be it racial, ethnic, or gender related, as we have seen in the Introduction.

The hierarchical ranking changes from place to place as a result of different historical circumstances. Thus one will not expect to find in Los Angeles the same racist ranking that can be found in New York.

By explaining the different patterns of integration of Italians on the East and West coast, Di Leonardo (1984:56) observes that "the significant presence of racial minorities, largely Chinese and Japanese in this period [1890s], but including Mexicans and Native Americans, clearly acted to displace white racial animosities from white ethnics." On the West Coast Italians found a well established lower status group upon which to develop feelings of racial superiority. On the East Coast, on the other hand, they were still sharing with the Irish the position that Mexicans, Native Americans, and Asians were sharing on the West Coast. While on the West Coast they could even develop feelings of racial superiority in relation to lower-status groups, on the East coast they were still the "niggers". Di Leonardo's example confirms Wallerstein's theory about what he calls "neo-racist" politics. In other words, any social segmentation, be it based on ethnicity, race or gender, has to be understood within the limits of the capitalist need for producing and maintaining differences to justify inequality and exploitation. João Cândido, age 48, gives his impressions about this game:

> Because of our tawny color and the fact of being immigrants here we are classified as Latinos, or as Hispanics. I relate well with them, the Latinos, the Mexicans. The only thing that I see in the Mexicans is that they don't know how to assert themselves, have you thought that they are the majority? If we were to consider merely their numbers they would rule here in California. As such they work for free for everybody, and we lose our opportunities because of them. You are kept from better earnings, you live badly here because of them. Because the American will never do the work that we do. Look, there are Mexican babysitters who charge 1 or 2 dollars per hour, understand? So if a Brazilian wants to work as a babysitter she will have to fill her house with children because the people are already used to paying little to the Mexicans.

The consequences of being born in Brazil and thus connected to the Latino population reach all Brazilians regardless of the social class from which they came. In fact, these two factors can be reduced to just one. They are Brazilians and Brazil is a Third World country. In the United States, whether they like it or not, Brazilians only make sense to the extent in which they are seen as Latinos.

But social class certainly matters and, as we will see in the following chapters, ethnic discrimination is expressed differently according to the social class to which the individual belongs. The compensatory politics for minorities also benefits individuals differently. Giménez (1992:13) states:

> Latin Americans as a whole benefit if they choose to play the minority role. While civil rights legislation and affirmative action are indifferent to class, protecting everyone from illiterate peasants to scientists, professionals, and the wealthy from discrimination in economic, political and social activities, it is the upper strata that are likely to benefit the most. Working-class Central and South Americans are likely to be over-represented in low-paid, undesirable employment;

affirmative action is not relevant to their chances of finding jobs. It is possible to hypothesize, consequently, that while all Latin-American immigrants are potentially subject to stereotyping and racial discrimination, racism is likely to be most strongly felt among those who are working-class, poor, and/or of mixed non-European ancestry. Those with high socioeconomic status and high levels of education are better equipped to make the system work for them and to protect their children from the racism of teachers and peers.

To Gimenez's assertion, I would add the following: loading the term Latino with negative connotations is a need of the international job market which, as we have stressed before, benefits from these hierarchies of power. Despite these general needs, which are met hierarchically, it is necessary to distinguish the different roles played by different Latinos. Even though all of them are submitted to the same general racist constraints, some Latinos benefit from playing a more valued role in the system, as Giménez states. It is a mistake, however, to expect a solid group equally benefiting from the cleavage established between Brazil and the United States, or between upper middle-classes and working classes. There is a hierarchy of advantages ranging from one position to the next. In the case of the Brazilians in Los Angeles, there are some that play a role similar to the one that Brazilian elites play in Brazil. They are generally part of these elites and work as middlemen, doing here what they used to do in Brazil. They work to make sure that Brazilian population, despite its place in the capitalist wheel of fortune, never doubts the benefits of its inclusion in capitalist civilization.

These middlemen can eventually play the role of Brazilian representatives in Los Angeles. However, this is a less important part considering the size of the Brazilian population there. Their main role, I would contend, is the role of strengthening the ties between Brazil and United States, as we have seen in Chapter One.

Community, Communities

One of the most interesting methodologies designed to study immigrant assimilation was proposed almost a century ago by Thomas and Znaniecki's *The Polish Peasant in Europe and America*. By studying

Polish immigrant integration into American society during the first decades of this century, Thomas and Znaniecki observed that, beyond problems of individual assimilation or non-assimilation, it is crucial to understand the way immigrants make their passage between the society where they are coming from and the new society into which they are being absorbed.

In the case of the Poles, where assimilation was not an individual but group phenomenon, Thomas and Znaniecki observed that during the transitional period a new society is created. In such a society the individual does not stand isolated in the midst of a culturally different group. He is part of a homogeneous group in contact with a civilization which influences in various degrees all of the members. The new society, they say (1996:108),

> ...is neither Polish nor American, but constitutes a specific new product whose raw materials have been partly drawn from Polish traditions, partly from the new conditions in which the immigrants live, and partly from American social values as the immigrant sees and interprets them. It is this Polish-American society, not American society, that constitutes the social milieu into which the immigrant who comes from Poland becomes incorporated and to whose standards and institutions he must adapt himself.

I will be referring to this particular way of integration as "the community-based pattern of integration," opposed to the "individual pattern" where the immigrant, isolated from his compatriots, lives in the midst of American society and substitutes (or re-elaborates) values and attitudes connected to the old country into the ones required by the new environment at a faster pace. There are no actual correspondents to these two patterns as they are defined. That is, they are models and, as such, useful tools for our understanding of reality, but they cannot be mistaken for reality. In truth, the contours between the two patterns are not always as clear as our logical thought would like them to be. There are different communities, and the way they operate, I argue, depends on both the class position of its members in their societies of origin and the way their networks operate when they arrive in the United States. Additionally, the internal differentiation within these communities produces different opportunities of integration for their members. Thus, even though more dynamic than models that oppose assimilation to non-assimilation (and do not take into account collective processes), Thomas and Znanieck's model misses the issue of class differentiation. Thus the community-based pattern employed by Thomas and Znanieck, and still used by many anthropologists, relies on the notion that communities are made up of similar people. Such an idea, whose American version was proposed by Redfield on his work on folk societies (1940, 1947, 1955), gave support to a concept of culture based on homogeneity, whose corollary is the understanding of acculturation processes as having the same consequences over a specific tribe, nation or immigrant group. The idea of community as a homogeneous whole, however, has since been questioned (Silverman 1979). Steward's *The People of Puerto Rico* exemplifies the anthropological enterprise that was required to broaden anthropology's concepts and scope, especially since the methodological tools and theories applied to study "small communities" would not work properly when trying to understand larger contexts and processes. Steward's students, particularly Wolf (1955, 1957, 1966, 1986) and Mintz (1973) further developed the idea that processes of acculturation and integration cannot be understood outside the context of the productive relations that generate them. That is why Mintz (ibid: 96-7) rejects cognitive views of culture and insists that what men see is at least to some degree a function of their own position within a structure of power, wealth, status and authority.

In this sense the term "Brazilians," as suggesting a common experience and a shared vision, is only meaningful when Brazilians are generally opposed to other nationalities. In this perspective, there is always some criteria that will allow the lumping together of very different people and yet will consider them part of a determined community. A very broad concept of community, which is mainly useful to understand national identities, but can also work to interpret broad ethnic, gender or racial identities, is provided by Anderson's *Imagined Communities* (1984), which defines the nation as "an imagined political community." In this case all nationals, whether living at home or abroad, are included in such a concept. For a foreigner, whether an immigrant or not, nationality is the most salient identity. However, this works only when we are speaking in abstract terms. In other words, being Brazilian, Peruvian, Indian, or Pakistani does not say much about a certain person besides providing elements for a general classification according to the international ranking of values conferred to people.

Ascertaining, for instance, that the dominant pattern of Brazilian immigrant integration into Los Angeles society is the community-based pattern does not mean that Brazilians in Los Angeles comprise a community such as, for instance, the one comprised by Indians in Artesia [Los Angeles county], which is territorially based. There are huge differences between the Brazilian and other older structured ethnic communities in Los Angeles, such as the Chinese, Indian, Mexican, etc. There are many reasons why Brazilians do not comprise a community in the terms that these most "classic" groups do. But it is a mistake to suppose that it is because the Brazilian immigrant population is less homogeneous than the above mentioned ones.

As Bonacich (1990) proposes, not much empirical evidence supports the belief that people of the same ethnicity always comprise homogeneous and highly cooperative communities. Contrary to that, the existence of these immigrant communities is generally mostly based on internal differentiation. Studies developed about these groups as economic enclaves definitely question romanticized ideas about the supposed homogeneity within them.

But Brazilians neither comprise an ethnic enclave nor a geographically based community, such as many ethnic communities in Los Angeles do. First, Brazilians are not as numerous as the mentioned groups; second, they are not as physically distinguishable, and, third, they have a very recent immigrant history, and have therefore not yet built an immigrant "know-how" the way many of these communities have.

However, there are other explanations. Margolis' *Little Brazil* (1994:195-219) questions if the term "community" fits the case of the Brazilian immigrant population in New York. By giving examples of American social life or examples of several different immigrant communities in New York, Margolis concludes that the "disunity" among Brazilians in New York does not allow researchers to think about a Brazilian immigrant community. She also argues that one of the most likely reasons why Brazilians have not made up a community

comparable to those of other immigrant groups is because they refuse
to see themselves as immigrants. If they are here only for a little while,
then why should they waste time with community organizations?
Margolis herself observes that despite the disunity among
Brazilians, their introduction and survival in New York's world is all
processed through Brazilian friends and acquaintances. She says that
two-thirds of the Brazilians in her sample received help from other
Brazilians in finding a place to live, and over one-third had help in
locating a job, and, even long after arrival, the informal immigrant
employment network continues to operate (ibid: 201).

Why are Brazilians expected to form an ethnic community as many
other ethnic groups do? I think that Margolis' explanation that
Brazilians refuse to see themselves as immigrants is a reasonable one.
However, I think that it misses the main point. That is, she observes
that Brazilians survive through Brazilian networks. Everything they
acquire or learn is through the help of other Brazilians. I would not have
a problem with calling these networks communities. Complaints,
conflicts, and so forth would only be part of any close relationship.
However, the problem remains. Even though they live within Brazilian
communities or networks, Brazilians complain about the lack of union
between them. I have noticed, among those Brazilians who are not
strongly connected to any Brazilian association, a refusal to publicly
associate or to admit affiliation with other fellow citizens. In these
cases, Brazilian communities, groups, or associations are considered to
slow down the process of assimilation. In other words, the Brazilians
who reject association with other compatriots are those who believe
that their assimilation into American society can be complete and that
it is only a matter of individual effort. Dissociation from other
Brazilians therefore seems to be an important requirement. Why would
that be so? After three months living in a Brazilian network in New
York, Henfil (1985:120) observed,

> Brazilians don't form ghettos. All of them want to integrate
> for real, and what we most often hear is that we should avoid
> living among other Brazilians, with each one trying to
> integrate by himself, to become a legitimate American. It
> seems to me that there is a general failure, but nobody notices.

There is also impatience with speaking Portuguese, as if one was retarding or impeding the learning of legitimate English. The need and urgency of assimilation is nothing but the need to get rid of the destiny of the colonized, which all Brazilians share. If Memmi (1991:74) is right when he says that "nothing can ever save the colonized," then the self-denial that Brazilians impose on themselves is absolutely useless.

I have observed that the attitude of avoiding other Brazilians is more common among those who belong to the Brazilian middle and upper classes. And, generally, among those who understand that they have greater chances to pass for white Americans and, consequently, assimilate completely into American society. These Brazilians generally think of "community" as a synonym for low class people.

In any case, there is no such thing as a mythological ethnic community fully embedded in American policies of immigrant integration, a community where everybody sees and cooperates with everybody on a daily basis (Di Leonardo 1994). In fact, there is hardly such thing anywhere, even less in Los Angeles, and not even among traditional ethnic neighborhoods. Los Angeles' rhythm hardly leaves room for a familiar existence, at least as far as the working class members are concerned. João and Sônia Cândido, for instance, told me that during their first ten months living in Los Angeles they would see their children only on Saturdays, and that was because they are Seventh Day Adventists and keep Saturdays as a holiday. Other than that they would spend a third of their 24-hour day commuting to their jobs. They would leave home around 5 a.m. and get back between 11 p.m. and midnight, when their children would be already asleep. Even where it is not necessary to commute long distances, it is still hard to develop what Margolis calls a community life in urban sites, especially in geographies like Los Angeles'.

Non-working class Brazilians also have a hard time getting around to see other Brazilians in Los Angeles. Meeting Brazilians on a systematic basis has to be an organized enterprise. The discourses below exemplify these difficulties.

It's very difficult to meet people here casually. It's crazy how spread apart Los Angeles is. Everything is far from everything, and people live two hundred miles from each other. If you want to meet people you always have to organize something, there is no casualness. Hey, I was just passing by and decided to stop and chat (Derek, age 48).

When the girls invited me to participate in the group, they knew of my experience with a group of women in Colombia, in Bogota. But I have always thought that here everything is more difficult. First Los Angeles is very large, and I thought that it was difficult for you to gather people like this here. Everywhere you go is at least 40 minutes away. Everything has to be done one hour earlier so that you can be on time (Marina, age 45).

I find Los Angeles tranquil. Calm. But very big. It took a while to get used to it because it is not an open city, where you go and find things easily. You go to New York and it has a city center. Here there is no center where you can go and find everything. My difficulty in Los Angeles was finding a center of the city where things are happening. Later, of course, I discovered that it doesn't exist. Here, every neighborhood, every city has its own little downtown. And this is very large; it takes time to assimilate the whole thing, to go out without the fear of getting lost. To take a car and go out. In New York I would go out on foot. So Los Angeles is a difficult city for integration. And one of the reasons why we created the group of Brazilians was because each one lived in a distant neighborhood, and so the need emerged to meet friendly people, right? So that you could meet and relax. It had to be organized because everything is very far (Nilce, age 47).

Indeed Los Angeles does not have only a heart, but several. Los Angeles is a monstrous conurbation linked by endless freeways. Geographical limitations prevent Brazilians from meeting casually; on the other hand, they promote the need for organized meetings.

In general, however, it is not simple to organize communities in a city like Los Angeles if there are not very good and clear reasons to do so. This does not mean, though, that there are no Brazilian communities in Los Angeles.

What I refer to as a community does not have the same meaning or the same scope as those communities that are organized into neighborhoods, forming enclaves within the bigger city. As a matter of fact, what I call community in this case can be simply called a network. In this sense, there are several Brazilian networks in Los Angeles. But they are hardly organized around the abstract category of "Brazilian." In real life, Brazilians do not extract their survival from their abstract Brazilianness. Thus, those Brazilians who come together and develop a systematic relationship have very good reasons to do so, and these reasons are not necessarily connected to their class position, since a few Brazilian associations join both "rich" and "poor" Brazilians.

My questions are mostly in regards to the ways different communities process integration. What do they teach their members? What are their ideas about themselves and about those with whom they have to interact in their daily lives? Even though I have known and occasionally participated in other Brazilian communities' gatherings in Los Angeles, as I already pointed out, I focused my study on the Portuguese-speaking Seventh Day Adventist Church of Chino and on the Brazilian Women's Group. Through the observation of these two communities it is possible to concretely understand the differences between the two patterns of immigrant integration and the ways in which class position (in Brazil) affects such integration.

CHAPTER 3
The Brazilian Adventists in Chino

The Portuguese-speaking Seventh Day Adventist Church of Chino comprises one of the largest and most permanent groups of Brazilians in the greater Los Angeles area. The October 17, 1999 wedding of two of its members, Isaac and Jaidete, brought together some 300 Brazilians.

Church members meet every Saturday for service and on Wednesday evenings for prayer. The group is composed of both Brazilian and Portuguese members. With children included, the church has about 200 congregates, around 180 are Brazilians and some 20 Portuguese. Excluding children under 10 years of age, the majority of the members are first generation immigrants whose adult children are generally not members of Chino. The latter follow their spouses or friends and associate mainly with Adventist American churches. Out of some 20 couples who have grownup children, only four of them have offspring that frequent Chino. Yet they have particular reasons for doing so: they have married among themselves, and the ones who have not married Brazilians, have married other Latinos.

Brazilians who started coming to Riverside, Loma Linda, and Glendale in the early 1950s formed the original nucleus of the present church. Even though the Brazilian Adventists moved to the area where it is currently located in 1994, their history is much older. Adair Souza, born in 1929, came to Riverside in 1963. La Sierra Adventist church was the first church he attended. He says that he was well received there, but he never really felt he belonged to the congregation. He never felt comfortable enough to volunteer to help with church work, and always felt somewhat useless for not being an active member of the church. Fortunately, he met other Brazilians in a similar situation. During the idle times between Bible School and services, Adair would talk about superficial things to a couple of Americans, but would mostly hang out with a couple of other Brazilian immigrants. Noticing that a satisfying integration into the mainstream group was impossible, the Brazilian group talked to the Pastor and was offered a little room so that it could conduct Bible school in Portuguese. For many years this group stayed in La Sierra, but never received any special attention from the mainstream congregation.

Just a handful of people composed the original group: Adair Souza, Áurea and Oscar Fonseca, Dirce and Samuel Holland, Celina Benjamin, Vicente Ribeiro, and Ilka dos Reis. Adair says that it is thanks to Ilka that a Portuguese-speaking Seventh Day Adventist church exists today in Southern California. She was acquainted with a large population of Portuguese immigrants in Norco who were not able to speak English, and proposed to move the Brazilian group from Riverside there. They got a much larger room at the church of Norco and were received with more consideration than at La Sierra. In fact, they had been so ignored there, that even after being a member for more than 15 years, Mrs. Fonseca was once mistaken for a newcomer. The pastor approached her to introduce himself and asked who she was. She said, "you don't know yet who I am? I have been here for 15 years!"

The plan of this Brazilian Adventist group in Norco was to spread the word of God to those Portuguese immigrants who could not speak English. Even though they were able to convert a couple of Portuguese immigrant families in Norco, the group has always had a large Brazilian majority because, Adair explains, "the Portuguese immigrant community is very Catholic and conservative, and prefer to be without any word of God than to switch churches." Considering that their aim in Norco was to reach the Portuguese settlement there, it can be said they failed. However, more Brazilians kept coming and the group finally grew large enough to afford their own pastor.

When Ilka dos Reis died in 1990 and left her inheritance to the church, the group was already large enough to afford their own place and support their own pastor. It was thanks to the money she left and a substantial donation by pastor Palmer Harder, who had been a missionary in Brazil for 62 years, that the church members were able to move the place to where it is today.[31] The establishment of the church was not free of conflicts. And even though it has a very recent history in Chino, it has been full of ups and downs. When Pastor Edilson, the second pastor, assumed his position, he and some other members started enforcing a policy that made some families leave. Controversy surrounded the creation of spaces for socialization and amusement versus the enforcement of activities connected to evangelization. Pastor Edilson was transferred to another church as a consequence of these conflicts. Pastor Claudiner Mockiuti assumed his position in 1995.[32]

When I started my fieldwork in Chino, Pastor Mockiuti had already been there for two years, during which the church had almost doubled its number of members. He was aware of the prior problems and was willing to work them out. In our first conversation he explained the dynamics of a church composed of immigrants and the content of his policies:

> I'm going to explain something to you. The difference between Hispanic immigration and Brazilian or Portuguese or Chinese, or any other, is that here we have this border. The first generation of Hispanics, (when I say the first I mean those which left there and came here), is being constantly renewed today. You go to a Hispanic Adventist church and you will find that the first generation is the strongest group. The second generation is a little like this. But what happens to the second generation? It is either assimilated into the culture, and goes to an American Adventist church, or does not go to church at all. But they keep growing because the first generation keeps coming. ...Well, what is happening with the Brazilian, the Portuguese, the Italian? We don't have a border, we have an ocean, a great distance, this is one of the factors. Fine, what happens to the Portuguese from Portugal? They stopped coming a long time ago. The first generation has diminished day by day. The second generation is already disappearing, and the third you don't know, but you talk to them, they don't even tell you they are children of Portuguese. I go to a Portuguese home and see the father, the son, and the

grandson. In church you only see the father and the son. We
had to have a class in English for the second generation. Our
church has not received anyone lately. What happens is that
we need to work to attract the second generation. Today I have
a great number of people from the second generation and I am
going against the principles of those from the first. That is, I
have to accept American customs to maintain them within.
Music, clothing, everything. Why? Because if we don't do
something to keep the second generation we will not keep the
third generation inside. Because all of the third generation that
was here is already out. So now we are maintaining a second
generation hoping that the third will stay. I have the third
generation returning, because the second and third maintain a
tie, they speak perfect English. The third has already forgotten
Portuguese. Sunday I had a young man visiting. I say a
young man, but he is already married. Motorcycle, long hair,
tattoos. I approached him in conversation and asked him if he
spoke Portuguese: "Yes." I asked him if he preferred to speak
in Portuguese or English and he said, "You can speak in
Portuguese." I said, " I can speak in English, but I don't think
I could express myself to you as I would like to." I noticed
the following: good will. We have to consider this opening
and invest in it. Then every time you see an individual with a
headphone in church it's because he doesn't understand
Portuguese, but wants to be there. I have simultaneous
translations of all the sermons. If you want to hear my
sermon in English, all you have to do is put on a wireless
headphone, sit wherever you want and I have a person
translating everything that is being said. Why do I do this?
First, thinking about the third generation. The second
generation wants to come, but it becomes attached to the third
who are their children... so this story about the language really
is impressive. When I arrived here the people said this is a
church that only speaks Portuguese, no one speaks English.
But we observed that the children didn't understand the story
when it was told in Portuguese. Besides this, it is not only
Brazilians and Portuguese that we have in our church. I have

in my church an Argentine who lived in Brazil for thirty years. And there are Mexicans in the church because they are married to Brazilians, and there are Americans because they are married to Brazilians, and there are Americans who date Brazilians. So we have to open up. I suffer with the first generation because I am also first generation. It's almost impossible to convince them of our policies, I have elderly members who are literally sick with all these changes. I tell them that if they had children they would understand it better. I also didn't accept long hair, earrings. An earring to me was a challenge. This is the way I used to think. So my major argument with the first generation is to ask them to put themselves in the place of the parents whose children are here. What would you do to help, what is the church doing to help? The first generation only likes classical music and with the second it's contemporary music. Our church is somewhere in between. We have a little of the contemporary but we still maintain the traditional. But to keep these two cultures in the same environment is a constant conflict, I am always having problems.

Besides being the Pastor in Chino, Mockiuti is also the representative of the Portuguese-speaking churches on the West Coast. In 1997, as a result of his performance at the church of Chino, the Seventh Day Adventist congregation invited him to switch to a Hispanic church in Glendale where there was already a group of about 50 Brazilians. This is a much larger church with some 500 members. The church was going through organizational problems, and Pastor Mockiuti was chosen as a strong candidate because of his work at Chino. It was a very sad and distressing time because he was extremely divided. The members of Chino who had become used to him and his wife, who is also a very charismatic person, were feeling somewhat abandoned. He finally decided to move, and for about a month there were several farewell parties and many tears.

Chino: A Profile

Before discussing in what terms the Brazilian members of the church of Chino constitute a community or what kind of community they are, I want to present a profile that I elaborated based on information collected through interviews and conversations during my two years of participant observation. Not all people in my sample are members of the church, some of them are visitors who I met there several times. All these individuals are included in the general profile for Brazilians in Los Angeles presented on page 8.

Table 1 - Birthplaces of Chino Members by Region in Brazil

Region	Frequency	Percent
Central West	4	4.8
Northeast	7	8.4
North	5	6.0
Southeast	40	48.2
South	27	32.6
Total	83	100.0

As table 1 shows, the largest percentage (48.2) of Chino members were born in the Southeast, mostly in the cities of São Paulo and Rio de Janeiro. This Brazilian region took the lead in industrialization, and also established permanent contacts with foreign countries because it received a considerable influx of immigrants between the last decades of the nineteenth century and the first five decades of the twentieth. In second place is the South, which has received waves of immigrants from Germany, Italy, Japan, Poland, and Portugal (Azores) since the last decades of the nineteenth century, and has therefore kept a much closer contact with the outside world. The Northeast, in contrast, is considered an area of early colonization, with its last influx of European immigration occurring in the seventeenth century, when the Dutch and French were still disputing parts of the Brazilian territory with Portugal. Even though there is a new flow of immigrants to this region brought by the tourist industry, the phenomenon is too recent to have already promoted an immigrant flow from Brazil to the countries from where these immigrants come. The regions of the North and Central West were colonized by national immigrants from the Northeast and South. These are, I believe, the reasons why Southern Brazil has closer relationship with the United States and other countries of Europe.

In the specific case of the church of Chino, I would say that besides the above factors, the strong presence of Southern Brazilians has to do with the fact that Seventh Day Adventism in Brazil developed in the Southern states, especially among German immigrants who were already Protestants. Also, many American missionaries had German ancestry, which facilitated their insertion among German immigrants in Brazil. I suppose that as a consequence of this proselytizing, stronger links were established between American missionaries and the first converts, and produced an incipient immigrant flow to the United States.

The church members who were born in the Southern and Southeast regions represent 80.8 percent of the group. The other 19.2 percent are from the North, the Northeast, and the Central West. It is important to note that the distribution of Brazilian immigrant population by region of birth in Brazil does not reflect the absolute and/or relative populations of these regions in Brazil as we can see below.

Table 2 - Brazilian Population by Region

Region	Population	Percent
North	11,288,259	7.19
Northeast	44,766,851	28.50
Southeast	67,000,738	42.66
South	23,513,736	14.97
Central West	10,500,579	6.69
Total	157,070,163	100.00

1996 IBGE Census – Brazilian Institute of Geography

Table 2 allows us to see that even though Southeast is the most populated region of Brazil, the percentage of immigrants coming from there is relatively higher than the percentage of its population in relation to the Brazilian general population. The Northeast is the opposite case: even though it represents 28.5 percent of the Brazilian population, it contributes only with 8.4 percent of the Brazilian immigrants in Los Angeles.

Table 3 - Residence of Chino Members by Region in Brazil

Region	Frequency	Percent
Central West	3	3.6
Northeast	7	8.4
Southeast	49	59.0
South	24	28.0
Total	83	100.0

Comparing Tables 1 and 3, we see that the percentages of birthplaces and residence before immigration of Chino members are the same overall, but it is worth noting that some individuals born in the regions of the North and Northeast had already immigrated to Rio de Janeiro and São Paulo (Southeast) before emigrating to the United States. This fact suggests that immigration to the United States and, I should also add, the First World countries in general, is connected to the ways in which capitalism has penetrated the country as a whole. Areas that have developed in a tighter connection to the United States are the areas that contribute the most immigrants to the United States.

Table 4 - Sex of Chino Members

Gender	Frequency	Percent
Females	47	56.6
Males	36	43.4
Total	83	100.0

As table 4 shows, 56.6 percent of Chino is female. The greater number of females is a result of the following factors: 18.3 percent of the total sample are women who are married to non-Brazilian men, as table 7 indicates; there are only two Brazilian men married to non-Brazilian women, and 16.9 percent of the total sample are divorced women. There are no single men who are divorced or widowed in the sample.

Table 5 - Age of Chino Members

Age (in years)	Frequency	Percent
11-20	6	7.2
21-30	11	13.3
31-40	18	21.7
41-50	18	21.7
>50	30	36.1
Total	83	100.0

As shown in table 5, approximately one-third (36.1 percent) of the sample is made up of members older than 51, and this has to do with the fact that the church of Chino is mostly comprised of first-generation immigrants. The relatively small number of individuals aged 11-20 years (7.2 percent) and 21-30 years (13.3 percent) shows that there is a remarkable absence of second and third generation immigrants. These individuals, who are the children of the first generation, mostly attend American Adventist churches, since their husbands and wives are mostly Americans, and their children are educated accordingly. The small number of younger members also has to do with the reduced influx of immigrants, as well as the limited marriage market for both males and females. There are not enough members of a marriageable age; thus, as several persons explained, potential members would rather attend bigger churches where their chances of meeting a mate are greater.

Table 6 - Marital Status of Chino Members

Marital Status	Frequency	Percent
Single	12	14.5
Married	54	65.1
Divorced	14	16.9
Widowed	3	3.5
Total	83	100.0

As table 6 indicates, the majority (65.1 percent) of the members of Chino are married. Those whose husbands or wives are non-Brazilians usually have no children, have children who are already married, or have children under 10 years old.

Table 7 - Nationality of the Spouses of Women in Chino

Nationality	Frequency	Percent
Brazilian	58	81.7
American	6	8.5
Portuguese	2	2.8
Bolivian	1	1.4
Canadian	1	1.4
Chilean	1	1.4
Mexican	1	1.4
Ecuadoran	1	1.4
Total	71	100.0

As shown in table 7, the majority of the married members (81.7 percent) is or was wedded to Brazilians. Most of them came to the United States already married and with children. In the case of those members who are wedded to non-Brazilians, their partners are usually Brazilian American, or American, or people from other nationalities who have lived in Brazil. Among those who are married to foreigners, only one of them met his wife in the United States. If the members of the church of Chino comprise an endogamous community from the viewpoint of the nationality of their spouses, the same does not apply to their children, that is, to the second generation. These will be marrying white and black Americans, and Hispanics or other ethnic groups according to where they live and what schools and churches they attend, and also depending on their physical and social characteristics.

Table 8 - Number of Children per Couple or Divorced Parents among Chino Members

No. of Children	Frequency	Percent
0	11	22.4
1	6	12.2
2	20	40.8
3	8	16.4
4	2	4.1
5	2	4.1
Total	49	100.0

As table 8 shows, 77.6 percent of Chino couples or divorced parents have children. The median and mode for those who have children are two children. The four couples that have more than three children are those that immigrated between the late 50s and early 60s. The considerable majority of the couples who have three children are also part of the first newcomers. New couples usually have two children.

Table 9 - Year of Immigration of Chino Members to the United States

Year	Frequency	Percent	# of Years in interval	% per year
1995-99	6	7.2	5	1.4
1988-94	32	38.6	7	5.5
1978-87	18	21.7	10	2.1
1968-77	6	7.2	10	0.7
Prior to 1968	21	25.3	-	-
Total	83	100.0		

Table 9 indicates that only 7.2 percent of the total group is made up of newcomers, which shows that immigration of Chino members has slowed down for the last five years. Either that or Brazilian Adventist newcomers prefer to join other Adventist churches, either American or Hispanic. The highest percentage of members (38.6 percent) came here between 1988 and 1994.

Table 10 - Level of Education of Chino Members

Level of Education	Frequency	Percent
Elementary	15	18.1
High School	33	39.8
College	35	42.1
Total	83	100.0

Table 11 - Employment Status of Chino Members in the United States

Employment Status	Frequency	Percent
Student	12	14.5
Blue Collar	46	55.4
White Collar	25	30.1
Total	83	100.0

There is a relative congruency between the educational level of Chino members and the type of job they hold in the United States. For example, considering that most white-collar jobs require college degrees, only 42.1 percent of the members, as shown in table 10, would be expected to hold white-collar jobs. The actual percentage of members holding white collar jobs is 30.1 percent, as shown in table 11. This indicates a difference of 12.1 percent. However, under the category college (table 10) I also included the members who are still students attending college. Therefore, if we only consider the members who actually hold college degrees, the difference is negative. That is, there are more people holding white-collar positions than expected. This happens because under the category "white-collar" I also included self-employed workers who do not need college degrees.

Under the white-collar category the most common jobs among Chino members are lawyer, accountant, doctor, nurse, teacher, and self-employed. Under the blue-collar category I included jobs as different as mechanic, truck-driver, babysitter, housekeeper, agricultural worker, nurse's aide, and janitor. Mechanics and nurse's aides require a grade 12 level of schooling.

Therefore, overqualification is infrequent among them. Instead Chino members undergo a period of transition in which they have to validate whatever educational degree they acquired in Brazil. This period lasts in general five to ten years. A shorter or longer process depends on concrete possibilities of investing time and money on the validation of these degrees. The only way to avoid the need for such validation is to have an American company hire Brazilian workers in Brazil. They go to Brazil to recruit workers so that they can fill a shortage in the American job market, as in the case of computer analysts and programmers. However, no one in my sample fits this case.

Meeting in the Intersection of Freeways

About half of the members of Chino live in Riverside, near La Sierra University, which is one of the Seventh Day Adventist universities in Southern California. The other half of the members is spread around the greater Los Angeles area. They say that they chose to locate the church in Chino because the city of Chino is a central place for everybody. Wherever they live, most of the members drive about half an hour to get there. The other reason why they chose Chino is because real estate prices are lower there than in Riverside. However, commuting 20 to 30 minutes to go to church does not seem to be a problem for a population used to commuting daily to their jobs, which are usually far more distant than the church. Commuting becomes a problem only when excuses for being late are needed. But generally, driving long distances is as much a part of Southern California life as shopping is part of American life.

What Kind of Community is this?

After a few encounters and chats with members of Chino, and after understanding the proportion between Brazilians and Portuguese in the composition of the church, I asked some of them about its name. That is, if the majority of the church is comprised of Brazilians, why is there no indication of that in their designation? Some Brazilian members to whom I talked about this issue told me that the name was a request of the Portuguese group. They would not accept being part of a church whose name did not indicate their presence. In this case, why not Luso-Brazilian instead? Since Luso means Portuguese, Luso-Brazilian would encompass both groups. It seems that the Brazilian members are so secure about their place in the church that the name of the church has not been an issue. On the other hand, being simply identified by the language instead of a country or specific nationality or ethnicity makes their spectrum larger. That is, the church is potentially a place for any Portuguese speaker regardless of being Brazilian, Portuguese, Angolan, Mozambican, and so forth. During the period I observed the church gatherings I was introduced to visitors from several African ex-colonies, as well as from the Azores. However, there is no member from any other Portuguese-speaking country besides Brazil and Portugal.

The question of the language as the basis of the Portuguese-speaking Seventh Day Adventist Church of Chino is not only stated by its name. We have seen that the idea of congregating Portuguese speakers who did not speak English was part of this church's original plan, when they moved from La Sierra, Riverside, to Norco. But I am not totally sure about the weight of the language factor in keeping this community together. Thus, how important is the question of the language in producing this community? I have got different answers, which make me question the weight of the language issue.

I think our church was created mostly to preserve the language and ... to help many Brazilians who come from Brazil without knowing English, and cannot go to an American Church. So they come to our church and in time they learn English...(Maria, 77 years).

This Portuguese church exists for one sole reason: the majority of the Portuguese who are here are persons without an education, who do not speak English. If they don't have a Portuguese-language church, they are without religion, practically speaking. For me, for example, this church is dispensable because I can go to an American church and take much more advantage of it. There are churches of better quality, but I am here to help, to be a part of it. That is, speaking Portuguese is not fundamental for me, but it is fundamental for Manoel because he doesn't speak English. My mother-in-law doesn't speak it and neither do others. We also have a large part of Brazilians who do not speak it, and even if they do speak a little English, they do not have the conditions to go to an American church and benefit, and participate in what is being transmitted. They will lose out on a lot (David, age 35).

This church is not only about a question of language, no. Because look at Pittau, he and his wife are Argentines. Therefore, their mother tongue is Spanish. But they lived a great part of their adult lives in Brazil and feel more comfortable among us here than in a Hispanic church. My experience in American and Hispanic churches has always been frustrating. The service would end, and if there was no lunch or some other special commemoration, everyone would go home. There is none of this pleasant endless conversation that we have here. The Hispanics also, pass by us, Buenos dias Hermano and that's it. There's no one else like our own people, isn't it? We like the same food, laugh at the same jokes, like the same conversation and have the same problems (Omar, age 62).

Despite thinking sometimes that younger couples find it hard to relate to us, the singles, and despite Chino being a small church where we don't have many opportunities to find girlfriends, I prefer coming here rather than to any other American or Hispanic church. It's not that I have any problems understanding English, I understand everything perfectly and I also communicate. But I don't feel at home like I feel here, you know? Here I feel at home and like I truly contribute to the group. And I also feel that there is more space for my own growth as a person, I'm free to speak, sing. Besides this, why would I frequent non-Brazilian churches if I haven't the slightest interest in marrying a woman who is not Brazilian? Good or bad, here there are always visitors from Brazil (Robson, age 35).

Nobody has ever told me that language is the only factor that makes Chino a community. There is also the faith and other common interests, as Omar pointed out. Food, behaviors, and other elements of Brazilian culture are also important factors. It is not only by chance that most of the Portuguese members have also lived in Brazil and in a sense are already acquainted with Brazilian culture. In spite of the faith that brings them together, the relationship between Brazilians and Portuguese in Chino has some characteristics that must be pointed out.

I became aware of the Portuguese members by observing that during the service a certain group of people always sat on the same chairs. After the first four times I attended the Saturday service, I decided to arrive earlier to observe members' integration during the study of the Bible. Thus, for about eight weeks, I kept switching from group to group in order to make myself known to everyone and also to observe their reactions to Bible texts under discussion.

The church is composed of two separate buildings. The one where the service takes place fits about 150 people. The other building has a large dining room, a kitchen, two classrooms for the children's Bible School, and two bathrooms. It is in this building that the youth develop their own program and Bible School until 11 a.m., when they join the adults at the main building for the service.

The Saturday activities for adults, youngsters, and children start at 9:30 a.m., when a particular person, who changes weekly, welcomes everyone. I did not know about the youngsters' activities until September 1998, when Pastor Wagner Kuhn was leaving to spend the following four years working for the Adventist Development Relief Agency (ADRA) in Azerbaijan. The youngsters had prepared a special farewell program for him and his family (wife and child) and that is when I found out that the youngsters are not avoiding Bible School and the other activities before service, they simply develop their own activities apart.

For the first couple of months of participant observation I only attended the adult activities and developed a closer relationship with them. And in order to allow everyone to participate in the Bible School discussion, four groups of about seven to twelve people are formed. Each one has a teacher, who changes every couple of months. It was by moving from group to group that I found out that one of the groups never has visitors or rotates people. They are always the same people, all of them apparently above fifty. Also, they usually look very serious and focused on their prayers. Before experiencing a Bible School class with them I had already been told that they were Portuguese. Since my focus was on Brazilians, I never participated of their debates of Bible texts. However, I talked to most of them during the monthly lunch potlucks. It was through these occasional conversations that I learned that most of them had immigrated to Brazil before definitely immigrating to the United States.

I think that there are different reasons why they keep themselves apart from the Brazilians, even though I have witnessed true cooperation between them in different occasions. For instance, when a daughter of one of these Portuguese families married, her wedding party was a result of the collaboration of most members of the church. The decoration of the church and community center, the preparation and serving of food, and afterwards cleaning were all tasks performed by members of the church, whether Brazilian or Portuguese, (though mostly by Brazilians because they comprise the huge majority, as we have seen).

The solidarity and affection that exists between them, however, is not expressed in touching or prolonged conversation during these weekly encounters. That is, Brazilians act differently when interacting among themselves than with the Portuguese.

Pastor David Bravo, a Chilean married to a Brazilian, has the following ideas about this relationship:

> I think what joins the Portuguese to the Brazilians is only and exclusively the language. The culture and history separates them. In Chile we have a phenomenon similar to that of Brazil. We also speak of Mother Spain, but deep down we don't have a lot of respect for Spain. Brazil doesn't have respect for Portugal either. The phenomenon is that Brazil advanced, the Spanish colonies also advanced, and their mother and father stayed the way they were, although they don't want to accept this. But the church has the mission of reaching all languages, all peoples, all nations. Our task is to also reach the immigrants of the Portuguese language. Me and my wife were the first to initiate this work among the Brazilians and Portuguese here in North America and we have done this for more that two decades. We know that what unites us is the language. Now, to desire that they participate, feel, and believe in the same way complicates things a little because they are different in many aspects.
>
> If in Brazil the history of the regions makes things a little difficult, in Portugal things are even more fragmented. Because for them the Portuguese from Portugal, from the continent, is one thing. Azorian Portuguese is another, and there are those from Angola, Mozambique, and Madeira. In that case there is already great discrimination between

themselves. Our idea is to promote unity within diversity, but
in truth all would rather have their own churches...
The Brazilian is different from the Portuguese, another history,
another philosophy. He has ease in adapting to everything.
And he also has an incontestable creativity, right? The
"jeitinho brasileiro"[the Brazilian way]. This exists and it is
very positive. Also the temperament, the Brazilian personality
has that sweetness, amiability, goodness, a disposition to
always serve, help, support. The problem is that Brazilians
don't take rules seriously. Commitments in general. Those
Brazilians whom we met abroad are generally not taken
seriously. I wouldn't say by the majority, but by a good
number. This is in marked contrast to the Portuguese. The
Portuguese see things with another mental framework. For
example, time. With a Brazilian you set it for 4 in the
afternoon, and there is one that will get there at 4. The
Portuguese person has been there since 3:45. The Brazilians
then arrive at 4, 4:30, 5, 5:30. They get there calmly,
casually, don't explain themselves, don't apologize, for them
this is not a problem. What's important is that he's arrived,
and so, what's the problem? Is there anything to be done? If
others did it in an hour and a half, he can do it in five or ten
minutes. On the other hand, the Brazilian is more transparent
than the Portuguese, who is more reserved. Brazilians go
more by feelings than by reason, with the Portuguese it is the
opposite.

   We go through many difficulties when we try to integrate
Portuguese with Brazilians because at times the conflicts are
very great. The Portuguese is sincere and he is quite frank, but
he is also sensitive, so he speaks sternly with you. But if you
speak sternly to him, he may become offended and be hurt
forever. Not the Brazilian. With the Brazilian you can be
sincere, frank, and speak sternly, but later you are hugging,
kissing, and everything is ok. A Brazilian forgives much
easier. He admits that he was wrong, asks you to forget it, let
it be, let's go forward. Not the Portuguese. I would say that
this has to do with the personality of the Brazilian, which is

different from the Portuguese from a socio-political and cultural perspective. Brazil had a dictatorship, but the Portuguese dictatorship was even longer, lasted five decades and this was reflected strongly on Portuguese culture, and made them a very controlled and submissive people. Now, the Portuguese has no problem with discipline, and in this way he identifies well with the American and the Canadian. I believe it is due to an almost natural submission which is natural to the Portuguese. That is, he also has his revolts and fights for his rights, but because he is more disciplined that the Latino in general he adapts better in American and Canadian culture. So if an American asks a Portuguese to hammer a nail in a certain way, he will hit it that way his entire life. After a year, two, or three, he will still be hitting the nail the same way. Now the Brazilian is more creative, he bends the nail, changes the nail, hits it anywhere, soon takes a break and finds another way, right? If the boss gives the Portuguese fifty nails and tells him to economize, he does everything to economize correctly. But the Brazilian doesn't submit to this pressure, because if twenty five come out bent, and if twenty five are right, he will find a way of finding twenty five other nails to complete the job. This is why I think the Portuguese adapts very well here because he accepts discipline and structure without questioning it. The Brazilian seeks always for a better place, is always in search for something better, different, but, of course, runs the risk of never settling himself down, never getting there.

[Look at] the very way in which one and the other come to the United States. I know that the Brazilian comes principally for adventure or in search of better opportunities, but you never see him in as favorable a position as he could have been, because his heart is always divided between returning to his beloved country, Brazil, or in staying here. And by not creating roots they never establish themselves economically or professionally. Not the Portuguese. He crosses the Atlantic and then burns his ships. Because he has no vessels to return, he never even dreams of going back. For the Brazilian, Brazil continues to be very important. He is capable of giving his life for Brazil. In the sense of family, friendships, the way we are understood, helped, and supported in Brazil. On the other hand, Brazil also allows more opportunities both to the Brazilian and to the foreigner, more than the Portuguese fatherland... Brazil creates in the citizen a truly larger involvement, the environment, the climate, the food, the social life, the beaches... these cannot be forgotten, right?

I also discussed the relationship between Brazilians and Portuguese in the United States with a Luso Brazilian, Ricardo, who migrated with his parents and siblings to the United States when he was five years old. His mother, a Brazilian born in the state of Paraná, in the South, met and married his father, a Portuguese immigrant, in Rio de Janeiro, where she was studying. Encouraged by his father's brothers who were living in the United States, they also decided to try their luck here. From the time they arrived in the United States, the family always lived in Artesia, which used to be one of the most important Portuguese ethnic neighborhoods in Southern California. His mother was a Brazilian living among the Portuguese and their family was the only one who had a Brazilian member. As his mother always insisted on keeping her Brazilian identity, the other Portuguese families somehow kept them at a distance. However, this was not really pronounced because his mother played some leadership roles and was much needed to organize activities for the community.

Ricardo suggests that those Portuguese immigrants who have lived in Brazil before coming to the States change their attitude towards Brazil and Brazilians when they are here because here they have a stronger immigrant community and there is no point - especially 30 years ago - in trying to replace a Portuguese identity with a Brazilian one. Mainly because a Brazilian identity was, and still is, connected to carnival (Mardi Gras) and its playfulness and excesses, and it is not the most appropriate identity to be linked to when one is part of a conservative community in a Protestant country. Furthermore, living in the United States allows the opportunity to vent some possible bad feelings the Portuguese (mostly those who had immigrated before to Brazil) might have about Brazil.

Considering the age of the Portuguese immigrant communities in California - they have been here since the end of the nineteenth century - it is understandable that the church is not their only space of socialization. They have a larger network of relatives, clubs, and other associations more common to massive immigrant flows. The situation is a little different, however, in the case of those Portuguese who convert to Protestant churches, as pointed out a Portuguese lady member of Chino. In this case, she suggests, they become a little isolated from the Catholic majority that comprises the Portuguese immigrant population and the new church becomes one of the most important spaces of socialization for them.

Yet the church of Chino is such an important space for the socialization of their Brazilian members that when Pastor Edilson wanted to replace spaces of entertainment with spaces of evangelization, several families withdrew. As Thomas & Znanieck (1996:115) observed in their studies about Polish immigration, one should be careful not to ascribe too much significance to external forms and official purposes of immigrant institutions. Referring to Polish-American parishes, the authors say that the parish comprises much more than a religious association for common worship under the leadership of a priest.

Thus, the church is expected to provide far more than spiritual guidance and a pastor willing to listen to individual or family problems. The church is supposed to care for many other interests of the group by organizing potlucks, picnics, short trips to visit other Brazilian or Portuguese-speaking Adventist churches nearby. Fishing trips, barbecues, carnivals, garage sales, and fairs are also activities organized occasionally. In the case of Chino, the youngsters organize most of these outdoor events.

Moving Down the Social Ladder?

The functions of the church go far beyond those already mentioned. The church is also a center of information for newcomers, visitors, and travelers. It is a permanent open channel of communication with Brazil and the Portuguese world, the Hispanic world and the world as a whole. As I discussed in Chapter One, Brazilian Adventists do not migrate to the United States through the few Portuguese-speaking or Luso-

Brazilian Adventist churches spread through this country. Many times they find out about them after they are here. Once connected to them, their networks expand considerably. Nonetheless, no matter how much their networks may expand, they are still very restricted considering that this is a small and scattered population.

In fact, this is a quite restricted network when one looks at the little variety of jobs. Even so, there is some chance of mobility in spite of the lack of alternatives. For the female members of Chino, for example, there is mainly a way of improving financially: working towards becoming a registered nurse. Such an enterprise is not easy because it demands time and dedication, and requires having some money saved to invest in it. Besides requiring a reasonable knowledge of English, the board test for nurses requires specific knowledge of the profession. This is hardly possible for newcomers, especially in the case of those who have small children. Until their children are old enough to go to school, they baby-sit other kids helping in that way with the household income. Chances are that single women or married women with no children will achieve their goal of becoming a registered nurse sooner. The possibility of accomplishing this goal is also connected to one's age of immigration, social background and friendships here. In general, women are more willing to work to improve professionally between the ages of twenty-five and thirty-five years old, when they have yet had no children or when their effort may reflect on their children's education.

Housekeeping is like a rite of passage for many women in this community. It is the most easily available job and it does not require papers or language skills. Staying a housekeeper is nobody's goal, but it is the reality of many female members of Chino. They are usually the ones who only have an elementary school education, and come here when they are over thirty years old. They are usually single, divorced, or have grown children, and their social identity, in this case, is more connected with their children's accomplishments than with their own. The situation is quite similar for those men who work as janitors. These are the ones who, according to Pastor David Bravo, come here with no clear plans, but mainly to try their luck.

Edson Couto is about fifty-five years old and came a few years ago because his wife got a job as a registered nurse. The only time that we met I asked him what his job was and he answered, an economist. My question was not really clear, but he mentioned first his profession in Brazil; a few minutes later I learned that he works here as a janitor. I asked him how he feels about it. That is, how does he reconcile such different identities? In Brazil he worked as an economist for the São Paulo government. He said that he prefers not to think about it and always looks at himself in terms of his previous identity.[33] He is still an economist. He does not see himself as a janitor and, even though he does not feel like struggling to get a job closer to his qualifications, he believes that his work as a janitor is temporary. However, he has no plans to go back to Brazil since they have bought a nice house and their daughter is pretty much integrated into American life. I did not ask him what other factors made them come to the United States. That is, I do not know if working as an economist for the São Paulo government provided them with material conditions similar to the ones they have here.

Besides him and a few other newcomers, I only met two other people whose professional qualification in Brazil apparently contrasts with their jobs here. One of them was a high school teacher in the southern state of Rio Grande do Sul. The other one was a physician. The former has been working as a housekeeper since she came here, eleven years ago. The other one delivers pizza and has been here for about the same amount of time. These cases are rare, however. What is common in cases similar to these is that they will hold this kind of job only temporarily while working on a new degree or getting the necessary credentials to exercise the same professions they had in Brazil. That is, in general, the members of Chino will try to carve a living close to the one that they held in Brazil. In this case, their social background really matters because they feel they are going as far as their personal history will allow them. As Bourdieu proposes (1983:63),

> Whoever I am, if I may have the vocation to study but do not have the money to dedicate to it, I do not really have the vocation to study, that is, an effective vocation, a true one. All practices are subject always to receiving negative sanctions, therefore a secondary negative reinforcement, when the environment they face really is very distant from that to which they are objectively adapted. We may understand, by this

logic, that the conflicts between generations posit not opposing classes of ages separated by forces of nature, but by habits which are the fruit of different modes of production; that is, of conditions of existence that, by imposing different definitions of the impossible, the possible, the probable, or the certain, make some feel as natural or as reasonable practices or aspirations which others feel as unthinkable or scandalous, and vice-versa.

There are always other possibilities for those whose level of education is higher. Pedro Schneider, age 42, came to the United States through his in-laws. He met his wife and in-laws in Rondônia, northern Brazil. They moved there to start a business because their chances of success were higher than in their native states. At that time Rondônia and other northern states of Brazil were seen as a land of opportunities, the "last" Brazilian frontier. Things did not work as well as they expected, but they had yet one more "frontier" to try: the in-laws had a sister who had been living in Riverside for a couple of years and she urged them to join her and her family here. Despite having a Pastor's education, for seven years Pedro worked here at menial jobs. Last year, encouraged by one of his friends who is going to spend four years in Azerbaijan, he applied to work for the same period of time as a missionary. Besides being a prestigious experience among the Adventists, it is a unique opportunity to save money. Missionaries generally receive several times more than the amount they need to survive, and thus end up saving a considerable amount of money.

The disparity between their professions and educational backgrounds in Brazil, and their jobs and way of life here is not only a problem for individuals in particular, but also for the Church. To provide means to motivate immigrants to pursue their professional goals, or something in between their goals and their concrete chances in a foreign world, is another function that the church is supposed to perform. Pastor David Bravo says,

> The church, besides being a meeting place for men and women with common goals, is also transformed into a type of therapeutic center. You go there to somehow surrender what you have or what you would like to have had and don't have,

and your frustrations, traumas. In this way the church is also transformed into a hospital. I observe that the majority of those who already bring their titles [degrees] from there and cannot integrate here in the same field live in a constant frustration. And we can't say that prayer, the Bible, or going to church will solve things. The thing is to try, and with some of them we have succeeded; they enter school to take some course where they might in some way reach a better level. And many of them go back to Brazil. But their return is not that great because after a certain while the person has started to set roots here. Either he married, had children, or acquired something which holds him here. And also the economic question, which is always difficult in Brazil. So he might even go back, but when he notices that the money which they took isn't enough to get what they would like or even already had here, then they try to come back and some go through a lot of suffering, because few can reenter America. But I think that the majority of those who go back are doing well in Brazil. Even if they haven't reached the dreams they had, they're in Brazil, right?

Regardless of social background in Brazil, the members of Chino are generally motivated to take a computer course, or something similar, in order to change jobs and improve chances of applying for permanent residence. However, the first generation usually ends up sticking forever to a job that provides them with the material comfort they consider indispensable, regardless of its status, and transfer their professional and material ideals to their children. Therefore, they start to rely on their children to achieve realization and to justify their enterprise of coming to the United States, which is a common phenomenon also among other immigrant groups.[34]

Jacob and Mirtes Hirsch came to the United States in 1964 with their five children. In Brazil he had gotten a college degree and worked as the manager of a coffee plantation. Things were going fine for them in Brazil, but they had a friend in Riverside who convinced them to come, arguing that here they would have more chances to succeed than in Brazil.

Here he has had different jobs but has spent most of the time working as a truck-driver. Although he questions the immigration process from the restricted point of view of his particular situation, he feels proud of his children's achievements. He took his time telling the story of one of his daughters, who got accepted at Harvard for a degree in Architecture and received a six thousand dollar award at the end of the course for being the best student of her class. Thus, if the first generation immigrants do not succeed in the terms they expected but their children do, they consider that they were right about their choice of coming. Educated in an American environment, their children will certainly be better prepared to realize their parent's American dream.

Coping with Illegality and Discrimination

Another aspect that has to be dealt with is the issue of illegality. Pastor Mockiuti has observed the following throughout his experiences with illegal immigrants in the United States:

> Illegality transforms the lives of people into an unknown, a constant insecurity. It generates a set of situations in the family which are tremendously bad. Fear, insecurity. You know that if an illegal [alien] is caught there on the street corner he is deported. So he doesn't feel secure to establish roots here. If he goes to buy anything, he thinks, this here, if I am caught, will I take it with me or leave it behind? So he deprives himself of many things because he is insecure. He has money to take a trip, to see Canada, for example, or another state, but just because of the fact that he has to cross the border, he doesn't go. He may want to go by plane, but he may be checked on the plane. He is a trapped individual, he has no liberty to do what he likes, even though he might have some money to do it.

Even under the pressure that the condition of being illegal imposes on people there are different ways of coping. Pastor Bravo calls attention to different ways of dealing with the problem according to the individual's social position in Brazil. He says,

I would say that the background of the individual is very important in determining his integration here in the United States. What the individual was there, the education he received will help him for good or bad to face any reality, including that of being an illegal. So he says either "I face illegality like many, I hide, dodging it and finding a way," or if the individual is more enlightened, he saves 3 or 4 thousand dollars and finds a lawyer to get him residency. Or before this he may get a student visa. With this visa he can work and study, he can join a company and after he concludes his studies he can get a job contract which will end up normalizing the situation.

Some members who have been illegal at some point of their trajectories here suggest that there is a certain discrimination from the legalized members of the Church against the ones who are not legalized yet. It seems that there is a certain fear of having the image of the church connected with illegal immigration, but there is also a certain acceptance of the idea that laws are correct no matter whom they benefit.

João Cândido, whose legal residence is being processed, told me that he has never been discriminated against in regards to color, or to the region where he lives in Brazil and so forth. The only thing that made him feel uncomfortable was the question of illegality. He says, "I felt discrimination from people in relation to this question of illegality. They kept wanting to know how we were, showing concern, but deep down we thought that they were only testing us. It's as if they were always thinking of our situation, understand? And theirs too, of course."

These aspects aside, illegality also lowers a person's self esteem. For instance, several times I tried to schedule an interview with Mari Costa, age 52, and an immigrant since 1992. She would always find an excuse not to meet me. One day, tired of looking for excuses, she looked at me and said, "why the hell do you want to interview me? I have nothing to tell, I'm not even legal!"

If the issue of legality constitutes a huge problem for some people, it does not seem to bother others much. Here I am no longer referring to the members of Chino, where legality seems to be an important issue. I am broadening my reference group and talking about other Brazilians I interviewed in Los Angeles. Paulo Castro is thirty-five years old and has lived in the United States for eighteen years. His father is a businessman in Brazil and has an upper middle-class status. He told me that illegality never prevented him from doing anything he wanted. He says, "This story about not doing something because one is an illegal [alien] also works as an excuse, see? I was here illegally until I married and I always did everything I wanted and I sincerely think that I had worse problems on account of my English than because I didn't have a visa. I acted as if I was as legal as any American – who would doubt someone with such a straight face?"

Magali Cademartori, age 31, a Brazilian journalist, shares with Paulo the same ideas about illegality. She says,

> There are a lot of "jet set" people [bacana], daddy's kids, living here without any documents. You don't believe it? People who are the children of famous people in Brazil. ...They are so sure of themselves, they go anywhere... They dress well, generally have good English. ...Tell me, will it cross anyone's mind that they are illegal [aliens]?

Antônio Carlos, age 46, who works in the Brazilian cultural business in Los Angeles, told me the following when we were discussing the issue of legality: "You can bring all those unemployed illegal [aliens] you may have and I guarantee I will find work for everybody. ...Whether the job is better or worse will not depend on them being legal or illegal, it depends on their education and the talents they may have. But don't believe that story about not finding something good because they're illegal [aliens]."

I would say that these different ways of dealing with the issue of illegality depend on each individual's background and the ways their class histories have carved out their personalities, or rather, concrete chances of surviving well in both places. After all, living in the United States for a time is an adventure that is worthwhile regardless of how it may end. Brazil will always have a place to fit these people when they, for any reason, return. This situation is totally different from that of those who are gambling everything on a trip to the United States.

In any case, going back to the specific case of the church of Chino, the chances of obtaining success through Chino network do not depend only on the network itself, but also on the social background of each one of its members. After divorcing and selling her house in Brazil, Goretti Souza, age 38, decided to come to the United States. She came with her two boys, the youngest with Down's syndrome. She had learned that she would find here the best treatment for his problem. She came as a student, enrolled in the Graduate Program in Education at La Sierra University. She had never met anybody from the Church of Chino, but as soon as she came to Riverside, she was told about the "Brazilian" Adventist church of Chino. A couple who are friends of mine, who usually help newcomers start organizing their lives here, helped her get a social security card for herself and her children, gave her directions on how to obtain her driver's license, and also gave her many other tips about renting apartments, buying a car, about cheap places to buy groceries, where to find Brazilian food and so forth. I met her at Chino a few times. I was told later that she considered it too far away to attend and preferred attending La Sierra church because it is located near her home. She brought some ten thousand dollars with her to start her life here. After the first quarter less than half of that amount was left. She had to start looking for something to do in order to save her money. The only job that her Brazilian friends could get her was housekeeping. She did not feel comfortable with such an idea. The money would not be enough to keep up with her budgetary needs and, besides, what good was her Brazilian degree in education? Altogether disregarding the suggested alternative, she started investing in a nursing career. Meanwhile she has gotten help from several people. The church of Chino itself promoted a fundraising event to help her pay her rent. Now, my friends told me, they are praying for her to get a husband because they do not think that she can make it otherwise. The couple of times that I met her I did not notice the willingness and submission that usually move most of the immigrants. She has always been very critical about everything in Riverside, which is her experience of the United States. It seems that what she had nourished for many years as a dream turned out to be a nightmare, and the main reason for this, I would say, was her lack of information about immigrant life in the United States. In any case, she has been here for almost two years, spent already all the money she brought with her, quit studying, but has not yet worked on the available menial jobs. I was told that she is managing to survive because her ex-husband recently immigrated to New York and has sent her some money.

The need to also have the church as a space for entertainment has to do with the socio-economic limitations of these immigrants. First of all, the ones who have been here for a shorter time and are still struggling for a secure job, work all week long and do not have other spaces or the time for entertainment. Their workload is such that many times they do not even have time to socialize with their own family.

The Pastor of a recently founded Brazilian Adventist church in Las Vegas, while on a visit to Chino, compared the life of an immigrant with the life of an American citizen. He said that everybody else works, eats, sleeps, and has some fun. An immigrant works, works, works and still has to work. The situation worsens a great deal in the case of illegal immigrants with no special skills. Pastor Mockiuti says,

> The jobs of illegals are the worst, not only in terms of wages or quality but also in hours. They work the worst hours, they work all night long, till day-break, or after midnight. So what happens is that the very job impedes a tie and a relationship with other members of the family. So Sunday comes around and the father could be at home, but he is working. On Saturday he is working too. The child is at home, but the father isn't, because he is a low-income earner, and he has to work not only one job, but two, three. He works full-time during the week and a second job on the weekends, just to be safe. Normally this happens with illegals because they earn very little. And if he gives himself the luxury of being in America and wanting to live in a good house because he is in America, and that is the idea we have, I'm going to America to live in a good house, then he will kill himself. He dies, and he dies from materialism.

In many cases, the church becomes the immigrants' only space for entertainment. However, providing the word of God and amusement is not the only way Chino works. Chino is also a space for learning about how to get by as an immigrant and how to widen networks. It is a space to learn about American society as its members interpret it.

Even though there is not a variety of jobs and professions among Chino members, their socialization in American society is broader and more varied that one would expect. It is worth noting that the universe of their jobs is not the only means of interaction with Americans or of being connected to the American way of life. Through their children and their schools they also have other spaces of interaction with Americans. And they soon understand, as I did, that it is more appropriate to refer to American "ways" of life instead of an American "way" of life. In other words, as soon as they arrive here they find out that their expectations about the United States will never be more than expectations. Reality is going to consist of each particular way of getting by in order to achieve something somehow connected to their expectations.

Diane has been in Riverside since 1993. When she came she knew no English and had no children. Now she has two children and knows enough English to take the certified nursing assistant test. During these years she has worked as a baby-sitter and a housekeeper for both Americans and Brazilians. Lately, after learning some English, she has started working with a building management company, and she is also working toward becoming a registered nurse. When I asked about her feelings toward the United States and Americans she explained that at first, when she did not know any English, she would feel intimidated and totally uncomfortable with their way of relating to her. Now she simply says,

I got used to Americans and I don't really care about them. It's as if they didn't exist, understand? They are not part of my world, and neither am I part of theirs. They are very strange. Their lives are from work to home. We Brazilians are very different from Americans, they are more distant. Their way is different, they're not into parties, they don't like a lot of conversation. If they have a TV, then everything is ok. But I am satisfied here. There's the people from the church, and me and my husband are buying a house that we would never have dreamed of in Brazil! In Brazil, no way did we have the economic level to own a house like this! I was poor in Brazil.

Here I am poor but I have a house, a car and I don't need to wash my clothes by hand!

In the case of those who come here to try their luck, the relationship with white Americans is basically a relationship between employer and employee, as João Cândido notes:

I haven't had good relationships with white Americans. Those who were my supervisors always discriminated me tremendously. They think that because we are foreigners we have no rights. For example, I have 2 days off each week, and she found ways of calling me for the smallest things on my days off. And in our company when you are on your day off they can only call you in case of an emergency, and an emergency means water, fire, and blood. Nothing else justifies being called. And on Fridays, when I was at prayer services with my family, she would knock on my door to talk about things for the next Monday. I'd say I wouldn't answer, but one day she even came into my house. Oh, I hate this woman so much that I lose my mind when I speak about her and remember what she used to do to me. It was hell, everything I did she thought was badly done. This supervisor now also hates Brazilians. Nobody knows why. She looks as if she's Jewish. I also see in white Americans a great falseness. That American smile scares me a lot, you know? That doesn't come from deep inside in any way. But if you think about their lives. ...When they are small they spend the whole day with a babysitter. ...Then they grow, they are alone when they come home from school. They have no friendship within their own family, who will they be friends with? The other thing also, I think they are so isolated and are afraid to interact because they don't trust other people's feelings. It seems as if they are afraid of being rejected.

The quotation above, however, does not represent the average experience that members in Chino have had with white Americans. It generally seems that those who came here a long time ago had fewer problems than the newcomers. Yet, even just considering the newcomers, the situation varies in each case and depending on where each one goes. For instance, Pastor Wagner Kuhn is here to get a doctorate in Theology at Fuller Theological Institute. Most of his colleagues come from other countries, so the environment is quite international and the relationships between people do not necessarily follow the American way. His wife, on the other hand, has had a different experience while working as a nurse at Loma Linda hospital. She felt stronger discrimination on the part of white Americans, but also on the part of other organized ethnic groups that work there, such as Filipinos. I would speculate a bit further and propose that racism and discrimination are expressed differently depending on the physical features and personal character of each immigrant. I am not suggesting that the weight of racism can be neutralized in determined cases, but I am saying that those who do not succumb easily are more likely to make it. These, of course, are the ones whose previous histories and social references give them strength.

Sara Cruz, age 59, who has a law diploma from Brazil, and has been in California for ten years, started working as a baby-sitter and bought the house where she lives because her employer signed the necessary papers for her to obtain a loan. She is deeply grateful to him. But in her current job she basically feels mistreated by everybody: whites, blacks, Hispanics. She explains, "that's my position, I am a teacher's helper, which is the lowest position at school, and everyone feels that they can step on me."

There are specific reasons why a person holding a law degree cannot find a job better than the one Sara has: 1. Not all law degrees have the same value. 2. She was almost 50 when she moved to the United States, and not really willing to invest in validating her degree here. 3. Her English is not good enough to allow her to explore better alternatives. And finally, she is dark skinned. Nonetheless, I argue that the discrimination that she experiences at her workplace is much more connected with her position there than with any other factor. The problem of racist discrimination against immigrants, as Castles and Kosack propose (1973:2), must be interpreted as connected to the function that immigrants generally have in the socio-economic structure, and not the other way around. In other words, color or ethnicity cannot be regarded as the determinants of immigrants' social position because their position has been already determined beforehand.

That is, immigration is motivated to supply specific labor demands (Piore 1979). This confirms what I have been arguing, i.e., that integration into the receiving society is a process seriously influenced by the class position of the immigrant in his native country. A certain general discrimination against all immigrants results from the belief (and ignorance) that they are all the same.

Brazilianness in a Brazilian-Portuguese-American Protestant Community

It was potluck day when I first went to the church of Chino. After several months without seeing and eating a complete Brazilian lunch, I could not feel happier seeing all that food displayed on that long and large table. There were black beans, rice, green salad, farofa (manioc flour fried with oil and garlic), and an assortment of vegetarian soufflés and pies. Generally the potluck is a monthly activity and it is always scheduled for the third Saturday of the month. However, whenever the members of Chino have a special reason, they offer extra potlucks. For instance, the first day that I was there members of the church were involved in a scavenger hunt that lasted about three months. The three groups competing were constantly organizing special events to raise money. There were barbecues, garage sales, and many other activities. All these occasions were very opportune ones to meet new people or engage in longer conversations with some of them. The competition in itself brought about hidden disputes or problems between members. Simultaneously, however, it promoted a constant atmosphere of feasting. Almost everyday something was going on. It was by listening to the complaints of some people that I learned about Seventh Day Adventists' vegetarianism. Even though vegetarianism is not a requirement of the Seventh Day Adventist church, it strongly recommends abstinence from meat, as well as alcohol and tobacco. The youngsters, particularly those coming from Rio Grande do Sul, still maintain meat in their diets and have barbecues as the center of most of their gatherings. Those members who have been able to change diets or have been raised in vegetarian families would not miss a chance to criticize the "carnivores." The newly converted are also quite radical in relation to what the church theoretically recommends.

The competition also opened space for the rise of new leaderships, which caused envy and jealousy among already settled leaders. However, it was not serious enough to prevent the game from being rejuvenating and agreeable, and despite a certain tension because all three groups wanted to win, when the competition ended there was a felling of nostalgia. Everybody was saying that they enjoyed the game very much. So did I.

By the way of games, in contrast with many other Brazilian communities in Los Angeles, the Brazilians of Chino did not arrange meetings involving all members of the church to watch the 1998 World Cup Soccer games. I talked to some of them about this issue and they said that they did form small gatherings to watch certain games. However, it is complicated to have more people for several reasons, such as their work schedules, ages, and drinking and eating habits. In other words, when Brazil is playing and winning in world cup soccer championships even the Adventists feel like celebrating with a bottle of beer or some wine. The ones who feel like doing so will not watch the match with those who disapprove of drinking alcohol. In general, the world cup atmosphere took over everybody considerably, even though once in a while the Pastor and other invited ministers would criticize the frantic spirit that possesses everybody in those circumstances. These occasions are also very opportune moments to observe how differences between generations are expressed.

The issue of Brazilianness and/or Americanization is always brought about through the dialogue between generations. The youngsters and their attitudes are always a problem or a reason for the older members to apologize to outsiders. At the end of one wedding party I attended, the so-called youngsters started to dance the Macarena. Pastor Mockiuti approached me and said, "please do not jump to conclusions because they are excitedly dancing and so forth, this is a surprise for me too. Besides, this does not say much about who they really are."

Several times I heard reproachful comments about the clothes that female teenagers wear. Dresses which cling to the body so much that the outline of their panties is visible, dresses with low cut backs or fronts, or even mini-skirts are all seen as indecent and inappropriate. Attire, and the forms that relationships with boyfriends take, are the aspects of Americanization that most concern the Brazilian parents. It is interesting to observe that Americanization still has a pejorative connotation among the parents, regardless of their age. For them, Americanizing means becoming "way too modern," especially in terms of sexual freedom for women.

The strong reaction against certain values of the American way of life seems paradoxical considering that in general all parents are striving to get closer to mainstream values, or hoping that their children will accomplish assimilation as they could not. Therefore it seems acceptable to have comfortable houses, cars and other consumer items, but the adoption of other "American" values is a problem still. In other words, they accept American patterns of consumerism as desirable and reasonable, but they reject certain behaviors connected to the same patterns, such as sexual experience for women before marriage, a phenomenon that is observed also among other immigrant communities (Brodkin 1988).

Pastor Mockiuti talks about problems between parents and children produced by the faster assimilation of their children into mainstream values and behavior.

I think that one of the biggest problems we have to face is the problem of the culture. Most of us were not prepared to be here because the culture is very different. For example, here at 18 the father tells his own son that it's time to take care of life. This is a consensus, the son already grows up knowing that when he is 18 there will be no more space for him in that house. He has to make it on his own. So our children who are used to our paternalism see the Americans like this and become totally confused. This causes a very difficult situation in their minds. I have here cases in which the children continue thinking like Brazilians in regards to their background, but who have adopted the culture from here. For example, the question of the relationship of the young man with his girlfriend: here it is much more common for the boy to live with the girl. This generates an anguished situation with his parents, the parents see this, and they complain. The son, on the other hand, we speak with him, and he says, I know I am wrong, but here things are like this. I believe therefore that acculturation is a great source of problems. Because we want to maintain our culture, but it doesn't make sense in the world where we are. In short, this whole story of acculturation is very hard for us, the parents. Early on, when we arrived but had not yet dominated the language, we would unite more, talk more, remain closer. But I have noticed that from the moment in which we begin dominating the language, this link which was created is lost. And this generates a problem inside the family. Because for the parents who learn, as is our case, to raise their children closely, it seems as if we are losing our children. There it looked as if they were simply fulfilling a normal cycle, but since this is a country which is not ours, it looks as if we are losing our children. They are going out with people who are not of our culture, don't speak our language, are from families whose values we do not know, so this generates a large anxiety. Without mentioning that in this story where everyone here has to work, the mother is not as present as she used to be in Brazil.

Regular problems of acculturation such as the ones described above worsen when children do not physically identify either with the mainstream white American group or with other "ethnics." Lucas, whose mother is a white Brazilian and father is a black Brazilian, had difficulty finding the right group to socialize with. He was born here, and now he is about six feet tall and has an appearance that fit both the Chicano or African-American stereotypes. But his family would not allow him to identify with either group because they were seen as "marginal" and his parents did not want to raise him as marginal. Thus he was constantly dissuaded from hanging out with those groups that he could more naturally approach. On the other hand, he never felt accepted among white Americans. Against his parents' will he went through a phase in which he adopted and was adopted by the black community. Later he switched to the Chicanos, and now, after getting in trouble for consorting with the "wrong kind," he is finally taking advantage of his ambiguous ethnicity to socialize with "all kinds."

I saw other Brazilian parents with dark skinned children who expected them to assimilate into American society through their association with white Americans. They hardly understand that the process of "whitening" that is so common to Brazilian racist ideology does not work in the United States. Thus, in general, the children are personally blamed for being unable to succeed through the channels their parents expect them to, which, again, is well explained by Stolcke (1993:33): "if the self-determining individual, through persistent social inferiority, seemed to be incapable of making the most of the opportunities society offered to him, this then had to be due to some essential, innate and therefore hereditary deficiency. The person, or better even, his or her biological endowment, rather than the socioeconomic order was to be blamed for this."

CHAPTER 4

The Brazilian Women's Group: A Place to Feel at Home

The Brazilian Women's Group began almost by chance. Six Brazilian friends who usually had dinner together once a month started inviting other Brazilian friends to join them. Before they knew it they were too many to comfortably have dinner together in a restaurant. That is when they decided that their monthly dinner would be held in their own houses. Today, almost four years since the first informal meetings, the group has grown, and become a non-profit organization that brings together some 200 Brazilian women, although only one fourth of them are active members.[35] The monthly dinner has become a tradition and the group already has a history to tell. That story can be approached in different ways, but I will start by taking a quick look at some issues of its monthly newsletter, which has accompanied and briefly recorded the history of the group since September 1996. The first newsletter, for instance, brings comments about the September party, announces the host house for the following month and has also a short section of tips and another with classified announcements. In the section that reviews the previous party there is some indication of the social position of these women: "Our last party, held at BB's cozy house located in the Bel Air Mountains, was a total success. Thirty-five members of our group showed up at the nice wine and cheese meeting."

Even though the group has had its composition slightly changed over its four years of existence, it still keeps the imprint of the social position of its original nucleus. Despite efforts against this, the group is still identified as being composed of Brazilian women who belong to the middle or the upper-middle classes. Either married to Brazilians or Americans, these women are seemingly nostalgic for a space to exchange ideas, tips, and to converse in Brazilian Portuguese. Still commenting on September's party they say: "It was a very agreeable night where many ideas to invigorate the group came out, such as Portuguese classes for children, the celebration of Brazilian traditional feasts, and the creation of a classified section and a section for tips in the monthly newsletter."

A desire to create spaces to cultivate Brazilian identity is clearly seen when they show concern about teaching Portuguese to their children or celebrating Brazilian traditional feasts. This is emphasized by the idea of creating and expanding a network for exchange and support. The newsletter that I have been referring to, for instance, offers tips for Brazilian newcomers on how to choose schools for their children in Los Angeles (they suggest buying the *Parent's Guide to LA*), and where to buy household items (*Bed, Bath & Beyond* and *Pier 1*). They also suggest a Gym Club (*for Women Only*) for those Brazilian women who live in the San Fernando Valley. The last tip is about a Brazilian market in Culver City where Brazilians can "kill" their homesickness by buying Brazilian traditional food, drinks, and spices. Finally, the classified announcements are about Portuguese classes for children.

The content of the newsletter suggests that the group was formed as a space to feed and affirm Brazilianness by connecting people whose different ways of integrating into Los Angeles' world have led them to be somehow isolated from their Brazilian identity. Offering Portuguese classes for children, for instance, suggests that many Brazilian women have not been able to teach Portuguese to their Brazilian-American children, probably because they integrated into American society individually and somehow became disconnected from Brazil and Brazilian culture. What would lead them to undertake now the enterprise of teaching their mother tongue to their children? What would justify this return to their roots? Also, which Brazilian women would put together a group interested in affirming Brazilian identity in Los

Angeles? What Brazilian identity do they divulge and advertise? And what are the dynamics of the group? [36]

Brazilian Women's Group: A Profile

The Brazilian Women's Group members and guests are concentrated in the city or county of Los Angeles.[37] There are also members scattered throughout Orange, Ventura and San Bernardino counties.[38]

Most of the data used to build the following tables was obtained through informal conversations with the Brazilian Women's Group participants that I met at the fifteen monthly gatherings I attended between November 1997 and July 1999. I am also using information obtained through long tape-recorded interviews with fifteen of these women. About 40 out of the 65 women surveyed are actual members of the group. If I had built my tables based only on these 40 cases, the general profile would be closer to the "petit-bourgeois image" that the group has tried to get rid of and which I will discuss further on the next sections of this chapter.

Table 12 - Birthplaces of Brazilian Women's Group Participants by Region in Brazil

Region	Frequency	Percent
Central West	3	4.6
Northeast	12	18.5
Southeast	47	72.3
South	3	4.6
Total	65	100.0

Table 13 - Residence of Brazilian Women's Group Participants by Region in Brazil

Region	Frequency	Percent
Central West	4	6.2
Northeast	7	10.8
Southeast	51	78.5
South	3	4.5
Total	65	100.0

Although similar to the case of Chino, where the majority of the members come from the southern regions, the Brazilian Women's Group, as table 12 shows, concentrates more people born in the Southeast, which comprises the states of Rio de Janeiro, São Paulo, Minas Gerais and Espírito Santo. Unlike the case of the members of Chino, there is a considerable percentage of participants who are from the Northeast. Such a fact can be explained as a function of the special interest Americans have in Bahia and the networks established on such interest, and also because of the considerable presence of women connected to Odebrecht, a company headquartered in Salvador, Bahia. When tables 12 and 13 are compared, we still see the same pattern we observed in the case of Chino. That is, many people who were born in the Northeast had already migrated to the Southeast.

The increase of people in the Central West region is due to the Brazilian capital being located in the state of Goiás, therefore creating another pole for the concentration of power.

Table 14 - Age of Brazilian Women's Group Participants

Age (in years)	Frequency	Percent
21-30	6	9.2
31-40	22	33.9
41-50	31	47.7
> 50	6	9.2
Total	65	100.0

The age mode of the participants is 44 years, but 81.6 percent of the participants have ages that vary between 31 and 50 years old. Most of them came when they were between 20 and 35 years old. I found only two cases who came at the ages of 47 and 58 respectively. The first case came after divorcing her Brazilian husband,

Sometime after my marriage ended I came to spend a few months here with a Pentecostal church. I had always been Catholic, but I was curious to know Pentecostalism in the United States. When I returned to Brazil, after three months, I got a job as a tour guide. I would visit here and Europe. I came here in the summer, and I began to see that things went better here, and that my way out was to stay here. I wanted to marry again, to make a life for myself again. I was born to be married, my mind was made to be married. I had no chance of either a good job or a new marriage in Brazil, with my age, 47 years! (Elizabeth, age 67).

After a year of living in the United States she married an American man who was a member of the same church she attended. Among the participants of the group a second marriage to an American man is also a relatively common event. In fact, a second marriage represents 10.8 percent of the women's marital status, as table 15 shows.

Table 15 - Marital Status of Brazilian Women's Group participants

Marital Status	Frequency	Percent
Single	5	7.7
1st Marriage	45	69.2
2nd Marriage	7	10.8
3rd Marriage	1	1.5
Divorced	4	6.2
Widowed	3	4.6
Total	65	100.0

There are interesting facts to observe on table 15. The first is that 92.3 percent of the participants are or have been married. The second is that the percentage of women who are in their second marriage is higher than that of single women. Third, a total of 18.5 percent of the participants have gone through divorce. The difference between the Brazilian Women's Group and Chino in regards to marital status is that in Chino I did not find the second marriage category, even though they recently celebrated two marriages where one of the partners had had a divorce. I would suggest that the almost total absence of second marriages among the members of Chino has to do with the fact that the divorced people are just recently divorced, but I would also suggest that it has to do with the limits of their network.

Table 16 - Nationality of Spouses of Brazilian Women's Group   Participants

Nationality	Frequency	Percent
Brazilian	20	33.3
American	36	60.0
Argentine	2	3.3
French	1	1.7
German	1	1.7
Total	60	100.0

The majority (66.7 percent) of the married women in the group are or were married to non-Brazilians. Sixty percent are married to American men. This is almost opposite to the situation in Chino, where 81.9 percent of the members (not only women) are married to Brazilians. This fact might be helpful in understanding why these women invest in creating a space where they can express and cultivate their Brazilianness. The high percentage of marriage between the Brazilian Women's Group participants and American men also suggests that their process of integration into the world of Los Angeles is, in contrast with the Chino members' case, an example of individual integration, where assimilation occurs faster and is seemingly more complete.

Table 17 - Number of Children of Brazilian Women's Group Participants

No. of Children	Frequency	Percent
0	25	41.6
1	9	15.0
2	16	26.7
3	6	10.0
4	3	5.0
5	1	1.7
Total	60	100.0

As table 17 shows, 41.6 percent of the group participants do not have children. There is no connection between not having children and the spouse's nationality. In other words, the percentage of women with no children is similar whether they are married to Brazilian or American men. Based on interviews and casual conversations, I am led to believe that this considerably high percentage of women without children is mostly due to the fact that 1) Brazilian Women's Group members prioritize their careers and thus postpone their child-bearing age, and 2) Many of them have decided not to have children at all.

Table 18 - Year of Immigration of Brazilian Women's Group Participants to the United States

Year	Frequency	Percent	# of years in interval	% per year
1995-99	15	23.1	5	4.6
1988-94	25	38.5	7	5.5
1978-87	15	23.1	10	2.3
1968-77	9	13.8	10	1.4
Prior to 1968	1	1.5	-	-
Total	65	100.0		

Table 18 indicates that like the members of Chino, most of the Brazilian Women's Group members immigrated to the United States between 1988 and 1994. The percentage of newcomers is nearly half that of the period of highest immigration, which is significant especially when compared to the other group. That is, the percentage of newcomers in the group is three times larger than the percentage of newcomers in Chino. I believe that this difference is connected to the fact that a considerable number of newcomers are either students or spouses of Brazilian men working for Brazilian companies whose period of stay is limited to less than five years. Another reason is that Brazilian Women's Group network is broader and this favors the possibility of more newcomers.

Table 19 - Level of Education of Brazilian Women's Group Participants

Level of Education	Frequency	Percent
Elementary	8	12.3
High School	23	35.4
College	34	52.3
Total	65	100.0

Table 20 - Employment Status of Brazilian Women's Group Participants in the United States

Employment Status	Frequency	Percent
Housewife	25	38.5
Blue Collar	14	21.5
White Collar	26	40.0
Total	65	100.0

As in the case of Chino, there is also a relative congruency between educational levels of Brazilian Women's Group members and the type of job they hold in the United States. Out of the 52.3 percent expected to hold white-collar jobs, 40 percent effectively do. However, many of them work for Brazilian companies, which means that they do not really have to compete for jobs with Americans. The difference between the percentage of members holding college degrees and the members holding white-collar jobs is 12.3 percent. I would suggest that part of these women are those whose expectation of living in the United States for good does not justify their investing much on validating their Brazilian degrees and competing for jobs in the American market. Thus, while living in the United States, they focus on their tasks as mothers and housewives.

The most evident difference between this group and Chino is that the latter cannot afford unemployed housewives. That is, their wage is low enough to require both partners to work.

"A Space to Feel at Home..."

"The aim of the Brazilian Women's Group is to be a space where one can feel at home." Marina closed her farewell discourse at the meeting of July, 1999, with these words. She was leaving her unfinished term as president of the group to move to Brazil because her husband had been transferred.

Many other members referred to the monthly meetings as a space that should be preserved because it is a space where they *all* feel at home.

> I don't know if the group has reached its ideal maturity. That is, I don't know if they have achieved the goals that they are proposing. For now, I think they are crawling, trying to get somewhere. But I think the idea of getting together every month is a very good one to relieve the longing for that body language, the laughs, the jokes, the food; in short, that Brazilian atmosphere (Elizabeth, age 67).

> I don't go every month, but I like it very much when I do. I always meet someone interesting with whom I talk about interesting things. The marvelous food, the gossip, the jokes, the laughter, all this is very pleasant and rejuvenating (Mara, age 48).

> For me the monthly dinner is the best break I can have from my routine as a wife, mother, and homemaker. I tell my husband (a Brazilian), "today you take care of the children because I'm going to have some fun." And how much fun I have! I like the gossip, I like to see how the people are dressed. I think some of the women are a bit annoying, putting on airs, but we find that anywhere. I like most of them (Alice, age 35).

Even though most of the members or visitors whom I interviewed agreed that the meetings are a space to feel at home, a few women said that they never really felt at home at the monthly dinner. These women are generally those who go once or twice and give up participating because they do not feel comfortable enough among the members of the group. They feel somehow inadequate because are not treated with the warmth and attention they expected:

> I never felt comfortable at those dinners. I might have had the bad luck of only finding and talking to the wrong people. But

for the love of God, I went there twice, and everybody to
whom I was introduced looked at me with that air of
superiority and asked "And you, child, what are you doing
here?" "How long have you been here?" The feeling I had was
that there was either something wrong with me or with them.
I became fed up and quit completely. Well now, if the idea of
going to this type of event is to have fun, why would I submit
myself to those kinds of constraints? (Denise, age 27).

I don't feel comfortable with the majority of those people.
That is, I meet a friend here and gossip a while, laugh a little.
But I always have the feeling that they are measuring me up,
testing me out, and deep down, I don't believe that they see me
as an equal. Some try to treat me as an equal, but I think that
they still see themselves as superior, measuring me by the
same standards used in Brazil (Telma, age 46).

The two women above have different social backgrounds, which
prevent me from immediately connecting their feelings of discomfort to
their social position. The first one has a college degree, was born and
lived all her life in São Paulo, and comes from an upper middle-class
family. She met her American husband when on vacation in Europe. I
met her only once at a meeting organized by a mutual friend to talk
about "our" immigrant experiences and my research. She dressed in
casual name-brand clothes, wore simple fine jewelry and had a modest,
cheerful and self-confident attitude. Her education and upbringing can be
perceived through her manners and clothing. In other words, any person
able to classify social position by manners, fashion, speech and other
apparent elements in Brazil would classify her as belonging to upper
middle-class. There is, however, an element that might suggest a
different classification: her accent. She is from the interior of São Paulo
state, and where you come from is an important sign of distinction. In
any case, I am not proposing that the group members and visitors give
the same treatment to everybody regardless of the way they present
themselves. Appearance, an important indicator of social position,
really matters. What is chic? What is tacky? Who is eccentric? When
only elements of appearance are at stake the chances of accurate
classification decrease, as the following explanations suggest:

Here in the United States it is harder to distinguish who is who than in Brazil. Here you go to Ross and buy a name-brand blazer for 15 dollars. In Brazil there is no Ross, and you can easily distinguish people merely by the clothes they are wearing. Of course, a lower class person would not even know how to take advantage of what a Ross has to offer. Because this story of class depends on the education, family education, and not on the kind of education you acquire by going to school, understand? You know the saying that one does not learn how to samba by going to regular school? After all, it is not only the clothes that matter, it is the hair, the way one walks, sits, eats. It's in the way one converses and also about what one speaks of. It is in one's [personality]. But here in the United States you have in general the false impression that everyone is or could be middle class. This is good in one way, it seems more democratic. But if you seek distinctiveness it is very bothersome (Virginia, age 48).

I like living here in the United States because everyone is equal. Everyone has the ability to dress decently. But there are many haughty Brazilians who come here and don't like this very much because in Brazil only the rich dress well (Telma, age 46).

Americans have this cult of the middle-class, democracy, and such, but all of them are impressed when you include a few French words in your speech. And in terms of clothing the secret is this, you can follow the policy of being like everyone else and put on these stodgy, or elegant, clothes, following the colors of the season and such. Or you can dress more casually and throw a *fois* around your neck and there, you are elegant; everyone treats you well (Lícia, age 36).

She told me she preferred living in France because the French are more refined, traditional, and polite. She said the difference between France and the United States is that France has a history, tradition, and a sense of taste which has been perfecting itself through many centuries, and the United States has economic power, but no pedigree. She came here because of her husband's job and because she thinks it is important that her children speak English fluently, because English is the language of business, isn't it? But she says she'll return to living in France (Sônia, age 38).

What is considered good or bad taste in the United States and Brazil is always discussed in the group. There is also a certain general understanding among some members that Brazilian fashion follows more closely French fashion, which is supposedly more sophisticated than the American. Despite these general and vague considerations, I observed distinction and social position being established based on levels of integration, or, say, Americanization. In this case, Americanization means skillfulness in American culture. Therefore, social position in Brazil would not guarantee by itself an immediate transference and/or acknowledgement of status for many different reasons. First, even though the industrial areas, São Paulo and Rio de Janeiro, have centralized money, fashion, and the means of mass communication, different parameters are still used to determine social status in different regions in Brazil. Elements that define taste vary from place to place, and the words "tacky" and "sophisticated" have different contents in different regions. Second, what is true in relation to regional variations of determinants of social status in Brazil is also true for the United States. That is, there are also several standards for measuring social status in the United States (Bourdieu 1984). Third, other elements particular to the condition of immigrants are added to the usual elements of distinction operating in either or both societies. And fourth, different upbringing and social status produces different classifications.

There are different explanations for the discomfort that Denise felt when she twice attended the group monthly meetings. I shall attempt the following explanations: 1) She did meet the "wrong" people – meaning that she met women whose social position, both in the United States and Brazil, prevent them from recognizing tastes beyond the limits of what is tasteful in their social positions. 2) She met women whose status in the group is superior to their social status. This gives them confidence to act superior within the boundaries of the group and, sometimes, even take vengeance on those who are higher socially. In this last case, what motivates action x or y is not ignorance/arrogance, but the knowledge of a provisory advantage. Still, like she asked, "what is the point of wasting my time in a place where I do not feel at home?"

Thus, the Brazilian Women's Group is a space where Brazilian women can hypothetically feel at home, but they do not necessarily feel that way for the reasons discussed above. In the case of Telma (see quote on page 126) the constraint is produced by her belief that the members of the group pretend that their environment is free of prejudice when in fact it is not. That is, she feels that her social position is an obstacle to feeling accepted in the group.

I talked to older members of the group as well as current members of the board of directors about these different complaints, and they interpret them as follows:

C – Unfortunately, we have never been able to change the image of the group; many people think the group is a group of *dondocas* [hoity-toity matrons], a group for the elite, and, they say, what am I going to do there? But I don't consider myself elite, for the love of Christ!

M – Neither do I.

B – But you are elite, at least within the group, even if you don't want to be.

C – No, the group has a place for every one of us. On the other hand, each one of us makes a position for ourselves. For example, I'm not going to go to a dinner party and sit in a corner and feel inferior because I'm participating in a group where the majority is supposedly elite and I don't belong to that group. And so, because of this, I'm not going to take up the cause of the group? A cause which pays respect not only to the elite but to all us women as Brazilians? Am I going to merely continue criticizing the group without contributing anything? Of course not; you have to look at yourself, analyze and see what you effectively want to do, independently of what class you're in. I don't see why a person who works here [in the U.S.] as a janitor or a manicurist can't come and join us.

M – Creuza is a nanny.

B – But Creuza is probably well received because she cooks well, and...

M – But she is what she is.

C – She treats people well and is interested in helping out, and that's why.

M – Creuza is Creuza and she does not change because she joins the group or doesn't join us because she is working or because she isn't . . .

C – And neither is she treated differently because she is a good cook, no! Each one of us is good at something. Do you understand? Why isn't the girl who does your nails with us? She is an excellent manicurist, she could be here, why not? Therefore I think it is other people who create this type of barrier, we don't create it, or at least I don't feel this way, quite the contrary. At the same time I continue asking myself why we still haven't gotten it right.

I want to stress two points of their interpretation. The question of social position and correspondent spaces in the group and the question of not having "gotten right" the politics of the group. According to the above conversation, the group has available space for all women who want to join the group. In principle, everybody is equally accepted and their differences are equally appreciated, as long as one uses her talents to benefit the group. However, the group, according to their own evaluation, has not achieved the expected success. We have also seen that there are discordant opinions among different members and visitors to the group. In other words, some of them do not even feel comfortable going more than a few times to the monthly gatherings.

But I want to insist further on the difference between the reasons presented by Denise and Telma. The first one felt annoyed by the superficial way in which some members of the group want to establish distinction.

The second one apparently accepts the terms of the distinction such as established, and the reason why she does not feel comfortable there is because she believes that she does not belong to the group. That is, she does not fulfill the "required" criteria; she does not belong to the elite.

On the other hand, I observed for over two years that several members of the group, usually a part of the board of directors, make a sincere and steady effort towards increasing membership by motivating the invitation of as many women as possible and by developing policies that induce the visitors to join the group. In this fashion, one of the new features of the monthly newsletter is to list the name of the visitors present at the previous meeting. Names are listed again when the annual membership fee is paid and occasionally when a person writes an article, poem, short story, or special report, as well as when a person or somebody related to her has been granted an award or performed an exceptional deed.

Based on my readings of different opinions about the group and its dynamics, as well as on my experience as a member for two years, I am led to conclude that the group is a success from the perspective of certain members and a failure from the perspective of others. Therefore, there is a problem of a common collective identity that remains to be solved in order to put everybody at ease with respect to the ways that they will meet their plans and dreams. Again, the question is what kind of group (or community) do these women propose, and what kind of group have they been able to be?

From a Space to Chat to a Space for Politics: The Challenge of Changing Identity

While the Brazilian Women's Group was only a group of Brazilian friends meeting monthly to dine and chat, everything was apparently fine. Marina Cavalcanti, age 45, says that, "our problems began from the moment it was proposed that we transform that group of friends into a non-profit organization, without lucrative ends, and with specific goals. From that moment I saw that it was something that might turn out well or not."

Why would a group of Brazilian friends be suddenly interested in becoming a non-profit organization with certain aims and a plan of action? Claudia Capelo, age 43, explains that she was the one who proposed to drive the spontaneous energy of such a considerable number of women to something more useful and pragmatic. She says,

> The idea of transforming the group into a non-profit organization was mine. I proposed it because the group didn't address my expectations, and I was not satisfied in going every

month to meetings only to socialize, only to talk, only to
speak about the son who is in school or what one is doing in
L. A. and such. I thought that this was too little and that we
could take advantage of that energy, that large number of
women, to do something more besides making friends. And
so, I wanted something more. Ever since I arrived here in L.
A. in 1992, I always dreamed of seeing the Brazilian
community doing something for which they could be
recognized. And when I saw that this could be achieved
through this, I personally dove in. And I'm in this precisely
with this expectation of seeing us being able to do some work
with real repercussions for the Brazilian community. Well, at
that moment I was taking part in the Council of Citizens, at
the Consulate. That was the first year of the Council, which
was an initiative of the Brazilian government to motivate a
closer contact between the Brazilian consulates and the diverse
Brazilian communities throughout the world. The idea is to
have a council made up of people who serve in some way as a
link between the community and the consulate. I was part of
the council in the first and second year. So, at the council, we
would sit and speak together with the Ambassador about what
was happening in the community and this and that. And
within the group of Brazilian women I could see an enormous
number of them, and I began insisting that we needed to do
something more. The Ambassador himself one day suggested
it, why don't try to form a more organized group? Nowadays I
think that maybe 80 percent of the people who are part of this
group do not have this same interest. No one has effectively
spoken against the idea, but with time we began noticing that
if people don't volunteer to become more involved, to help out
more, it is because they are not really 100 percent in
agreement.

Indeed, transforming a spontaneous group of friends who meet
monthly to chat freely into a non-profit organization with the ambition
of promoting the Brazilian community in Los Angeles is a huge step
and demands an organization that is hard to accomplish when the
components of the groups are not really tuned in many aspects.

Thus, Claudia had the dream of promoting the Brazilian community in Los Angeles and convinced a few other participants that it was worth trying out this possibility. From May of 1997 on the group of Brazilian friends began the process of becoming the non-profit organization Brazilian Women's Group. Its purpose, they wrote in a flyer distributed in August of 1998, "is to promote the Brazilian culture to the American community and organize charitable events to help the less fortunate in Brazil and the United States."

Its goals are the following:
> To increase public awareness of the Brazilian culture.
> To work together with Brazilian businesses in L.A., helping them grow.
> To engage in activities that will promote the Brazilian community in Los Angeles.
> To organize charitable events.
> To promote cultural and social activities for the Group members.

The group has been promoting Brazilian culture in Los Angeles since 1997 by organizing public events such as festivals, shows, parties and other related activities in order to expand the understanding that Americans in general have of Brazilian culture. Claudia explains,

> The idea was to join and promote events that would pass on to Americans a broader idea of Brazil. We could put together a book fair, [or other] events which showed off a bit of our culture. Even the June Festival is something that I personally find tacky. I like the June festivals there in the Northeast [Brazil], out in the countryside and such. But in large cities in general, Los Angeles or São Paulo, Salvador, I always thought it somewhat tacky, out of place. (. . . .) I think that the Northeast, Ceará, Campina Grande, should really be the place for this. It's like carnival in Bahia that goes on all year. I think that the June festivals there are a part of the soul of the people. Thus the June festival outside these places is a bit forced [fake]. Even so it is something traditional, you know? It is part of our culture as a whole, and so I think it is nice that we have it, as long as we do it in organized fashion. Anything we do in organized fashion, which is pretty, and

professional, is something that we are showing to the outside, to Americans, something else Brazil has besides naked women. Because everybody has the idea that Brazil is beautiful women with exuberant bodies in small bikinis dancing on top of a stage.

It was, therefore, with this desire of promoting a knowledge of Brazilian culture beyond Carnival that the group started organizing its events. The first fundraising act was a joint event organized with City of Hope in October of 1997. "A Night in Rio" at the Beverly Hills Country Club drew 485 guests and raised $21,000.00, which was donated in its entirety to the City of Hope.

The event was evidently successful but it raised conflicting issues among the members. The main question was, "Why are we, Brazilians, working to give money to American institutions if they do not need it?"

Marta, ex-president of the group, explained to me the controversy over this issue as follows:

> The problem is the following. There is a faction among the directors of the group that thinks that we should primarily initiate campaigns to help Brazilian institutions in Brazil. I don't agree because I think that we are a very new group that has only recently been formed as an institution, and I think we still need to gain the confidence of the American so that we can ask the American to aid Brazil. So my strategy is to construct an institutional curriculum, and to shape an institution which promotes the image of Brazil in a positive way. And we are here to embrace any cause which we think is important. Like the City of Hope. They don't work with anybody, they work alone. We are together only because I had the good luck of meeting some people who were in love with Brazil and wanted to do something with Brazil. So the great disagreement is that there are people who think we should only carry out projects for Brazil. Why? Because Brazil is poor, and the U. S. already does a lot of fundraising and they don't need it. I say, people, in order to promote campaigns for Brazil, in order to be able to do anything, we first have to

create a name for ourselves here, and to create a name we must work with American enterprises. And by the way, for me, diabetics, cancer and aids patients, and the poor and hungry have no nationality. They may be from wherever. They are all in need. Second, we are learning how to run things with these guys. Because the way things are done in the United States are different from in Brazil. You may have been a fundraiser all your life, but here things are different. I even said this in the message to the president [of the City of Hope], "we profit and learn from those who know." So first we learn from those who know, and second, we are establishing a résumé. It's not easy, see? We wanted to do a project with Caring for Babies with Aids (CBA). We wanted to hold a June festival and donate the money to them. My friend, we had to submit ourselves to a complete interrogation, the president there asked me for a letter from the City of Hope, stating that we had worked with them, what we had done and how much money we had raised. Do you know what these institutions fear in supporting us? That we will want to promote ourselves at their expense. They don't want to muddy their names with just any group. This is why I said, people, we have to build ourselves a résumé!

Marta proposes going beyond nationalist claims of poverty or wealth in order to acquire the knowledge to operate and build a respectable résumé. However I have not found a single person who really agrees with her ideas, not even as a strategy to get started. In general, all members believe that everything that results from the work of the group should be donated to Brazilian institutions, not American. The argument is the same that Marta presented when discussing the reactions of some members of the board of directors "Americans do not need us, they have enough already!"

Like it or not, promoting events to raise money to donate to Brazilian charitable institutions seems to be the only appeal capable of motivating the action of some of these women. I witnessed inflamed debates over this issue. One of them told me "I won't employ a second of my time to work to donate money to American institutions, no way Jose! Plus, I think that Marta is particularly benefiting from the work of the group. I mean, she is working more for her self-promotion than for the group as a whole."

As far as I can see the person who told me this has never put in any time to do anything for the group anyway. She goes sporadically to the monthly gatherings. However, her general understanding of the purpose of the group, and destiny of its efforts is shared with several other members. But this is not all. In order to operate as professionally as Marta and Claudia want, the group needs the commitment of its members to other tasks beyond organizing and attending the monthly gatherings. The group could only succeed if other members besides those who make up the board of directors helped with all the work needed to organize events bigger than a monthly potluck. Counting on the help of other members revealed itself a very complicated enterprise. The lack of cooperation shows itself in different ways. Many of the participants of the monthly gatherings would not even contribute with the annual membership fee of 60 dollars. Marta says,

> The people don't pay! There are people who have been coming for three years and have never paid. I said, "people, this is a donation." There are some members in the board of directors who are more radical: they no longer send out bulletins!! They don't invite them here any more. I said, "people, if the person wants to come to all the dinners and not pay, that's on their conscience."

But there is lack of cooperation in other aspects too. Claudia explains,

> I spend a lot of time writing the newsletter, sending out millions of messages asking for help, opinions. In the matter of the election, we began advertising three months earlier, Contribute! Nobody called to say either yes or no, don't take a vote, disband the group. It is an impressive lack of commitment, totally. Only the board of directors is committed. For this reason I have increasingly asked myself if it is worth continuing to do this. Is it worth continuing the group? This is because the people are not clearly interested. When they go to the dinners they love it! Ah, this month's party was excellent, I saw so-and-so again! That's it!

Claudia is saying that the only support that she can expect from the majority of the participants is their occasional presence in the monthly gatherings. More than this is very rare and accidental. On the other hand, she is not willing to invest her time in maintaining a group whose only purpose is to get together once per month to chat, gossip, eat and laugh. She interprets the lack of interest in cooperating as a trait of the Brazilian character. She says, "the Brazilians are very competitive and only stick to something if they can take immediate advantage of it, otherwise they don't bother investing one second of their time." She adds,

> What I have been noticing is that some people come to the group with a particular interest. You, for example, came and stayed only because of your research. If their needs are in any way attended, these persons remain; they stick with it. Otherwise they disappear. We have examples of persons who come because they want to show some product by I don't know who, and so they offer their home, we set it up, but the real interest is in advertising the product. The next month they disappear! "Ah, I'll go there to see if there is some mother who will read stories to my child..." And so, you find it or not, but you give yourself the opportunity and give an opportunity to the group to meet other people. No one meets, or falls in love like that the first time with everybody else, understand? If only these same people were more open. You tried to do something and it didn't work, but, darn it, you discover that that group is a community, set aside your commercial side for a while, and try to have a little more emotion, be a little more united. And insist a bit more. We have a chance of doing something more. There are millions of people from various fields, we are all in some sort of activity. We would be able to do many other things, if this union existed, this mentality. And I ask if in our case, now, here in the board of directors, if we don't know how to pass on this message to people. Maybe we don't know how to do this, we are not getting it right. On the other hand, I see that every time someone calls me asking for something its with some ulterior motive, understand? That's fine, perfect, the group

functions also on this exchange of interests. We will not say, "No, don't come because your interests are different." In no way. We open the door so everybody can come in. And we ask people to come, insist that they participate.

When Marta left the presidency, her strategy of building up a résumé for the group by producing joint events with American institutions was left aside. But it seems that the main reason was not the members' disagreement with her politics, but the general unwillingness to help. In other words, the constituted group does not have the structure to support becoming a non-profit organization as dreamed by Claudia and Marta. Claudia explains: "My dream is to put together a larger event, something more substantial, more professional. The events that we hold are very basic, very homemaker-like. This thing about potlucks, every one bringing a dish, is something very small, you know? We have managed a few things, but they weren't what I would have liked them to be."

A question remains: why have they not been able to create a group closer to the one of their dreams? What is needed to operate at the level Marta wants?

Ever since the first president left, the production of public events has been reduced, and other money raising activities inside the group have been created, such as bingos, the production of shows, etc. The amount of money raised has diminished, but it is now being sent entirely to charitable institutions in Brazil. In 1999, for instance, the group donated $5,000.00 to a Brazilian orphanage. Yet, contrary to what Claudia dreams, the Brazilian Women's Group of today seems further away from the possibility of putting on events of the size she wants. I think that several explanations can be presented for understanding why Claudia's dream has not yet been realized.

There is a general concern among the group actual and potential members about their work or other kind of collaboration benefiting particular members, in this case, particularly benefiting the president and other members of the board of directors. Such concern is used to justify the unwillingness to collaborate with the group. However, I propose that it is not the action of a particular president or member of the board of directors that motivates these feelings. Instead, they seem to have been developed in the context of social relations in Brazil and that get reproduced here, especially in businesses among Brazilians. In Brazil or abroad, Brazilians seem to be followed by the ghosts created by a highly hierarchical and discriminatory society, a society whose elites have always survived at the expense of popular classes. Thus the feeling that somebody is, or might be taking advantage of us follows us like our own shadow. I want to convey that, in the case of the Brazilian Women's Group, the ones who take the pride also take the pain. In other words, if the members of the board of directors benefit at all from their status in the group, this is just one of the consequences of their work and dedication. Marta says,

> This work that I do with the group. . . My husband sometimes says, "My, if you only earned money for all the work you do for the group, [or even for] the time you answer phones!" "Look, I've heard of your group," "I don't know anybody around here and wanted to know if I could join your group." If you had any idea how much work it is to organize a group like this. It's monthly meetings, it's deciding what to do. The treasurer tells me how much money we have, what it is we can do. Make cards. Make banners. Let's work with this company, let's help that charity. How are we going to organize the event? Who is going to help? All the meetings I had with the City of Hope alone were crazy!

Thus, the Brazilian Women's Group is mostly a result of the work of a few Brazilian women who have the time and the determination to organize such an enterprise. The group has not relied on a systematic effort of many but on the extraordinary effort of a few. Whether coincidentally or not, these few are mostly married to Brazilians living here (either temporarily or permanently) in a position to claim or feel proud about Brazilian culture. A group with such a purpose could hardly be created by Brazilian women married to American men because these women have, in one way or another, given up their Brazilian identity for a more complete assimilation, except in those cases where their husbands maintain business connections with Brazil.

The Individual Pattern of Integration

Even though complete assimilation into American culture is more likely in the cases of those Brazilian immigrants married to Americans, assimilation is the quest of all who have chances of achieving it. One of the members of the board of directors, for example, only speaks English with her children even though her husband is also a Brazilian. No one is, in principle, against assimilation, but those women married to Brazilian men who are here because of their husbands' jobs, realize that their assimilation is very limited, as we can see from the following statements:

N - Here each person joins with his own culture, that's the way I see it. For example, I have a Korean neighbor, the other is Mexican, I talk to them for half an hour and that is it, more than that and I have nothing else to say to them.... That's why there's the need to get together with our own people.

C – I agree that we must dive into American culture. If we are living here, we have to adapt ourselves 100 percent here, but without forgetting that our country is Brazil and in what ways we can unite and do some things for ourselves. Do you know why? Because despite our trying to dive into this culture, we feel the need for that human warmth that the Brazilian has, we feel the need to share those experiences which are ours, and that is why we have to help ourselves in some mutual way....

N – But this is a problem only for us first generation immigrants, the second generation feels no connection at all to Brazil. They have neither the patience nor the interest. Stay here five more years to see if your children will want to play with the children of Brazilians. Of course not, no way! They find it bothersome....

B – But why do those from other communities play, the Jews, Mexicans, why not us?

N – I don't know, maybe because the Brazilians who find themselves here are very different from each other. We keep talking about the unity among Brazilians and such, but what we seek here has never existed in Brazil. Inside Brazil proper we have this thing, the Northeast thinks the best place in

Brazil is the Northeast. The South thinks it is the South. Minas Gerais thinks it is Minas Gerais, and so forth.

On the other hand, it is interesting to observe that even in the case of the members of a group interested in affirming Brazilianness, the integration happens at the expense of Brazilian culture. In most cases the children of Brazilian women with American men do not speak Portuguese and do not develop any special relationship to Brazil.

I was once interviewing a Brazilian woman, age 48, who has been here for 25 years and is married to a Jewish American. While we were talking the phone rang and she answered it. It was her husband. He seemed to have asked what she was doing and she said, "there is a Brazilian lady here interviewing me. She wants to know about my life in the 'jungle,' and also about my life here."

Her metaphor suggested to me those primitive tragedies where the little girl is rescued from a backward, primitive, and violent place and is offered the paradise of modernity with its tons of goods. Despite referring to Brazil as "the jungle," she said that she would like to visit Brazil more often, but she cannot because her son, age 16, does not feel comfortable being in a place where he cannot speak the language. "Why didn't you teach him Portuguese?" - I asked. She said, "Because he does not need Portuguese!"

The following quote also tells about other outcomes of the individual process of integration,

C – Maybe it's difficult to put these people together because there are many Brazilian women married to Americans, and sometimes Americans hate being near Brazilians! Why? Because when Brazilians get together they start speaking Portuguese. So the guy starts feeling isolated, so he prefers not to go.
B – He isolated his wife his entire life, but there was no problem because she submitted and accepted this...
C – Exactly, she learned English, accepted it and such. Let's see, in this other case, I met a Brazilian woman last year at a gift fair at the convention center. I saw some marvelous painted ceramics there. I thought, "Wow, what beautiful workmanship!" Because I was with my husband, we were

speaking in Portuguese, and then she asked, "Ah are you Brazilian?" "Yes I am." "Me too." Well, she's a Brazilian, was displaying her work there, has been here for 15 years, and so forth. So I told the group about her. This was exactly at the same time that we were putting on the first event for the City of Hope. She donated a piece for the event and said, "Ah, I would love to come." I went to her studio, and she told me she would love to take part in our group, have some contact with Brazilians, because she's been here for a long time and such. But her husband hates to be near Brazilians for those reasons I just said. It's obvious, she never came to the event we threw for the City of Hope and she never showed up again. So, like her there are so many others, whose husbands can't handle the Brazilian community.

What we see is that Brazilian culture and traditions are not considered important when what is at stake is, for instance, the education of the children. Thus, my hypothesis is that, regardless of their social position in Brazil, but especially when they come from lower middle class, these women are integrated into American life in an evidently subservient position and this is connected with the position of Brazil in the international division of labor, as I have discussed in the Introduction and Chapter One.

Dynamics of the Monthly Gatherings

The Brazilian Women's Group members usually gather for the monthly dinner on the third Thursday of the month. A member of the group offers her house and all guests are supposed to bring a dish and drinks. All women interested in attending the meeting are supposed to call the hostess and arrange with her what dish to bring. Some of the hostesses have organized their potlucks around themes of Brazilian regional cuisine. In general, however, the hostess only makes sure that the basic components of the main course and desserts will be there, asking each guest to bring items according to what is needed.

I talked to a couple of women who, like me, would bring simpler or more sophisticated dishes according to their inspiration at each meeting. The most complicated dish that I ever made to take to the monthly dinner was stroganoff, which takes about two hours to prepare. In general, however, I took easier dishes such as salads, rice, and flans. A few women, however, took their time preparing very special dishes, and harvested much praise during dinnertime.

Dinnertime is sighing time. Diets are broken and homesickness arrives, especially for those who do not have a chance to eat Brazilian food on a daily basis. The highest point of the dinner is the dessert. Oh God, there is a certain passion fruit mousse that reminds me of the gods of Olympus. But one is supposed to be patient because the dinner is the last thing to come and there is no exact time for it to be served. By the way, punctuality has been always a matter of concern for the hostesses and for the members of the board of directors, especially when there is a guest speaker. In the meeting of March 1998, for instance, the dinner was served about 9 p.m. because two different activities had been scheduled before dinner. First, a Brazilian masseur talked about his special technique and did a public demonstration of his massage. After that, Pastor Isaías, from the Brazilian Evangelic Community - Salvation Army, Torrance, presented a videotape about the history of the Salvation Army and talked about the Brazilian group in Torrance. When we finally ate, there was not much time left to chat.

The monthly gatherings do not have a schedule to follow. The different things going on at each meeting have always surprised me. Usually, however, the hostess and older members of the group, or the members of the board of directors receive the guests. First-time visitors usually come accompanied by the person who invited them and this person introduces her to other members she knows. Older members go from one group to the next greeting everybody and talking longer to friends they apparently have not had a chance to meet elsewhere. There is generally a member of the board of directors taking pictures. Selected pictures appear in the following newsletter with comments about the gathering. The quote below is from my description of my first meeting:

> Yesterday I went for the first time to the Brazilian Women's Group monthly gathering. It took place in Sherman Oaks and it took us about 70 minutes to get there. Clarice drove, of course. We got there half an hour late, rang the bell and the hostess herself received us. After leaving our purses and blazers in one of the bedrooms, we were guided to the kitchen where

we left the food that we were bringing for the potluck dinner. Most of the women were talking in small groups in the TV room, across the kitchen. Some 20 women were there already and many more were about to come, I learnt later on. Also, I learnt that we were not really late because there are some people who get there two hours after the scheduled time, which is 7 p.m. It was the first time I saw such a big gathering of Brazilian women. I could not help my excitement and curiosity to find out about all their migratory stories. What had brought them to LA? I estimate that some 40 women attended that specific meeting. I was introduced and talked to about ten of them. Soon after I arrived, I met, introduced myself and talked for a short while with the president, who was taking pictures.

She said that the Christmas Bazaar during the November meeting had already become one of the Brazilian Women's Group traditions. Members and guests buy and sell Christmas goods to each other. I did not even check what was on sale, interested as I was in talking to people. I only considered it opportune to talk about my research with Ana, a 25-year-old UCLA student. With the other women I talked about other issues such as marriage, children, physical exercises and so forth.

A demonstration of beauty products was going on while I was talking to Ana, but we did not pay much attention. Our conversation was interrupted when the hostess announced that dinner was served. After filling our plates we started looking for a place to sit and we finally sat at an 8-seat dining table in the dining room. There was another table in the kitchen and most of the guests sat on couches and chairs in the TV room. We were 8 women eating and talking. I had not been introduced yet to any of them, but I could easily distinguish the visitors from the members. The latter would feel much more comfortable about talking, asking, and laughing as well as commenting things about other members whom I had not yet met.

One of them, very talkative and confident, was talking about her work as a masseuse in a clinic that charges one hundred dollars per hour and pays her fifty per cent of that plus other benefits. Once in a while she would mention that such and such dish was excellent, but would especially comment about Vilma's dishes, the "official" cook of the group. The food was good, but not as Brazilian as I had dreamed. Probably because I was dreaming of a *feijoada* or *carne de sol com macaxeira*. After dinner I talked to a woman in her early forties who has been in the United States for more than 20 years. She lived most of this time in New York. She came to LA after getting married. She is an architect and we were talking about teaching Portuguese to children when one of the parents does not speak Portuguese. She said that when she had her first child she managed to teach some Portuguese to her. But after having two more children she decided to give it up because they only speak English among themselves and her husband was not really encouraging them with the Portuguese.

Clarice introduced me to other friends whose husbands, like Clarice's, also work for Odebrecht. And I also met a *gaucha* who is a member of a Pentecostal Brazilian church in Los Angeles. She is in her 60s and came to LA to live with one of her children who works for the movie industry. I got her phone number. Before I knew it, it was already time to come home.

The dynamics of the monthly meetings has varied as a result of the entrance of new members and the incorporation of their suggestions. After the successful talk presented about Feng Shui in November 1996, the group organizers decided to have a regular activity every meeting. This activity could be informative talks, demonstrations of products or services and so forth. However, some members started complaining and in the first newsletter of 1997 the organizers changed their minds and proposed the following: "due to a question of organization and a great necessity to catch up on our conversations, it was decided that we will have only one speaker per meeting, and only every other month."

As a matter of fact, the need to catch up with what is going on in everyone's life seems to be the very reason why everybody gets together. Thus, in general, in terms of dynamics, the current meetings are closer to the one that I attended first. That is, people started coming at 7 p.m. They chat, chat, chat before, during, and after dinnertime and start leaving about half an hour after dinnertime. At the meeting that I stayed the longest I left at 11 p.m. and a few women were still chatting with the hostess.

Nilce, age 47, gives some hints to understanding this "endless" chatting:

> The group arose exactly from the need for friends with whom you could talk about things concerning your origins. I have, for example, an American neighbor who is very friendly, very kind, but my conversation with her will last only one hour, half an hour. What will we talk about? About our neighborhood? I have nothing in common with her except the fact that she lives next to me and is friendly. But to have a friendship with her would be difficult because I would have to have some activity in common with her. In Brazil it's the same thing. You have to have something in common, school, a sport. Here [Redondo Beach] I am surrounded by Americans and Orientals. Orientals are even more difficult because even their English is difficult. So the idea is to make possible the encounter of interested persons and promote this pleasant and comfortable conversation we have when we get together. But I think there shouldn't be any pressure for the sale of things, because the Brazilian doesn't like this and stays away. To do, for example, a bazaar. Everyone goes there and shows off their lacework. This is too commercial! We want a meeting so we can talk. Some commercial meetings are fine, but too many are not. Many people distanced themselves when this thing of sales began. This is not what people want. You are already bombarded with sales here everywhere else.

What is all this chat about?

From cinema to diapers, these women talk pretty much about everything. With Marta I talk about cinema and Brazilian history. She always comes by with some novelty from the world of cinema. She reviews Hollywood movies for several Brazilian magazines here and in Brazil. With Nilce I talk about her last trips to Brazil, her and mine impressions about the "Americanization" of Brazilian teenagers and other issues connected to Brazilian and American lifestyles. But these conversations around specific themes started to happen later, only after we knew each other better. Spontaneous conversations involving more than three people generally bring about themes such as vacation trips, marriages, domestic duties, plastic surgery, nutrition and diets, physical fitness, new movies, Brazilian and American political scandals such as the Monica Lewinsky case, and so forth.

When members are just introduced to one another they generally ask each other more "standardized" questions such as,

1. What brought you to LA?
2. What nationality is your husband?
3. How long have you been here in the United States?
4. What part of Brazil are you from?
5. What school did you attend in Brazil? Or what school do you attend here?
6. Where do you live?

Of course nobody asks all these questions at once or follows the suggested order. I participated in a conversation that took place between first arrivals in one of the gatherings where one of the older members of the group was "leading" a conversation about nationality of husbands and advantages and disadvantages of being married to a Brazilian or an American man. Thus, she asked all of us one by one what was the nationality of our husbands. After this general survey the conversation focused on the characteristics of American husbands. Moral: the ones married to Americans concluded (without knowing much beyond the stereotype of the Brazilian male) that they are better off in terms of husbands because Americans at least help with domestic tasks. The conversation, however, did not contemplate other issues such as affection, sexuality, education, profession and so forth.

The number one question asked upon one's introduction regards the reasons for being in Los Angeles. For example, in my case, I would be introduced as follows: This is Bernadete (surname is rarely spelled out), she is doing research about Brazilians in LA for her Ph.D. in Anthropology (many times they said Master's). This statement reveals what I am doing right now but it does not really explain why I am in Los Angeles. So they usually ask: did you come just for your Ph.D.?

Other questions follow: are you married (since I do not wear a wedding band)? Do you have children? How many, etc?

Many times I was introduced as a *Paraibana*, a person born in the northeastern state of Paraíba. Being a *Paraibana* in the middle of so many *Cariocas* sounded sometimes like a joke. In this case, they would introduce me by imitating my accent, which, according to them, is slower, and sounds like it is sung instead of spoken. They would also joke about the reputation that we, *Paraibanas*, have of being *"mulher macho."* Of course, introducing me as such requires a certain intimacy and this only started happening after I had attended several meetings.[39]

Some members (see for instance quotes on page 126) referred to a certain annoying way some of these women have of asking introductory questions. It seems that after "reading" one's appearance they judge if their social place is at the same level, above, or below that of the observed person, and according to this judgment, they approach each person differently. As is expected, these evaluations are based on whatever educational resources each person who is evaluating has; that is, it is an evaluation that varies from person to person. That is why Denise assumed she might have met the "wrong" people. Wrong in the sense of being unable to interpret and treat her according to what she expected. This "inability" to judge and treat people "accordingly" can be explained in many ways: first, ignorance of the diversity of possibilities of being upper or middle-class; second, knowledge of these possibilities but the belief that their experience of middle or upper middle-class is the best, and so forth. Regardless of many possible explanations, these criteria seem to matter more than Claudia suggested when she said that each woman has to carve out her place in the group instead of expecting it be designated by other members. It is in this sense that I consider that there is a gap between the purposes of the group and its daily practices. In other words, if there is a strong purpose bringing these women together why would not they value each other for whatever they are, as Claudia (page 129) proposed the case was?

The second question, nationality of the husband, is asked when this information is not included in the answer of the first question. I have noticed that an American husband, regardless of his social position, is, in principle, valued as much as a Brazilian husband in a position of power. For example, most of the members married to Brazilians are married to Brazilians who work for the Brazilian government (Consulate and banks) or Brazilian multinational companies. These are people who generally hold college degrees and receive high wages, especially when compared with general wages in Brazil. The same homogeneity is not observed among the American husbands, although several of them also have higher education.

Time of immigration is also another important element of distinction, as the following dialogue suggests,

- How long have you been here?
- About two years.
- Only two years?!

In principle, having been here longer confers a certain superiority over those who are just arriving, but it generally depends on what is at stake. Let us suppose an upper-middle class Brazilian has a husband who gets a special offer to work in Los Angeles, so she suddenly has to face living in an English speaking world. She knows some English, but not as fluently as many lower middle-class Brazilians living in Los Angeles. I have heard comments like "the poor little one, so wealthy and with such bad English."

These "transnational" associations produce new values at the confluence of the current values in both societies to which the immigrant is connected. Occasionally, even if for a short while, members who have been longer in Los Angeles feel "superior" to others who have been here for less time, even if the latter has a higher social status than the first.

The four other questions [What part of Brazil are you from? What school did you attend in Brazil? What school do you attend here? Where do you live?] are only asked after one has exhausted the themes connected to the three first questions, unless the conversation starts with any of the issues connected to these latter questions. For example, if the other person is a student [as I am], we will naturally talk about schools here and in Brazil. Or if she notices my accent and asks what state I am from in Brazil, our conversation may be driven to issues connected to Brazilian regionalism and this sort of thing.

Finally, the few times when I was asked where I lived in Los Angeles was because I had to explain why I was leaving early.

- I got to go because I have a long drive ahead.

- Where do you live?
- Riverside.
- Where in the hell is Riverside?

Theoretically, all members are valued for their specific talents. As Claudia said, "the group has a place for each one of us." In general, however, I would say that the group members are very much concerned in ranking people according to the different types of "capital" they possess. Therefore, the following things are valued:

1. Properties and/or money invested in the financial market or savings (economic capital).

2. Diplomas and similar credentials preferentially concretized in prestigious jobs.

3. Special talents (sports, music, plastic arts, moviemaking, etc).

The social status is defined regardless of whether it is the member herself who possesses the mentioned qualities, her husband, or her family. All these elements are tradable, depending on what is stake in each circumstance. For example, I was once in a carnival party talking to one of the members, who was making comments about clothing. She was complaining about having to buy new clothes all the time because her husband's position requires them to host parties and meet "important" people very often. After saying that, she looked at me and said, "At least you do not have to worry about these matters because you're a student." I asked, "Why not?" She answered, "Nobody expects a student to dress accordingly. I mean, you're a professional in the making, you know? But you're not yet a professional."

Even though not yet a professional, being a student grants some privileges, besides an excuse to not dress properly. Being a student means being able to afford to pay fees and tuition or having enough talent (either intelligence or a network) to have been granted a fellowship. Furthermore, everybody understands that educational capital speeds the progress through the system.

Another time I was interviewing one of the members when she referred to another member who is a cook. She said, "you know, she is a cook, but she lives in a nice apartment in a reasonable neighborhood and has a nice car."

Many times I heard bits of conversation like the following, "I don't know what she does, but her husband is a retired actor and they own this amazing house in Hollywood Hills." Thus, one does not have to fulfill all criteria to be respected, but it seems that they are "more" respected if they do. Perhaps this is one of the reasons why the group needs more than the broad purpose of "promoting the Brazilian culture to the American community and organizing charitable events to help the less fortunate in Brazil and in the United States."

Despite complaints of some participants and the dispute over the purpose of the group, the Brazilian Women's Group works very efficiently in the sense of creating a space where Brazilian women "can feel at home" in Los Angeles. Therefore, either for those Brazilian women married to American men or for those married to Brazilians and living temporarily in Los Angeles, the group is an interesting space where the women are introduced to several possibilities of living in Los Angeles, possibilities that they would hardly be aware of otherwise. They widen their networks and receive different insights about many problems that they share as immigrants, mothers, wives, and women. Even if the group cannot accomplish their objective of divulging a non-essencialized image of Brazil, they certainly can learn how to deal with it better.

CHAPTER 5
Carving out a Place in Los Angeles

Searching for a Distinct Place

(Los Angeles, July 12, 1998)
Today was the most depressing day since I started my fieldwork in LA about a year ago. I have many times felt angry, irritated, bored and so forth. But today all I feel is sadness. It is not only because Brazil lost [the World Cup] to France. I wanted it to be otherwise, I even prayed for it to be otherwise. It did not happen, though. The Brazilian team was playing so badly that people were wondering if they had not been given money to let France win. Hardly considering the possibility of losing the game, Brazilians were ready to celebrate their fifth world championship. The LAPD had even reserved a few blocks on Venice Blvd because they were expecting a huge celebration and did not want to disrupt traffic, as had happened in the last few games Brazil had won. That is, if Brazilians made all that noise just for winning partial games, what was to be expected if they won the final?

After an endless 90 minutes of sighs and complaints Brazilians were faced with the defeat they did not want to bring home. I was watching the game in a Mexican pizzeria where Edna, a friend of mine, had taken me since I decided to watch Brazil's games in Los Angeles instead of Riverside. The

Brazilian bars and restaurants were packed from the first game and were reserved for those people who had been there since then. The Mexican pizzeria was always packed too. But today it was unbelievably crowded. Edna had asked me to get there earlier because it would be hard to get in after a certain point. When I got there with two more friends from Riverside the door was already closed and the manager was guarding the door to not let anybody in. It took some time until Edna finally convinced the guy to let us in. Finally we were all there, and I had video and photographic cameras ready to document the biggest Brazilian celebration that I would witness during my fieldwork.

Today, unlike the other times, there was too much disruption going on. There was a Mexican guy who was cheering for France and irritating everybody. He was drunk and would shout and whistle every time France scored or got close to score. He finally got into a fight with a Brazilian guy who was also drunk and pissed off with the guy and the game. There was also another guy dressed in the French uniform, but this one was quiet and people were sort of used to him since he had been there in previous games and always dressed in the uniform of Brazil's adversary. Other than that, everybody was cheering and there were many other nationalities besides the Brazilians themselves. Before the first half of the game, *Dona* Doris had already bitten off all her nails and was about to have a heart attack. By the end of the third quarter disappointment and sadness had already replaced anger and expectation. The drums had been put away. I hardly kept videotaping. It seemed that my interest in research could not surpass my solidarity with everybody's feelings. I was all disappointment and sadness too. What had happened to Ronaldinho? The game finally ended and nobody seemed to believe what had just happened. Even the LAPD cops on Venice Blvd seemed disappointed. Unlike other days, just a few people were surrounding Zabumba, a Brazilian bar and restaurant where Brazilians used to gather after Brazil's team victories in this World Cup. After Brazil's victory over Holland, for instance, the party went on for about five hours.

The closed blocks seemed like too much space for so little to celebrate. In any case, some people decided to take a chance to show that Brazilians are happy and funny regardless. Even though there was hardly anybody to show anything to, I heard a girl who was dancing samba say that we had to show that we are proud of ourselves regardless of soccer and that we also know how to have fun whether we win or lose. It did not seem like that, though. I was extremely tired and decided to leave the street and drink a cup of coffee. When I went back after about 40 minutes, the blocks that had been closed for the celebration were already open and traffic had resumed its regular flow. Once upon a time Brazil would have been the five-time champion. Perhaps in next World Cup?

What struck me the day Brazil lost to France was the effort that some Brazilians were still making to reinforce the *carnavalesco* stereotype according to which Brazilians are happy, funny, nice, warm, crazy, and beautiful people no matter what. In order to preserve such an image they seem to take advantage of any chance they have to reinforce it regardless of their true feelings. But why would it be so important to stick to the *carnavalesco* stereotype?

When Brazil won the game against Holland and became the potential champion of the 1998 World Cup, I was among the Brazilians who were dancing, singing, screaming around Zabumba. The LAPD was there controlling the crowd in order to guarantee the free flow of traffic. The enthusiasm was such, however, that many times the LAPD had to interfere, asking the frolickers to avoid disrupting the traffic. The cordial spirit between Brazilians and the LAPD cops was maintained until the end and I heard many Brazilians commenting about it.

- See? These cops were afraid of us making the same mess Mexicans did when Mexico won the game against the United States...

- Ah, but they know that we, Brazilians, like parties and celebrations, not violence, right?

- I don't know if they know, but they are always suspicious because for them we are all Latinos. Then, you've seen it, right?

- At least, we have a chance to show that we are a very special kind of Latinos.

Indeed, in relation to the existent ethnic mosaic in Los Angeles, Brazilians are nothing more than one kind of Latino. However, as the conversation above proposes, Brazilians comprise a very particular kind of Latino. **They are the exotic Brazilians.** Even though many Americans still remember Pelé, and the American Youth Soccer Organization (AYSO) brings together thousands and thousands of American children who play soccer, it is not through mastery in soccer that Brazil has built its reputation in the United States. It is carnival, instead, which is the most important key to understanding the basis of the Brazilian exotic image in the United States and how it has shaped Brazilian identity in LA. In other words, whether Brazilians like it or not, the word "Brazil" in LA often stands for carnival. Thus, it is by fighting or reinforcing it that Brazilians make their way through.

This chapter is about different ways of expressing Brazilianness and different ways of dealing with the Latino and Brazilian stereotypes in Los Angeles. I will be presenting and interpreting the particular ways in which Brazilians have carved out a place in Los Angeles. My hypothesis is that Brazilian image in the United States is not forged by Brazilians themselves, not even by Brazilian elites. In the United States, the construction of a Brazilian identity is connected to factors such as the position of Brazil in the international division of labor, the relative position of the Brazilian immigrant population in relation to other immigrant populations, and the specific needs of the American cultural market.

More concretely, the construction of a Brazilian identity in this country, particularly in Los Angeles, can only be grasped within the broader context of a Latin-American identity such as it has been constructed in this milieu of globalization in which Latin Americans particularly, and Third World people in general, have become the "other" in American domestic and international politics. It is in this ambiguous space that a Brazilian identity shifts between distinguishing itself from or allying itself to a Latino identity in order to conform to different circumstances that require one or the other kind of identification.

In order to be able to discuss the interface between particular experiences and public versions, I observed several "public" events and explored the issue of Brazilianness with everybody whom I interviewed, besides the systematic observation of the two Brazilian groups on which I focused. It is worth noting that I do not think these groups internally produce what I am calling here public versions of a certain Brazilian character. In other words, the events these groups promote in their daily lives are not "display cases" for Americans or other non-Brazilians, but spaces for Brazilians to interact among themselves. Unless they are participating in broader events or speaking about themselves to non-Brazilians, they are not interested in reinforcing any particular Brazilian identity. That is, if there are no "others", Brazilianness is forgotten and people concentrate on issues that have more to do with their daily lives, which are the issues that I discussed in the two last chapters.

Some Brazilians believe that the *carnavalesco* stereotype makes us a very distinct kind of Latinos and, in a certain way, connects us more easily with the colonizers because carnival is strongly rooted in Catholic Europe. Also, many Americans say that we have a "funny sort of French-sounding accent". However, things do not always happen according to this reasoning. Which groups of immigrants we are connected to usually depends on what roles we are performing and where. For more than four years I have tested two alternative answers when asked from where am I. First, I could promptly answer, "Brazil," to which 100 percent of people would respond: "Brazil? Wow!" Second, I could answer with another question: "Where do you think I am from?"

I have observed that the answer to my question varies according to the person being asked. If it is another Latino from the Caribbean or South America they usually guess someplace in South America. Some have guessed Argentina, and then I ask if I have a Spanish accent. They say not really, but your skin color suggests so. For the same reason - that is, because of my skin color and the way I do my hair - white and black Americans always guess some European country, mainly France, Russia, or other countries in Eastern Europe. I noticed once a man who asked me if I was French he looked a bit disappointed when I said I was Brazilian. The most peculiar episode happened in my own house when a cable repairman came to fix my television antenna. After noticing my accent, he (a young white American, about 25-30 years old) asked where I was from, and this time I promptly answered, Brazil. He said "Brazil?! I did not know that there were any Brazilians in Southern California!"

He kept staring at me as though I was some sort of *avis rare.* He even apologized and explained that this was his first time meeting a live Brazilian, and told me that he rents some cable channels that have special shows with Brazilian women. I did not even dare to ask what kind of show. Afterwards, I did not know if I should cry or laugh at the whole scene, but I certainly felt embarrassed and I think he ended up feeling uncomfortable too.

I collected similar tales from other Brazilian women. A journalist friend of mine told me that a Brazilian upper middle-class lady came to visit Los Angeles and when she was introduced to an American male she noticed his particular reaction: "Huh, Brazil?!"

She then turned to her Brazilian friend who had introduced them and said, in Portuguese, "Why is this guy so affected by learning that I am Brazilian? Is he assuming that we are all whores?"[40]

All Brazilian women I have talked to about this issue are aware of the stereotype and many of them consciously take advantage of it. Some of them do believe that the stereotype promotes the idea of prostitution. Others believe that the image is ambiguous and it is up to each Brazilian woman to ratify or deny its connections with prostitution. However, regardless of how these Brazilian women interpret and deal with the stereotype, most of them *truly* believe that Brazilian women are more erotically appealing than American women. The following discourses are samples of this perception:

> It's an advantage for a Brazilian woman to marry an American. Now, it is a disadvantage for a Brazilian man to marry an American woman. I'll explain. The American is not used to a homey, affectionate wife, okay? And the Brazilian is. And the American woman is not homey, is not affectionate, is not feminine, and they say that she is not good in bed. I know a Brazilian who married an American woman, and it was he who told me. But he got married mostly to stay in the country. He lived with her, would go out with her everywhere, and introduced her as his wife. But he says that the American women he met left much to be desired sexually speaking. I think they start with sex very early and then become like machines. You understand? There isn't the sensuality, the

charisma, the seductiveness that we Brazilian women have (Telma, age 46).

I think it is very natural for Americans to be attracted to the image of Brazilian women which is divulged here. Of course, they are gorgeous women, with marvelous bodies, fantastic! And they think that Brazil has a sensuality that they don't have, and I sincerely think they are right about this. In fact, the Brazilian woman is very sensual, especially when compared to the American! Anyone of us here is more sensual than any American. I know this, everybody knows this. It's not only Americans who know this, understand? My point is that we have much more than pretty bodies and sensuality, understand? And we want space to show the other things (Claudia, age 43).

I'm not bothered in the least by Americans taking advantage of the fact that I'm a Brazilian to dream a little about the sensuality that they don't have, the poor guys. They look at me as if I held some secret they would give everything to discover. I feed this stereotype a little, of course. I think deep down inside I also believe it (Paola, age 35).

I - I know that the American has the greatest fascination with Brazilian women. The collective fantasy of Americans is that women in Brazil are all topless. Nobody goes to the beach in Brazil topless, it is very rare, but they have this idea. They also think that Brazil is a big orgy, a non-stopping party. But, after all, it is a positive image they have of us.
A - No, but I think that this idea that the women are hot and this and that makes the image very distorted. When you say you are Brazilian, other Latinos look at you with such fascination: "Wow!" And Americans too. But I think it is an unreal image, bad for us. It has not bothered me much because I have a very serious attitude, and I am not a person who gives much of a chance for this type of thing. And when I see that someone is going to say something, or see that he'll come up with some truncated idea I change it quickly. I don't let

anyone bring up this subject with me, no. I don't give him a chance. I don't have this problem, normally. But I have friends who go through this. For example, it becomes much easier for them to flirt and to come on to you, you know how it is? Despite everything, I've been hit on. Every once in a while I hear something. When they ask me where I'm from and I tell them I am a Brazilian, people sometimes come on, and, apparently without pretensions, start "Ah, Brazilian, Ah the country of Carnival," then it starts. After Carnival there comes the question of whether you're married and such.

I - Ah, but all this is because you are pretty. I'm sure that if you were a hag it would matter little if you were from Transylvania or from Brussels.

A - Maybe, but I think that when they know we are Brazilian they become more fired up.

I - But its because this sex thing here is very heavy. The way we do it in Brazil enchants them because we can deal with the body and sensuality without becoming a seven-headed monster. The women wear bikinis on the streets, but no one is self-conscious... American men go crazy because they don't know how to deal with the body as generously, and for them it always has to mean something else... The Brazilian uses the body as one more space for expressing the personality... She doesn't have to take off her clothes to get a boyfriend, she will get the boyfriend anyway. She wants to show off her body because her body is hers and that's it! They go nuts over this, because they are so stingy with their bodies and we are so rich in expression with this body, right? (Ivan, age 44, and Annie, age 36).

Even though I quickly learned that Americans' positive reaction to the word Brazil is mostly grounded on their own fantasies about Brazilian carnival, it never really bothered me to the point where I had to lie about my nationality. On the contrary, most times I feel as if the word Brazil had the power to trigger day-dreaming. Innumerable times and in many different circumstances, I was told about peoples' dreams of visiting Brazil. A Mexican-American friend told me that she learned to like Brazil because of her grandmother. She said that the old lady stuck to her dream of visiting Brazil during Carnival until the day she died. Her grandma died without realizing her dream, but she told me once, "Who knows if I'm not the one who's supposed to do it for her?" Although I have other similar stories to tell, I would rather bring up one that contradicts the sort of positive perspective that I have been drawing here.

Elizabeth, age 67, married to an American man and living in Los Angeles for the last 15 years, says,

> In a general way the idea that Americans have of Brazil is of Carnival. Carnival and the most beautiful women in the world. Carnival means you are always ready for fun. That is, to say you're Brazilian is already giving them a green light. It's an invitation to play around. The greatest advertisement of Brazil is the rear end... if it was a billboard Brazil would be an enormous rear end. Now tell me, why is it that Brazil must forever be represented by rear ends? If its not only one behind it's thirty. The ad for the Hollywood Palladium Carnival was something horrible, I don't know how many *mulata*'s behinds were there. Until when will Brazil live off rear ends? Oh well, this is the market which Brazil offers here: rear ends, sexuality, carnival. That is, it is nothing serious. It's absurd! Many times I even say I am Portuguese. When I am among a more serious crowd I don't have the courage to say that I'm from Brazil because of this reputation. Everybody looks at my face and sees a rear end. I can't stand the quantity of rear ends that comes together with the idea of Brazil, it's not possible! It's like a nightmare! So it's like this, all over, if there aren't some thirty behinds, preferably of *mulatas*, it seems as if the message doesn't get through, it doesn't sell. Even the Brazilian consulate promotes this.

Some other Brazilian women that I interviewed agree with Elizabeth in that these images of Brazilian women have a negative impact over them in general and those living abroad in particular. However, some of them believe that these ideas attract non-Brazilian men to Brazilian women and may affect them positively when what is at stake is to find a non-Brazilian husband.

My husband had this fixation for black women. He had had a relationship with a black American whom he liked very much, but it was a very complicated relationship. He also felt very attracted to Brazil and all those fantasies related to carnival and mulatas. I think he was looking for this mulata when he found me (Jociclênia, age 42).

I don't know, I'm married to a Brazilian man, but I do think that many foreigners feed this belief that Brazilian women can offer them the ultimate sexual pleasure, the wildest, the most beautiful, whatever. But I don't think that this is the only reason why many American men choose Brazilian wives. I think that they also believe that Brazilian women are more submissive and traditional than American women, which is generally true. I mean, it is more than just sex and fun. Hello? Are we supposed to believe that all those Mormon missionaries marrying Brazilian women are looking for ultimate sexual pleasure? (Marta, age 45).

The Mormon missionaries that go to Brazil have a concrete chance to go beyond the limits of the stereotype and find many other reasons to marry Brazilian women, including the reason presented above – that is, Brazilian women are supposedly more submissive than American women and so forth. But Elizabeth, Marta, Ivan, Annie and I are referring to the way the stereotype works when far away from its sources. In other words, we are discussing and giving examples of how the myth of Brazilian women's sensuality works in Los Angeles.

In this case, during my fieldwork I had the chance to observe that some women who were complaining to me about the sexual content of the stereotype of Brazilian women abroad would reinforce it when interacting with non-Brazilians, especially when this interaction happened in Brazilian bars, clubs, or restaurants.

Brazilians and the Latino World in Los Angeles

The Brazilian immigrant population in Los Angeles is insignificant when compared, for instance, with the Mexican one.[41] According to the statistics presented by the U.S. Census of 1990, the proportion is one Brazilian to every two hundred and nineteen Mexicans. Considering the

Latino population as a whole - that is, people from Mexico, the Caribbean, and Central and South America - the proportion decreases to one Brazilian for every two hundred ninety nine other Latinos. Thus, Brazilians are numerically lost in the immense Latino world of Los Angeles. As Telma said, "here we are part of this race of Latinos." What other alternative is left? Brazil is located in South America, part of the immense world colonized by Portugal and Spain which became known as Latin America. Thus, Brazilians are Latin Americans or South Americans, but in the United States they become Latinos. Brazilians are Latinos and Latino is not a very nice thing to be in the United States because, as Telma wisely observed, "Latinos are like a lower class for the Americans."

Despite the rise of many Latinos to economically dominant classes in the United States, the content of the mainstream racist ideology that explains and determines the place of Latinos in American society has not yet changed.[42]

As we have seen in Chapter Two, the term Latino is too broad to satisfactorily represent all the particularities it contains. Colombians, for example, do not like to be mistaken for Peruvians or Argentines, and so forth. They know how differently each nationality was produced and they also know about social and regional differences. But if all Latin-American countries (except for Haiti, Belize, Suriname, and British and French Guianas) share the same language, the same cannot be said about Brazil. Therefore, beginning with the language, Brazil stands out among the South-American countries as the most distinct. This distinction should not merely be reduced to language or a few other idiosyncrasies that distinguish Portuguese from Spanish colonizers. The distinction is also a result of the characteristics of each colonial enterprise. Or rather, the differences between Latin nations were produced by the necessities of making different colonial enterprises work (Mintz 1973 and 1985). In this sense one would find greater cultural affinity between Brazil (especially the Northeast) and Cuba or Puerto Rico than with other countries whose histories were developed based on economic enterprises other than the plantation system.[43] That is, the plantation system was developed around certain elements whose dynamic relationship produced a people and a culture different from that of each one of its participants (Mintz 1985, Harris 1964, Ribeiro

1995). For the case of Brazil and Brazilians, Darcy Ribeiro (1995:19-20) proposes the following explanation:

> We [Brazilians] emerged from the confluence, the clash and the blending of the Portuguese invader with the Indians of the forest and the field and with the African Negroes subordinated as slaves.
>
> In this confluence, which takes place under the rule of the Portuguese, disparate racial origins, distinct cultural traditions, well-developed social formations confront each other and fuse to give way to a new people, in a new model of societal structuralization. New because it rises as a national ethnicity, culturally differentiated from its formative sources, strongly mixed, dynamized by a syncretic culture and singularized by the redefinition of cultural traces from which it is derived. Also new because it sees itself and is seen as a new people, a new genre of human different from others in existence. A new people, even, because it is a new model of societal structuralization, which inaugurates a singular form of socio-economic organization, founded on a renewed type of slavery and on a continued servitude to the global market. New, additionally, for the unlikely joy and astonishing vocation towards happiness, in a people so sacrificed, that encourages and moves all Brazilians.
>
> Old, however, because it is viable only as an external proletariat. That is, as an ultramarine implant of European expansion that does not exist for its own purposes, but to generate exportable profits by exercising its function as the colonial provider of goods for the world market, and through the devastation of the population it has recruited in the country, or has imported.

Brazilians have good reasons to be and to feel different from other Latin Americans, or to identify more or less with this or that country. However, I argue, this is not the reason why Brazilian immigrants generally avoid being identified with other Latinos in Los Angeles. The problem that causes the Brazilian fear of being identified as Latino is connected to what the mainstream ideology preaches, not to any experience that Brazilians have had with other Latinos in the United

States. Many Brazilians have had positive experiences with other Latinos, but whenever they have to generalize their impressions these are drowned out by the same racist Anglo-Saxon mainstream discourse. The difference, however, is that their discourse totally contradicts their practices. In other words, they do not really reinforce in practice what they generalize in discourse. During the summer of 1998, I met a Seventh Day Adventist Brazilian woman who was moving to New York. She was regretting having to move because she would really miss the Hispanic church where she had been a member for the last 6 years. She said,

> I am very sad about leaving my Church. I love this Hispanic church because I haven't had problems with anybody. With the Mexicans we don't have all the gossip that Brazilians do. They only talk about things when they can't be hidden any more. And the Brazilian, I don't know, if he's imagined it, he's already talking. The Brazilians *here* [emphasis mine] think that they are superior to the Mexicans, they say they hate the language, that the Mexicans are ignorant. And you know something? Ignorance has nothing to do with a country, with a nationality. You find ignorant people everywhere and from all nationalities.

Although she had a positive experience with Mexicans in California, she ended up reproducing the mainstream discourse when comparing what is good and bad about Los Angeles and New York, and saying, "at least New York does not have as many immigrants. I mean, to tell you the truth there is no place like this, the Mexicans are destroying California."

One can hypothesize that these discourses are not necessarily the product of American mainstream ideologies but must be first connected with Brazilian systems of classification and stratification. Indeed, immigrants generally process the understanding of the new culture through the eyes of their native culture. In this sense, they will be imputing old prejudices to new social actors. Or rather, they will renovate their anterior systems of stratification in light of the systems of stratification they find wherever they go. Thus, Brazilians observe that the words Hispanic and Latino, which are the social categories that encompass them, refer to both an identity and a social position.

Discovering that in most cases the Latino world will be "their world" in the United States is a big disappointment for Brazilians in general. Omar, age 62, states the following about the Brazilians he and his wife have helped settle here:

> I find the Brazilian race very separatist, he gets here and he decides that he doesn't want to learn Spanish, and why? Because of the Mexican. They say, I don't like the Mexican, I'm not going to learn Spanish and such and this is true ignorance. *He gets here and already starts with this, I don't like Mexicans*, I'm not going to learn Spanish, oh damned language [emphasis mine]. I don't want to learn this language, because only Mexicans speak it, Oh how many Mexicans are here! But there has to be, people! This land belonged to them and they were the owners here before the American arrived. There are lots of Brazilians who say this, that they don't like California because there are a lot of Mexicans and they don't like the sound of the Spanish language because of the Mexicans, and all that nonsense. Because many people in the world speak Spanish, not just Mexicans... The problem is that when you leave Brazil you leave with a vision of the United States as a Caucasian race. When you get here and you enter a community where you go to the supermarket and the largest population is Mexican, you go to work and it is Mexican, you go to college and it is Mexican. Then you say, well, I left Brazil to speak English, to meet the Americans, and so far I haven't seen an American!

I want to call attention to what Omar says in regards to the ways Brazilians deal with Mexicans. He says, "[Brazilians] get *here* and already start with this, I don't like Mexicans," which means that they did not bring those ideas from Brazil. They learn that there is a connection between Latinos and low status after coming here and in circumstances as different as those that I presented in Chapters Three and Four.

The first time I participated in a monthly meeting of the Brazilian Women's Group, I met Ana, a young Brazilian lady married to a Spanish man. She was about twenty-five years old and was taking classes at UCLA. I explained to her that I was interested in understanding the ways Brazilians are settling in Los Angeles. She began talking about her difficulties in approaching Americans in general, as well as people of other nationalities, such as Indians, Japanese and other Asians, and Arabs.[44] In her experience the contact with other Latinos had always been much easier. I asked her to which Latinos she was referring. She said, Italians, Argentines, Spaniards, etc, and she explained that she was still using the word Latino with the meaning that it has in Brazil.

> When I say Latinos I do not mean only Mexicans as people here do. I mean, people from Portugal, Spain, France, Italy and people from American countries colonized by them. In this sense I am a Latina, but I don't feel comfortable being a Latina here, understand? First, because there is way too much prejudice against Latinos here, and second, because I don't think that it is okay to lump into the same category people as different as Brazilians, Mexicans and Argentines. Plus, I don't think that I am what they expect a Latina to be.

Indeed, she was calling attention to the fact that the term Latino in the United States has a general connotation very different from the connotation it has in Brazil. Indeed, it is important to note that despite the last two hundred years of Anglo-Saxon hegemony |represented first by the British Empire, and secondly, after World War II, by the United States| and its systematic politics of misrepresentation of the Latin identity, Latino in Brazil still holds a general positive connotation. Connected to the previous hegemonic colonizing powers, Portugal and Spain, Latino is everything that refers to the Latin world and its consequences. As one of the most important elements of the Brazilian national character, the Latin-Iberian tradition is a source of pride. But it is also a source of shame and stratification when what is at stake is the comparison between the political economic position of Brazil and the United States. Without taking into consideration important facts connected to international imperialist politics, Brazil and the United States are generally compared as if they were simply a result of the adaptation of two different cultures (the Anglo-Saxon and Latin-Iberian) to a new environment, the American continent.

Thus, the category Latino in Brazil has a connotation totally different from its connotation in the United States. In the United States the category Latino generally refers to patterns of immigration and to social stratification. In other words, it refers to a particular social identity such as it has been produced by American history. In this case, Latino means an immigrant from any Latin-American country and his descendants born in the United States. Therefore, there is little connection to the meaning that the same term has in Brazil, since there it encompasses all people connected to the Latin culture and tradition including its European creators.

In the United States the category Latino is connected to an economic determination, the Third World, and to a social destiny, the immigration to, and low status in the United States.

But it would be a mistake to suppose that the Latino label only causes problems for Brazilian immigrants. Many Brazilians I interviewed referred to the advantages of being Latino/Hispanic in the world of Los Angeles. Even though many Brazilians benefit from affirmative action and other specific protections for minorities, when they referred to the benefits of being Latino they were speaking of other kinds of benefits. They suggested that Brazilians function as a sort of bridge between white Americans and other Latinos. In this way a few of them have been granted management positions in companies where the employees are mostly Spanish-speaking Latinos. The conversation I had with Ivan and Annie about this issue helps to clarify this idea.

A – During the first two years I worked making crafts with an American woman. I learned to speak Spanish before English and I would only speak English and Spanish the entire time at work. I painted and taught the Mexican women. So I was an intermediary between the employees and my boss.
B – How did you interact with these two groups?
A – My boss didn't treat me like she treated the Mexicans, but I knew that I was also an employee, despite being a worker who was slightly above the others. I earned more than the

others. My salary was different than theirs. The treatment was different from theirs, understand? But I was the intermediary between these two worlds. My boss didn't speak Spanish and neither did they speak English. I think the first year I was the bridge between these two worlds [...] A Mexican woman attained the same position as me, but she wasn't treated with the same respect. The fact that I speak Portuguese makes a difference; it makes a difference, to the Americans, that I am white. Ah, I also worked with a Jewish girl, and a higher value was given to her.

I – But she did an important job of interaction... She minimized the prejudice of the American woman, she served as the spokesperson for the Latinas who also did not know how to express their needs, their rights. There is no training for this. I'm not sure if any Brazilian would have done this. I think it has more to do with her personality. I have the impression that if she had been another spoilt Brazilian raised in a home full of thousands of maids she was used to exploiting, maybe she wouldn't have the interest in interacting [with the Mexicans].

I found similar examples in other areas. The case of Pastor Mockiuti, the former minister of the church of Chino is very revealing. He was invited by the Seventh Day Adventist congregation to serve a Hispanic church in Glendale because he represented the type of leadership that they needed at that moment. The church congregates Latinos of varied nationalities including Brazilians, but mainly Mexicans. He told me "Brazilians are seen as ideal leaders because we are Hispanics, but we are different, you know? So, sometimes it makes it easier to accept our leadership."

In any case, I want to stress that Brazilians distinguish themselves from other Hispanics or Latinos not only for the sake of Brazilian singularity, but to protect themselves from being lumped under a category whose most important function is that of discrimination against them. Consequently, they look for symbols that demonstrate Brazilian uniqueness.

There are many elements that make Brazil different from other Latin-American countries. But the elements most commonly chosen to show Brazilian identity are the ones connected to Carnival. In the next section I analyze how some of these elements are explored in the Brazilian annual carnival at the Hollywood Palladium in Los Angeles.

The Making of the Brazilian Carnival at the Hollywood Palladium in Los Angeles

Although there are many expressions of Brazilian Carnival in Los Angeles, the annual Mardi Gras Ball at the Hollywood Palladium is the largest and most famous carnival ball in Southern California. The event attracts some 4,000 people and its organization brings together individuals from several nationalities (Beserra 1999:22). Maria Lucien, organizer of the event since 1987, is a Portuguese immigrant, for instance. And, contrary to ethnic or nationalistic expectations, the main sponsor of the event is not a Brazilian company, but a Korean airline.[45] Though first created around Brazilians, the Hollywood Palladium Carnival is a party for all "races," ethnic groups and nationalities. At the last ball, for instance, I interviewed people from countries as varied as Syria, Greece, Lebanon, Yugoslavia, Mexico, Guatemala, Nicaragua, India, France and Peru, to say nothing about Brazilians and Americans.

In fact, the Hollywood Palladium Carnival has the reputation of being an international event. Eddie Sakaki, a Mexican journalist, about thirty-five years old, who has lived in the United States for the last twenty years, gives his impressions of the Hollywood Palladium Carnival: "When I am coming to the Hollywood Palladium Carnival, the last thing that crosses my mind is that I am coming to an ethnic celebration - that sort of thing. First the Hollywood Palladium is not an appropriate venue for ethnic events, and second, the idea that I see in Brazilian carnival is about moving beyond racial and ethnic segregation to celebrate the body."

Susan Cantine, a University of California employee, age 46, also points out the international character of the Hollywood Palladium Carnival. She says,

> From the first time I went I started noticing a lot of international people. I've met people from all around the world in that Carnival. One year it was a German, another year it was a Lebanese, you know? And that was something that appealed to me because I work here, around a lot of

international people. And, yes, there were people from all over the world and not just Latinos from other Latin American countries.

Maria Lucien, the organizer, also emphasizes the same aspect: "The Hollywood Palladium Carnival is mostly for Brazilians and Americans, but it is very international. We have Latin Americans, Persians, Israelis, and people from all kinds of countries. But mostly it is Brazilians, Americans and Hispanics, which is good for Latin Americans, isn't it?"

There is, in fact, a certain attempt to avoid the existing ethnic segregation and to create a truly international party. But it really does seem that the Los Angeles business world upholds such a proposal. In this sense, in order to have a big party every year, the organizer has had to look for the support of Latino businesses in Los Angeles. That is why she says that the Hollywood Palladium Carnival is mostly for Brazilians, Americans and Hispanics. Looking for the support of Latino businesses in Los Angeles may be good commercially speaking, but it jeopardizes the current reputation of being an international party, whose intent is to celebrate reunion instead of segregation.

In any case, even though it works in a direction different from that of other ethnic events in Los Angeles, the Brazilian carnival is still fed by the same logic of exotic consumerism that organizes the distribution of spaces and exotic markets in Los Angeles. In other words, the "universal celebration of the body" that it is proposed through the Hollywood Palladium Carnival is proposed through a specific culture, the Brazilian culture.

The problem lies in understanding why a Brazilian event would have a reputation for being non-ethnic whereas a Latino event would not. I attended two Brazilian carnival balls at the Hollywood Palladium, in 1998 and 1999. Even though the bands, the decorations, the costumes, and the public were relatively the same, the general dynamics were quite different.

What caused the difference was the Master of Ceremonies (MC). Indeed, the performance of a Brazilian carnival outside Brazil requires somehow teaching the audience about Carnival. Besides Brazilians and other non-Brazilians who have visited Brazil, not many people in the United States have been exposed to Carnival, since even that of New

Orleans represents the Catholic exception in a Protestant world. In that manner, the role of the Master of Ceremonies is extremely important. He is the one in charge of guiding the audience in the direction he and the organizers think the party should go. I observed a remarkable difference between the dynamics of the two balls just by considering the different ways the two Masters of Ceremonies performed their roles. In contrast to the Carnival of 1998, in 1999 the MC did not allow people to stand still for a long time. He kept inviting the spectators to become real participants of the party. People were invited to follow the music regardless of whether they knew or not the steps of the samba. "Come on, folks, let's move our bodies... Move your body as you please, only do not stand still... Carnival has to do with moving the body with sensuality... Let's go, you can do it!" His invitation was heard and after a short while almost everybody was dancing. Dancing and watching, of course. Even though I am a Brazilian who has been in several carnivals in Brazil, I have to confess that it was hard not to be enthralled with the show of music and dance that the Hollywood Palladium presents.[46]

What happened in 1998 was slightly different and produced reactions other than getting people into the spirit of communion that carnival proposes. I will briefly describe and analyze what happened at the first Hollywood Palladium carnival that I attended.

The performance of the 1998 Master of Ceremonies reminded me of the World Cup Games. Not only was he wearing the T-shirt of the Brazilian soccer team, but he kept repeatedly singing "Olê, Olê, Olê, Olá, Brazil, Brazil" as though he wanted to stress the Brazilianness of the Mardi Gras of Los Angeles. The refrain, similar to *Viva Brazil*, is usually sung when the Brazilian soccer team is playing international matches.

Instead of competitiveness, carnivals suppose a universal congregation of all with all, and an overturning of the rules of daily life. After a couple of "Olê, Olá, Brazil, Brazil," the MC started including the non-Brazilians by acknowledging the presence of people from different countries. He asked the audience, for instance, if there was anyone there from Cuba. If someone raised his or her hand or simply said "here" the MC would proceed to invite the audience to repeat "Viva" after yelling "Viva Cuba." He did this many times with people from different countries. "Viva the States! Viva! Viva China, Viva! Viva Peru, Viva!" Although he acknowledged the presence of many countries, the Latinos were the only ethnic group he reverenced. After saying Viva to a couple of Latin-American countries, the MC would repeat: "Viva os Latinos!" This created discomfort in a few people. I believe that this reaction had to do with different understandings of what is or should be the Brazilian Carnival in Los Angeles. But not only that, it also had to do with what is understood to be the place of Brazil and Brazilians in Los Angeles.

It does not matter much for the purposes of my reasoning to speculate over what was crossing the MC's mind when he was yelling *Viva os Latinos*. Nonetheless, the controversial reactions to his *vivas* are very revealing and deserve special attention. I first assumed that the MC was following a script defined a priori, but this was not what Maria Lucien, the organizer, said:

> Oh gosh, he started with all those Vivas to El Salvador, Cuba. I told him, quit cheering all these Hispanic countries, this is Brazil! (*So, he created this whole viva thing on his own?*) Yes, he did! It was all his idea, I think because Los Angeles is this very Latin city. But, there were some Brazilians who started to argue with me over this issue. What could I do with the man [MC]? Do you think that it is easy to control Brazilians? I asked the man to stop saying those things, but he kept saying the same things as though I had never asked him to quit!

The fact of not being a Brazilian puts Maria Lucien in a vulnerable position and in itself raises several issues: her right to represent Brazil, questions of authenticity, and so forth. Aware of these issues, she does all she can to avoid problems with Brazilians, since they are the ones who give Carnival its glamour. After all, she says, "how could a Brazilian Carnival be performed with no Brazilians?" That is one of the reasons why she asked the MC to stop cheering other Latin-American countries. "Can't you see? This is a Brazilian party!" As a matter of fact, the MC mentioned many other non-Latin countries. Yet the concern of some Brazilians who asked her to stop the MC was expressed only when there was a risk of Brazilians being mistaken for Latinos. And although she mentioned Hispanics in her interview, the MC never mentioned Hispanics. He said two or three times, "Viva os Latinos," which makes me wonder about his awareness of the political

significance of this ethnic label.[47]   Susan, who has attended the
Hollywood Palladium Carnival many times, shows that some
Brazilians and Americans shared the same concerns:

> I did see a larger influence this year of other Latin countries
> which were present, because I listened very deliberately and
> carefully. Every time that this guy [MC] with the microphone
> would come out and he would say Viva Peru! Or he would say
> who's here from Mexico? Who's here from, you know? There
> were just as many other Latinos, if not more, from some other
> countries, than Brazilians! And this never used to be like that,
> no, unh, unh. It is becoming a very large Latin population
> that is going. I don't know, I just think that it is less
> authentic from the times when I first used to go!

The concern is that the Brazilian Carnival in Los Angeles, which
used to be international, or at least, "authentically" Brazilian, is
becoming *Latinized*. This discourse clearly opposes internationalization
to *Latinization*, valuing the former and devaluing the latter.
Internationalization also seems to be a term that does not apply to all
circumstances that involve more than two nations. The presence of a
German or a Lebanese allowed her to consider the Hollywood Palladium
Carnival as an international event. However the presence of people from
different Latin-American nations led her to identify it as a different
phenomenon. In this case, instead of an international event, the
Brazilian carnival was becoming a Latino one.
   The fact is that under capitalist logic different regions of the world
are perceived in function of the political and economic role that the
internationally dominant powers confer to them within the universe of
international politics. That is, five or six countries from Latin America
do not seem enough to confer to any event an international character.
Following the logic of this discourse, the international character of the
Hollywood Palladium Carnival is conferred by the presence of
Americans (I would even say, white Americans) and other people from
countries that can stand on their own in the international panorama. In
other words, a Brazilian spectacle in Los Angeles or any other non-
Brazilian metropolis is not necessarily an international spectacle; such a
characterization depends mainly on who is in the audience. I could

contradict my own argument saying that a feast or any other event that has mostly people from European countries is an Europeanized event. But such a distinction would never have the negative connotation expressed through the terms "Latinized" and "Latinization," especially when spelled out in the context of Los Angeles.

The Master of Ceremonies not only accepted the inclusion of the Brazilian category within the Latino broader category, but also seemed to be proud of it. Taking all this into account, I would suggest that the MC's attitude of crying out *Viva os Latinos* in the context of that "international" event was a "revolutionary" one. He challenged the mainstream discourse of American society, which was so present in the quotes that we have analyzed. I have no way of measuring the scope of his discourse, nor of knowing his awareness about it. However, I suggest that the alliance that he is proposing between Brazilians and Latinos goes beyond the rhetoric of the occasion. He is a black Brazilian, and as such his possibilities of mobility in the ranking system are more limited, unless he has a special talent which could confer him special distinction. On the other hand, the ways in which race and racism have been constructed in the United States and Brazil do not really work toward motivating an immediate empathy between black Brazilians and black Americans.[48] In this case, and also as a function of the linguistic proximity between Spanish and Portuguese, the natural "colored" *allies* of black Brazilians would be the Latinos.

However, this is not an easy alliance. Maria Lucien stresses the resistance of Brazilians in joining other Latinos for the organization of the Hollywood Palladium Carnival:

> Brazilians are not really close to the Hispanics. It is almost like... they are crazy, do you know what I mean? They don't want to mix with Hispanics, but it is necessary to have unity to win. For example, for the Carnival, don't you think that we should have rehearsals with all the community? But everything that Brazilians do is always for money. And I say I cannot do everything. Can you do a little something for the love of Carnival, for the love of Brazil? And everybody is kind of like that, always. That's why it costs a fortune! There is no sponsor! Americans are not interested in this community and the Brazilians don't sponsor themselves! So, it is very

difficult! Latin Americans, the real Latin Americans, the
Hispanics, they are much more united. They are the ones who
really help me! They're the ones Brazilians should be grateful
to.

Despite her understanding that the place of Brazilians in Los
Angeles should be among other Latinos, Maria Lucien does not think
that it is necessary to spell that out in the context of the Hollywood
Palladium Carnival. I discussed this issue with her during an interview
and gave her the feedback from interviews that I had with other people
about the Hollywood Palladium carnival ball. When at the ball of 1999
the same MC as 1998 started again with his *vivas* to this or that
country, she immediately replaced him with another MC, who
performed his role of merely motivating people to dance and so forth.

The Latino issue was not the only one which the 1998 Master of
Ceremonies externalized. He also brought out one of the most
important pillars of Brazilian nationalism: the idea of racial mixture as
something positive. In the MC's discourse, samba works as a bridge,
"Hey Folks, here we will be celebrating with samba the union of races,
because samba is the symbol of the union of races." If samba is the
unifying link, Carnival is a special opportunity for this encounter, and
the Hollywood Palladium is a strategic space to insist upon the "union
of races" before a broader audience.

Though the MC's *vivas* to the Latinos produced controversial
responses, I would not say the same about his proselytism for racial
communion. As before, he was voicing a political discourse as loaded
as any other. How could I understand that even though he was making a
political statement similar to the first one, there was no response
against it? After all, in the United States the idea of racial mixture has a
connotation completely distinct, and even opposed, to the one that it
has in Brazil. American national ideology was built based upon the
power and superiority of the white colonizers and the high value placed
on racial purity. As a corollary, racial mixture, which is considered to
produce inferior human beings, has not been motivated, and racial
segregation has been the prevalent solution.[49]

Unlike the American, the Brazilian national ideology has valued
racial mixture as well as rhetorically acknowledged the role of the first
three important groups that participated of the formation of Brazilian

people: Indians, Portuguese, and Africans (Da Matta 1981, Freyre 1936, Ribeiro 1995).

Despite articulating similar empirical elements differently and producing extremely different forms of racial relationships, in both countries race has historically served as one of the most "natural" justifications for exploitation. Though in the case of the United States race has prevented kinship relationships, it has never prevented socio-economic relationships, which has made color an element to measure power, and a natural justification for the segmentation of the labor market and the rational explanation of social inequality. Therefore, color is considered the most important element of differentiation in American ideology (Harris 1964). However, what is clear in the case of Los Angeles' system of socioeconomic differentiation is that color is only one among many elements that are used to classify and subordinate people. Nationality, class, and gender, as well as other ethnic identities, are also used with the purpose of creating a cleavage to justify exploitation and inequality (Bonacich 1972; 1990).

The fact is that the discourse of Brazilian racial ideology gets lost within the playful space of the Hollywood Palladium Carnival. Still, a question remains. Why does the same thing not occur with the MC's cheers to Latinos?

I would say for now that a negative reaction to the discourse of racial communion did not come as promptly as in the case of the *Viva Latino* discourse because the ideology that feeds this discourse is an important part of the exoticized image of Brazil in the United States. In other words, as far as Brazilian ideology about racial mixture is only part of Brazilian cultural distinctiveness (wildness), it does not really affect American life or mainstream ideologies at all. It is only an isolated discourse in a restricted event. So why bother about ideas that have nothing to do with American reality? After all, Brazil and Brazilians are far away, lost somewhere below the equatorial line. Nonetheless, a condescending thought like this could not be developed in regards to Latinos in general, or Mexicans in particular in the case of California. Mexicans and other larger groups of Latinos are already part of the Los Angeles market of working exploitation which has created different versions for explaining inequality. All of them, however, stress the faults of the Mexicans or Latinos in general. Not being perceived as a part of Los Angeles' daily life, Brazilians are still seen as an exotic species whose political discourse can be taken lightly, and which American mainstream ideologies do not necessarily have to take seriously.

I have been led to believe that Carnival is, among other elements of Brazilian culture, the one that most easily stands out to establish the *necessary* distinction between Brazilian and the Latino identity and claim a more universal or more European identity. Despite all the problems that it might occasionally cause Brazilian women, carnival works as a positive distinction or capital when what is at stake is the search to distinguish oneself positively from a Latino identity.

In any case, using Brazilian Carnival as the main source of a Brazilian international identity or representation is limited and problematic because it means basing a representation, Brazilian identity, upon another representation, Carnival. Besides, carnival is a particular kind of representation in itself. First, it happens in a specific space and time. That is, carnival is not a daily life event, but an exceptional event. Second, as a ritual of reversal, the Brazilian Carnival's symbols and behaviors do not reflect reality as it is, but as Brazilians represent it for the purposes of the event. Third, the carnival of Rio de Janeiro, the reference for international versions, is only one out of several versions of carnival that Brazil has countrywide.[50] Fourth, even though women occupy the center of the party, Brazilian carnival is not only about women

I am not proposing the opposite view, that is, that Brazil has nothing to do with Carnival, or that these international representations are false. Representations are representations, that is, slices of reality with the purpose of representing the whole. I argue here that connecting the image of Brazil and Brazilians to Carnival produces consequences beyond interfering in the process of Brazilian immigrant integration into the world of Los Angeles. Indeed, exoticization makes Brazilian culture more saleable in the international market of exotic consumerism. However, it also makes Brazil more vulnerable to the political attacks from the hegemonic Protestant culture. That is, Brazilian exoticism can also work as a good excuse to justify the position of Brazil in the international division of labor. In other words, the same ideology that creates and commercializes exoticism uses it to justify the political position of exotic countries as a result of their "primitive" and non-changeable culture.[51]

While a transposed ritual, the Hollywood Palladium Carnival is not grounded in the same cosmological or ideological constructs that expressions of carnival in Brazil are.[52] My hypothesis is that the Hollywood Palladium Carnival is recreated according to the expectations of a public that is ignorant about carnival or whose only known version of it is the one promoted by the Hollywood movie industry. Perhaps that is why many Brazilian immigrants complain about it.

Paradoxically, the production of the event includes no a priori intentions of helping to sustain any specific ideologies. It ends up doing so to the extent that the ritual itself is connected with the context within which it is created. Thus the Hollywood Palladium Carnival is a creation of Brazilian immigrants eager for recreating in Los Angeles certain Brazilian national rituals to build up a tradition of gathering and socialization, as well as carving out a place for Brazil and Brazilians in Los Angeles. Thus, besides promoting Brazil and Brazilians in a broader scale in Los Angeles, the Hollywood Palladium Carnival also plays an important role as an arena where important alliances or circumstantial compromises can be established between Brazilians and Americans, as well as Brazilians and other immigrant groups, especially Latinos.

Surviving Los Angeles in the Brazilian Way (*Jeitinho Brasileiro*)

> I've just asked my husband how the American sees Brazil and he said: Irrelevant. Not in the picture (Elizabeth, age 67).

> But the younger American who goes to Brazil, for example, this friend of mine who went to study with Ivo Pitanguy.[53] People, he loves Brazil! You know what he most wanted? A Brazilian wife!!! He couldn't get one because our association ended and he didn't have enough time to find one. He was crushed! (Renato, age 30).

The place that the United States reserves for Brazilians is so insignificant that it usually does not take long for us to understand our position here. However, most Brazilians believe that it might take us forever to start behaving accordingly. Renato, age 30, living in the

United States for the last ten years, says "Brazil is just so big, so rich, so alive. Man – these gringos do not understand it, if they had a chance to immerse themselves in Brazil they'd never be the same, you know?" When comparing the behavior of Brazilians to Portuguese immigrants (Chapter Three), Pastor David Bravo insisted on how hard it is for Brazilians to fit into American society. He says that Brazilians do not follow rules seriously and cannot stand doing the same thing over and over again without adding some of their own creativity. According to him, Brazilians lack the most valued quality in the United States, consistency. Nonetheless, many other Brazilians believe that they are quite successful, especially considering the fact that, unlike the Portuguese, they have not "burnt their ships yet." That is, they still believe that if things do not work here as expected they can always go back home. Ivan, a journalist, age 44, explains what is special about Brazilians when compared to other Latinos,

> I think that Brazilians do better in America that most Latinos because of the attitude of the Brazilian. The Brazilian, maybe as a product of his own ignorance, is that which he is, and we, with all our defects, do not have a submissive attitude towards anyone. The average Brazilian doesn't feel he is less than anyone. He thinks he is Brazilian. And when he gets to those areas where he is good, then no one else comes close. Be it in soccer, samba, music, sex, in those things that we believe we are good at in our own positive image of ourselves. And the Brazilian, what do we believe the Brazilian is? We believe that all Brazilians are good ball players, every Brazilian is a good conversationist, every Brazilian is good at sex, at music, at partying. We are hot! We are the *quindins de iaiá* [Bahian dessert]. And the image that the world has of Brazil is that we are good with a ball, good at samba, good at fucking, good at everything, understand? It's exotic! Deep down they like it because they don't know much about us. So we aren't put in the same boat...you know? In a racist country such as this, the Brazilian even has a privileged position because we are not placed together with other Latinos. Brazilians are a separate category.

In general, however, as suggested by my observation and the explanation of Pastor David Bravo, *o jeitinho brasileiro* (the Brazilian way) is acceptable in certain social spaces more than in others, such as Paola, age 35, suggests:

Here in the United States everything has a lot to do with appearances and Americans vary the treatment towards the Brazilian, or toward any foreigner, according to his color. If you are Brazilian and you have a lighter skin, they treat you one way. If you are Brazilian and you have darker skin, they treat you a different way. It's always appearance. They think we are cute. They think Brazilians are interesting. But if the Brazilian has a darker skin they already classify him as another Hispanic. When they are not classified as Hispanics they receive the same treatment as a European. In that case, they find him interesting, fascinating, like they find the French and Italians fascinating.

As appearance is not only related to color but also to social position, I am led to believe that *jeitinho brasileiro* can be used as a trump card only when combined with other elements that allow one to rank different Brazilians into different social positions in American society. On the other hand, as suggested by Ivan and Pastor David Bravo, Brazilian patriotism produces in Brazilians a self-confidence that supposedly helps them dare more than other Latino nationalities in American society. As Ivan said above, "Brazilians do not feel they are less than anyone." Such self-esteem seemingly makes them generally stronger to endure discrimination in the United States. Otherwise, they believe, they can "always" go back to the "largest" and best country of the world.

CHAPTER 6

The Dilemma of Americanization and the Reinforcement of a Mythical Brazilianness

> In exile all attempts to put down roots look like treason: they are admissions of defeat (Salman Rusdhie, 1988:208).

> If [the United States] is a country apparently so cold, so dry, so straight-edged, but which still leaves us homesick for it, it can no longer be said that it is so straight-edged, so dry, so cold (Alceu Amoroso Lima, 1955:16).

To Be or Not to Be, is This the Question?

In this chapter, I deal with the dilemma of Americanization such as it presents itself to Brazilians in different social positions and at different moments in their history of integration. I address the question of returning migration and how either the decision to stay in the United States or the decision to go back to Brazil is connected with idealizations of Brazil and Brazilianness built from their concrete conditions of life here and there.

In Chapter One, I defined Americanization as the process of being acculturated by American society and ideologies. I also proposed that this process must be understood in the context of the expansion of the American economic project all over the world. In this sense, the "adoption" of American ideas and behaviors is less a matter of choice and more a matter of imposition. But the imposition of American ideas and behaviors should not be seen as disarticulated from other socioeconomic transformations produced within the expansion of the American political economic project. From this perspective, the adoption of certain American ideas and behaviors is better understood as *required* rather than imposed. In other words, a "modernized" society requires "modern" ideas and patterns of consumption.

Seen from this perspective, the phenomenon of Americanization is far beyond being consciously controlled by the individuals of a society submitted to such a process.

However, the ways in which Brazilians have reacted to the spread of American ideologies and behaviors in Brazil suggests that Americanization is a process that can be consciously and politically controlled, which is probably true. But it is also true that Americanization, as I have been proposing all along, is a phenomenon that affects individuals whether they maintain direct contact with Americans or not.

In Brazil, the issue of Americanization was brought out when the first famous Brazilian living in the United States was accused by sectors of the Brazilian media of not representing Brazil properly. Carmen Miranda tried to explain that the representation could be Americanized but she was still very Brazilian. She even inspired a song that became famous called *Disseram que eu voltei Americanizada* (They Said that I've Come Back Americanized), in which she argues that in spite of appearances she was still very Brazilian. The point, however, was not about her being Brazilian and keeping her Brazilianness to herself. The point was her submission in embodying an American version of Brazilian women and culture. Although her international success made Brazilians in general proud, many objected to her typification of Brazil. A São Paulo paper, *A Folha da Noite*, registered the disapproval: "So that's how Brazil shines in the United States: with a Portuguese woman singing bad-tasting black sambas. It is really like that! And so that's how it should be. Because there really aren't many people in this country who are worth as much as that Carmen, that great and excellent Carmen who left to sing nonsense abroad (Cited in Davis 1997:13)."

Decades have passed and it seems that Brazilians still feel uneasy about the idea of Americanization. Why would Brazilians resist so strongly such an idea? We have seen that whether Brazilian immigrants like it or not, their lives in the United States are quite different from their lives in Brazil. Even when their survival depends entirely on Brazilian networks and they only get around through their Brazilian friends and/or relatives, the outside scene is still American. We have seen in Chapters Three and Four that the attempts to reproduce Brazil in different environments and opportunities are only partially successful. Indeed, being a Brazilian in the United States is a situation totally different from being a Brazilian in Brazil. Even though Americanization is already in process long before Brazilians migrate to the United States, once here the process has a different dynamic, most of the time far different from what was expected, as we have seen in the previous chapters. In any case, after living in the United States for a while, whether eating tortillas, tacos, hamburgers, or *feijoada*, Brazilians are no longer what they were when they came. They have been transformed into immigrants and will forever be between two worlds. As proposed by Salman Rushdie's *Satanic Verses,* and by many studies on immigrant acculturation, immigrants are new beings whether or not they remain faithful to the traditions of their nation of birth. When their appearance allows it, they may either choose to be completely absorbed and integrated into the new world, or reinforce their links to their nation of birth. But this is a complicated process that involves feelings of all sorts, including the feeling of guilt when one chooses the new country.

"I Consider It an Act of Treason for the Person to Abandon his Country…"

Regardless of the reasons why Brazilians come, many of them decide to stay in the United States. There is no exact period of time after which it becomes more likely that a Brazilian would rather remain in the United States than go back to Brazil. However, some people have a few ideas about how long it takes to be "taken" by the American way of life (whatever that means for different people). When interacting with the members of the church of Chino I was asked several times how long I had been in the United States. I would answer, for example, three years. They would look at me and, nodding their heads, would predict: "you're not going back to Brazil. After two years here you cannot get used to life in Brazil anymore!"

There are many reasons why, after a certain period of living in the United States, Brazilians decide to stay for good. Marriage to

Americans, a career, and material comforts that they cannot afford in Brazil are some of the reasons Brazilians use to explain their decision to stay. However, even when none of these conditions are fulfilled, many of them still prefer to stay, and that is when the argument of "getting used to life in the United States" comes. This choice can hardly be understood by a Brazilian who has never left Brazil (or even by those Brazilians who have been in the United States only for a short-term visit). For them, the attitude of choosing the United States over Brazil sounds like treason.

In 1973, Henfil decided to spend some time in New York because he was tired of the Brazilian dictatorship censoring his artistic and intellectual output. He dreamed of working in an environment where he could create freely and he believed that the United States could provide him with that environment. Soon after, he found out that he was dead wrong. In any case, his friends could not feel worse about his decision, and heavily criticized it in a collective interview they did before he left for New York. Millor Fernandes, a Brazilian humorist, says:

> I want to say one thing: I think that travelling is a right everybody has. Me, when I travel for three months, I consider it exile. Every friend of mine who travels and says he is going to stay generally doesn't. I really consider it an act of treason. I'm not kidding. I consider it an act of treason for the person to abandon his country, especially for smaller reasons, to become famous, earn money, earn dollars. I think it an act of treason. All the more if in his country he has some type of fame, and a type of income which is already very adequate. [...] If he didn't have anything, suddenly we could take Brazil aside and say: "Here I didn't make it, but I will make it there." But you already have it here, what is your interest? You easily earn five thousand dollars here, why are you interested in getting 50 thousand there? This is stupid (Henfil:1983:58).

Throughout my life in the Brazilian Northeast I endorsed the idea that adopting American concepts or behaviors was a betrayal of my country and my self. My friends and I would even avoid Hollywood movies just to be faithful to our nationalist principles and not expose ourselves to American subliminal propaganda. Of course, we all had seen Westerns and such, but that had been before we understood the role they played in the spread of American imperialism. Even though we knew about Sacco & Vanzetti, Martin Luther King, and some interesting American leftists, these were exceptions we did not give much weight to when portraying the United States. In brief, the elites of the United States and Brazil were the ones to be blamed for the political situation in Brazil. Thanks to them we were living under a dictatorship that harmed the country to such an extent that we are still far from calculating the damage. In any case, we could not help but open a space for the English world with the Beatles and a couple of other revolutionary singers or writers, but England was already history. We were not aware that our lives were already impregnated with American goods and ideas. In any case, we believed we should consciously avoid co-optation. Thus, we too believed that Americanization was a process that depended solely on our agency. Yet the avoidance of American goods and ideas was not our only strategy of resistance. We were also helping to politically organize peasants, urban workers and others affected by the changes promoted by "modernization."

My experience does not represent the general experience of most Brazilians belonging to my generation. That is, my position was a particular one; my friends and I were Marxists and hoped for a working class revolution. For us, doing whatever would benefit the United States meant capitulation. "Go to the United States to study? Are you crazy? Look at me, that's a middle-class dream, I have self-respect and political consciousness."

However, the so-called communists were not the only ones to resist the penetration of American goods and ideas. Upper-class people had always looked down on American fashion and arts, and even today some of the people I interviewed here always complain about American taste, education, fashion and so forth. "We are far more sophisticated than they are. We have had the privilege of drinking from different springs, do you understand?"

It is a fact that the colonial position of Brazil makes it relatively open to the allure of different colonizers. When Brazilians affirm that they are more sophisticated than Americans they are mostly referring to the fact that Brazil has been exposed to several philosophies and possibilities of existence. But many times they are affirming that Paris is more sophisticated than London or New York, and that Brazil has had more influence from France (and the Latin world) than from England (and the Anglo-Saxon world). In any case, the argument generally used confirms the colonial spirit. That is, the question is more about choosing the colonizer than questioning or getting rid of colonization.

> I think that old folks in Brazil had much more of a European influence than an American one. If you look at the Brazil of 30 years ago, you see that the people of the higher classes first spoke French and then spoke English. Because French was the diplomatic language... You can see this in schools, I studied in a French school in Brazil. There's the Sion, there's the St. Claire de Marie... so I think that at the time when I was a girl Brazil had an American influence, but not as much as nowadays. For example, our fashions were much more influenced by European fashions, our songs were much more European, the movies. Of course we always had Hollywood, but I have the impression that life in general was closer to European than to American life. Nowadays you go to Brazil and everything is American: the clothes, the music. The kids of this generation today are much more turned toward the United States. To be very honest I always thought Europe was much more sophisticated than the United States. In terms of culture, tradition, the arts in general. Even movies. Nowadays I think that the Americans have excellent movies, but in my opinion the French and Italians were always more artistic in terms of the cinema than the Americans (Tania, age 51, divorced).

Many people, however, spent their lives dreaming of the paradise that the United States would be. I met here a colonel from the Brazilian Air Force who spent his life dreaming of the perfect world that he learnt the United States was. During his military career he came to the United States a couple of times for military training. He liked it so much that at the first opportunity he sent his two oldest children to learn English here. His children ended up marrying Americans and staying here for good. After his retirement he and his wife decided to join them here.

They mostly complained about everything on their first year. In one of our conversations he told me that his ideas about the United States had totally changed after living here:

> Before I came here I thought that the American was the most honest, polite, educated, and correct person in the world. I took a beating in the beginning and learned a lot in regards to American democracy, and today I have a completely different perspective on the subject. But my situation here is special: two of my three children have lived here more than 18 years. My sister-in-law, brother-in-law, and grandchild are American citizens. We have a green card and our youngest daughter may also plant her roots here. But today I have a different idea about what the American way of life really is, and I can guarantee you that I was completely wrong. And if I am living here it is purely because of the need to be close to my children, from whom we had been separated so many years.

I did not inquire deeper about the motivations for these feelings, although certain matters were noticeable at first sight. He had to cope with the loss of his position. That is, where he was a colonel in Brazil and benefited from all the honors connected to the position, here he could hardly make himself understood. Despite such qualifications the only work that he could find here was menial. In addition, his and his wife's relationship with their children, which they expected to be more like in Brazil, did not work out as such because the children were already acclimated to American customs, and hardly included anything from Brazilian culture in their daily lives.

Getting Used to the American Lifestyle

After a while, almost all immigrants get used to whatever American way of life they can afford and begin to stop noticing the differences between the countries. In any case, dreaming of the United States is quite different from living in the United States. For many people, however, living in the United States is everything that they had always wanted. Yet the same person who told me that she "was born in the

wrong country" also told me that "we, Brazilians, are more
sophisticated." Thus the question is far more complicated and its
understanding requires going beyond Manichean explanations: we have
seen that Brazilians come to the United States because of the expansion
of American imperialism, which has created needs that cannot be
fulfilled in Brazil for reasons already discussed in the Introduction and
Chapter One. They come and realize that things here are not as simple
as they supposed them to be. A friend of mine who has been here for
about ten years and has a considerably successful career in a highly
competitive area went to Brazil for six months. After coming back she
was telling me that she does not see herself spending the rest of her life
here. She said that the six months she spent in Brazil made her
understand what home is all about. She said, "you finally relax, you
know? You quit wondering about being appropriate or inappropriate. It
seems that no matter what, we, foreigners, are always inappropriate
here." She also referred to the professional competition that makes life
highly stressful in the United States. On the other hand, she says that
this is all very challenging too.

There are different reasons why Brazilians like or dislike the United
States, but most of them complain about similar things, such as those
things they believe Brazil has and the United States does not, or vice-
versa. In general, everybody wants to keep in touch with Brazil. For
instance, one of the reasons why everybody wants a green card is to be
able to visit Brazil at will. The first thing Ruth, age 52, and her family
did when they got their green cards after being here for fifteen years was
to visit Brazil. She does not contemplate the possibility of moving
back to Brazil because her three children are here and they will be
making their lives here. She says, "there is nothing left for us in
Brazil." But she was amazed to realize that even though her family here
earns three times more than one of her sisters in Brazil, her sister's
family seems to have accumulated more goods there than her family has
here.

> I found everything very expensive in Brazil, clothes and shoes
> are absurd! And food is more or less the same price as here. A
> dress I can buy here (at Ross) for 12 costs 100 in Brazil. But I
> don't understand things in Brazil. My sister, who is considered
> rich, who has a house and two cars, earns less than half of

what we earn here. Her husband earns little more than I earn, 1200 [at the time of the interview, 04/04/1998, the Brazilian currency was valuing as much as the dollar]. My husband earns 3 times what I earn and even so it looks like they have more things than we do. I don't know how we spend so much here.[54]

She was somewhat puzzled to conclude that even materially they are not better off than this sister to whom she is referring. Still, she concludes "there is nothing left for us in Brazil." Indeed, Ruth has several reasons to believe this. Two of her three children are already married to American citizens, and the third is going to college. When they came here, fifteen years ago, their children were quite young. Thus, all the expectations they created for their future were to be realized in the United States. Like most of the Brazilians living here, Ruth and her family did not intend to stay when they came. Her husband was a public employee in Brazil and they were not in any great need. He came first because he was the head of an Evangelical musical group in Brazil and was invited to tour the Brazilian Adventist churches in the United States. After a while he thought that it would be worth bringing the whole family and see what would happen. It would be just an "experiment."

Such an experiment, however, is one in which not all variables can be controlled. Both expected and unexpected things may happen and change initial plans totally, as we have seen in many cases I discuss here. Also, if our lives in the United States keep on changing, what can we expect about life in Brazil? Everybody wants, at any cost, to confine Brazil to our last experience of it, and hold on to it forever. Good or bad, it is our safe heaven, and it encourages us to pursue that for which we came here. The problem is that Brazil is not all the same and also changes like every other place. In the United States, Brazilians get involved in American consumerism, get used to American economic stability, organization, English and so forth. Our children grow, marry Americans and our grandchildren are now as American as any other American can be. They might be black Americans, Hispanics, white Americans and so forth, but Brazil seems to be gone. Commenting about the celebration of the Golden Anniversary of one of the members of Chino, Lúcia said:

Seeing all those Americanized people I thought, my God the Brazilian race is dying out here in the United States. Everyone is Americanized. There are children of parents in our generation who don't even speak Portuguese anymore. They married Americans, and became completely Americanized. Yesterday I was talking to Zoe, who was widowed last month, and she is seriously thinking about going back to Brazil to live with her sisters there. She is living in her daughter's house now, but she doesn't feel right because everything is Americanized, they only speak English and eat American food.

Missing a Mythical Brazil

In Chapter One I discussed how my position as a Brazilian with specific characteristics defined my choices and influenced my contacts and the results that I obtained in my research. My position as a Brazilian who was going back to Brazil and who clearly demonstrated affection for Brazil might have triggered the nostalgia of my interviewees and influenced their responses about the issue of return. Thus, these restrictions are probably even more applicable here than in the previous sections of this work.

Most of the Brazilians that I met in Los Angeles would like to go back to Brazil someday. Many of them already had plans to move back or spend part of the year there after retirement (in the case of those who have descendants in the United States).

When I think about old age here in the United States I freeze up. It's as if it was a death before death, you know? I'm already looking into the prices of apartments in Brazil. Who knows, maybe I might even go to Fortaleza? [teasing me because I live in Fortaleza] (Tania, age 51, divorced).

As soon as my husband dies, if he dies before me, that is, I'll pack up my bags and return to Brazil. The next day! God keep me from staying here and ending my life in one of these [retirement] homes they have here. Besides this, does it make sense to spend 3 thousand dollars a month on a home? I'm going back close to my kids in Brazil. If I can as easily die close to my children, why would I die among unknown old people? (Elizabeth, age 67, married).

Most of the Brazilians miss Brazilian warmth. It seems that a perfect life would have American material goods and a Brazilian spirit:

[If you ask me] if its more worth it living here than in Brazil, it is! But you don't have the same tenderness, here loneliness is much worse! We have friendships and everything, but each one lives for himself, each one has his own life. Here we live for our jobs. You go to sleep and wake up thinking about what you are going to do. The weekend arrives, and you enjoy it and such, but come Sunday night, and you are already thinking about work. And this is the story of why lately nobody sees me at parties: because any work I get I take advantage of it, because I have to work! Mainly now that I work by the hour and by the day.

In Brazil people complain that they don't see money, but at least we have fun with the little we have. You have a family, you go see your family, you argue, and make up. Not here. Here you are always alone, everyone fits into his own little world. And it is a very materialistic life. We live very much for material consumption. You can have everything here! A pretty carpet, a pretty sofa, and you live to have things. But you don't feel happy, understand? Another thing is that I got involved with domestic work because they pay well! So I spent 23 years here as a maid. But I feel something is missing. I like to cook, and do what I do, but this is not what I want! Even taking into consideration that the treatment that Americans show their domestic employees is totally different from Brazil. Here they treat you like a professional. I think this is what makes the difference for us. In the houses where I worked I never felt like their servant, you know? Here I never worked for any Brazilian! And even for Americans I don't do as I used to when I first got here. So, I plan to go back to Brazil and open a business in Brazil. I would want a wedding shop. It's something new that doesn't have a lot of competition. But I could even put aside this idea of opening a business, build two houses side by side, and live off the rent (Telma, age 46, divorced, no children).

Here things are very different, the customs are different, the relationship with friends is different. For example, I have these neighbors here and I never went over to their house, I say hello, but I never went over there. It's not like in Brazil where you go to each other's houses. There's a birthday, everybody goes. Here friendship is different, even Brazilians change, they become Americanized... [How?] They become worse (Sara, age 59, divorced, no children).

I have a few American friends, but [the friendship] is not as deep as it is with Brazilians. Americans always maintain what they call an *optimum distance*. And you cannot get in very easily, there is always that reservation. They don't open their houses like that, you can't knock at any time, no. You can't open yourself up either... Everybody becomes robotized, this comes from childhood. Everybody becomes a bunch of little robots... (Elizabeth, age 67).

Here there is this crazy consumerism which I didn't know and to which I was introduced to through my wife. She always wanted more and more and she didn't see how much I did to get this more. The more I worked the more she demanded. All kinds of demands. She demanded to live in a better place, to have more money, to spend more. But it was this business of showing off things we didn't have. To have everything and to give one's life paying the bills. That is, we don't eat like before, we don't live like before, we don't talk to each other like before, the conversation becomes solely about our debts. What to pay, our obligations, and this way the relationship starts to break up. I know that here the field is open for everybody. You know a little more about some type of work and suddenly you can get a lot of stuff. But you also lose a lot. You lose that side of the essence of life. For example, there are many people here who live for their jobs. Their jobs are the main thing. Then your kids are not important anymore, your wife is not important, your very health is not important, suddenly what is important is what he can get with the money he can earn, even if he can never enjoy it, understand? He doesn't eat well, doesn't sleep well, doesn't make love. In Brazil I never had half the things I have here, but I lived happy because I had my home, could put gas in the car, had the essentials to eat. I made money in the summer and hibernated in the winter, like a bear. But then I had time to write, to read, to watch movies, create new ideas for my work. I realized quickly that this life was distancing me from my dreams, but I believed that I had to continue because it was a new experience in my life and I didn't feel like I could let go without insisting a bit. Today I feel like a champion, for being alive and having gone through this great experience, which will mark my entire life, and will be the greatest lesson for my son. My future is still in Brazil. Here life goes quickly, it is a passage. I'm here because I have my son here, and if I didn't, I would be traveling to other countries and developing other tasks related to surfing.

One thing that American life instills in people is dependence to cities, to the system, to consumption, right there where you are. It's not easy to change. For example, I live here in this house, I have this car, if I don't do something I'll never leave here, never. As many Americans here don't even know Mexico. They don't even know Arizona, which is the neighboring state. When we speak of the international world, they close up and take on that attitude that the world starts and ends here. They don't want to know, ah South America... Is Brazil in Europe? The surfers are less like this because they like maps. But the majority are satisfied with being a part of society, and they are very good parts because they don't change, they continue consuming. This is not like me, you, or others who are just passing by here. We are like sponges, we absorb what good they have, and leave behind what is bad. So, why do we come here? Because they have the best technologies! We come, we learn, and we go back. So, living here in my old age is out of the question. I think that old age here, and it might even be as stable as it seems, but if you look inside the eyes and the heart of each one, they are all bitter, unhappy. They have houses, cars, and everything else they have put together, but they are bitter inside. They work their entire lives to attain this, but what they live seems as if it is not as gentle as old age in a country which is more free of obligations. So for me to live in this system here, I prefer to live in the system in Brazil. Living in Brazil, especially where I live, is much better than any other place in the world. Because we enjoy life and can pass on to future generations something better than the bitter side of moneyed tension (Romero, age 42, divorced).

There are as many representations of Brazil as there are different experiences. Therefore, what each Brazilian calls Brazil generally refers to a very particular experience of Brazil. And the same is also true in regards to their experience of the United States. The surfer above is talking about his life in Florianópolis, Santa Catarina. It is expected that the view Brazilians have of Brazil is strictly influenced by the kind of life they used to have there, and their decisions to live in the United States have to do with this. In other words, if they could live better (materially and emotionally) in Brazil they would have stayed there. But this is not always true. There are many Brazilians who can live (materially) better in Brazil than here, but they say that they like the challenge of living here.

I interviewed a young man from Rio de Janeiro, whose father, who owns a travel agency, sponsored him and his friends to come to celebrate his 12th birthday at Disneyworld, Florida. Later he came to California as a tourist and stayed. He married and divorced an American with whom he has a child. He told me that he loves Brazil but is used to the Californian way of life. "Is there anything better than driving on these freeways when they are really *free*? It is definitely worth paying any fine!"

There are many other Brazilians who can theoretically live anywhere because they can afford it. In these cases living here *or* there is not an issue because they live here *and* there. They are the transnational Brazilians who go as far as their money lets them. Although going through the same experiences as anybody else, they live them from a totally different perspective since they can give them up at any time. They do not have to be here. They are here because they like the Californian landscape, accent, weather, waves and general standard of consumption. This is totally different from the situation of those who believe that they have become entangled enough in the American style of life that they want to give up their standard of consumption here for the warmth of Brazilian people.

In general most Brazilians I interviewed long for Brazil and try to find hundreds of excuses (or motives) to justify staying here:

> Despite my being outside Brazil for 20 years, I continue to like Brazil very much, I go there every year, you know? This is interesting about the Brazilian, because I have spoken with Koreans, Vietnamese, and other immigrants; they have been here for twenty years and have never gone back to their countries, and never plan to go back. Now the Brazilian loves his country and never stops dreaming about it (Nilce, age 47).

It seems that regardless of all the ideas of spatial mobility which have spread through globalization, to choose living in the United States still sounds like a betrayal for many Brazilians, including some of those who have made this choice. Indeed, why would a Brazilian *choose* to leave such a beautiful, warmhearted and hopeful country?

I would not say that the images suggested above still hold true for most Brazilians. In fact, much has changed about the ways Brazilians perceive Brazil since the first president elected after the dictatorship, Fernando Color de Melo, was impeached. But the images of Brazil as a beautiful, warmhearted and hopeful country were widely trusted when the political exiles of the Military Coup of 1964 were forced to leave. Between the late 1960s and early 1980s the Brazilian singers in exile composed songs exalting the beauty of their country's nature and the warmth of its people. But they were not the first Brazilians to recognize the qualities of the country when living away in foreign lands.

Part of the literary and musical production that glorifies Brazil's land and people was produced by exiles, either voluntary or forced. Gonçalves Dias' *Song of Exile* is the prime example (reproduced from Haberly 1983:28-29):

Nosso céu tem mais estrelas,
Nossas várzeas têm mais flores
Nossos bosques têm mais vida,
Nossa vida mais amores
Em cismar sózinho à noite,
Mais prazer encontro eu lá;
Minha terra tem palmeiras,
Onde canta o sabiá

Minha terra tem primores,
Que tais não encontro eu cá;
Em cismar – sózinho, à noite –
Mais prazer encontro eu lá;
Minha terra tem palmeiras,
Onde canta o Sabiá.

Não permita Deus que eu morra,
Sem que eu volte para lá;
Sem que desfrute os primores
Que não encontro por cá;
Sem qu'inda aviste as palmeiras,

Onde canta o Sabiá.

Our heavens have more stars,
Our meadows have more flowers,
Our forests have more life,
Our life has much more love.
When I dream alone at night,
I find more pleasure there;
There are palm trees in my country
From which sings the Sabiá.

My country has a loveliness
That here I cannot find;
When I dream - alone, at night -
More pleasure I find there;
There are palm trees in my country,
From which sings the Sabiá.

May God not let me perish
Without returning there once more;
Without delighting in the loveliness
That here I cannot find;
Without another glimpse of the palm trees
From which sings the Sabiá.

Gonçalves Dias was idealizing Brazil, or rather, referring to a particular Brazil to which he was connected and which certainly many Brazilians of his time did not have the chance to know. Regardless of the several Brazils, or a Brazil for each circumstance, despite good or bad experiences of Brazil, many Brazilians seem still to believe that

Our heavens have more stars,
Our meadows far more flowers,
Our forests have more life,
Our life has much more love.

The corollary is "May God not let me perish/Without returning there once more/Without delighting in the loveliness that here I cannot find".

When Omar Santana, age 62, left Brazil thirty-six years ago, he was not sure that he would spend all these years in the United States. After a few years of living and working in Riverside, he believed he would never go back to Brazil. However, when visiting Brazil four years ago, he and his wife, Lúcia, age 55, decided that they would return to Brazil for good.

Omar and Lúcia have been married for twenty-eight years and have two sons, Tiago, age 25, and Lucas, age 22. As a Brazilian immigrant couple living in Riverside, in the greater Los Angeles area, they have socialized mostly with Brazilians, and have themselves educated their children as Brazilian Americans, because Lúcia has always lived a Brazilian life in the States, as she points out:

> I came as a maid for the family of a diplomat. My dream was to know this famous America which I so loved, understand? When I finished my contract with this family, I had the opportunity to come to California and one year later I got married. Then, when I married a Brazilian, my life returned to being Brazilian, only inside of America. I never felt myself very contaminated by this American materialism for electronic things that everybody thinks is so neat and such. Now, for example, despite the fact that everybody is buying 30-inch TVs, for me my 13-inch TV is still very good. So my way of life has always been Brazilian. First because I live among a church which is only of Brazilians speaking Portuguese. Inside my home, the food we eat is Brazilian. I only communicate with my children in Portuguese. That is, I continued being a Brazilian inside America... This is why my adaptation to Brazil will be easier. I won't say that I won't suffer, because after all, we were 30 years here!

Concerning their return to Brazil, they explain that their decision to move back has provoked surprise and indignation among both their Brazilian immigrant friends here and their relatives in Brazil. Omar says,

> My great desire, mine and hers, was always to return to our land. I know where I came from and I know where I'm going. The majority of people with whom we have spoken lately say: but how can you both return to that land? You aren't losing your head, are you? You won't adapt there. But how wouldn't I? I am a Brazilian! It is here that I am a foreigner. I may

encounter some difficulty, communication problems, but this will be for a short while, then I will adjust and it will be over! You know? There aren't any [problems], there aren't any, and we'll survive those there are! Understand? Even her sister asked her: "Are you both crazy? To leave the United States to come here to Brazil?"

This return to Brazil appears senseless because it is considered to be a backward move, a refusal of progress and its comforts. In principle and in a very Manichean way, Brazil is connected to everything that is bad and backward, whereas the United States symbolizes what is good and modern. Brazilians, unlike Americans, know very well that this is not true; there is nothing perfect about either country. They both have its good and bad points. The problem is that here, in the United States, Brazilians are foreigners, and a specific kind of foreigner, as I have explained previously. Thus, no matter what their specific paths of integration are they all know that there is at least one more way of living: the Brazilian way that they left behind.

Besides surprise and indignation, the return of Omar and Lúcia provoked envy, jealousy, and nostalgia among their Brazilian immigrant friends. I heard many people dreaming of going back to Brazil, being inspired by their return. There was also a feeling of abandonment. This is understandable because they have been part of the church since its beginnings, and not only as members who only attend Saturday services. Instead, they have unofficially shared with the Pastors the center around which the church spins. They have helped many Brazilians settle in Riverside. Their house is always full of people. The times that I have been there, there has always been somebody knocking on the door or phoning. They have always been ready to help everyone. Their farewell party gathered 200 Brazilians and a few non-Brazilians. Many of them took the microphone to talk about their connections with them and thank them for something they had done. There were tears, hugs and kisses in abundance.

Reconciling and Staying for Good in the United States

From our Brazilian perspective, life in the United States lacks warmth, creativity, and freedom. The excerpts of the article, below, by Arnaldo

Jabor, a Brazilian journalist and moviemaker, explain the dynamics of American life through the Brazilian perspective:

> The first thing that you have to get into your head, oh ineffable Brazilian, is that "you" is not important here [New York]. In fact, nobody is important in this city. Or even better, everybody is. Only that the "you" is not important. "You" or "I" - this word that wraps us up – does not have the same proud significance that it has in Brazil. We idealize the Americans; but they do not idealize themselves. The "I" here is part of a great "job" that everyone takes part in. Everything goes. Everything works, the TV, the telephone, you. That "you" is a part of a grand invisible orchestra that plays you. This is when you start becoming bored with democracy. You start to get nostalgia for your crazy ego, so full of magic and illusion. That's when there's danger of your tropical ego running into things, going against the rules of the game. For this reason, I will begin here my "psychological guide" for Brazilians in NY.
>
> Never look anyone in the eyes unless you have a reason to do so. Why? Because no one is anyone else's object, no one is anyone else's scenery. Why should you be allowed to continue observing someone without explaining why? Here you are simply the other of someone else. That's why no one looks at each other, to avoid being bothered. Loneliness is cutting. It makes little difference if you go out real cute-like or real sloppy. No one sees you. ...Only the blacks dress well, and even the sloppy ones try for an "attitude." The blacks have a vision of the world, though it may be made up of rap, baseball caps, and tennis shoes. ...And they make up what is best in NY, always struggling against the armies of sour whites in grayish suits.
>
> Be careful with the "excuse me." It doesn't hurt anyone, but it is irritating. The "excuse me" will exclude you. If you have stopped on a street to look up at a building and are in the way of pedestrians, you can be sure that someone will say to you "excuse me" with an acid tone of voice. They look for anyone who may be out of line and they go there, only for the

pleasure of pointing this out, made happy by your pale
humiliation. And then there is your "excuse me": say it with
a submissive intonation, like the Latinos in the movies.
[...] Here there is no such thing as "almost": "Gee, man,
I almost called you..." There is either yes or no. Nobody is
more or less. Here one is either a Republican or a Democrat.
There are only two categories.

[...] To complain without a purpose or a target is strictly
pointless. Try it: "This traffic is horrible... Why don't they
do something about it...?" If the driver is Pakistani, he'll
respond in Sanskrit; if he's an American he won't even look at
you; if he's Haitian he won't have the strength to respond.
You might be able to complain out loud with some Hispanics;
only that Hispanics never complain because that is their
merchandise: obedience. They look at you a bit startled and
smile: "Brasileño...Bebeto y Ronaldo..."

Don't smoke. If you smoke, don't come to NY and avoid
being humiliated.

A chapter on women. Don't flirt with anyone. Company
executives don't even have the guts to go down an elevator
with a secretary any more, not without having a third person
around for fear of being sued for sexual harassment. Women
will not smile at you. Only in singles bars. No one touches
each other. I don't know how they reproduce.

Here they only look forward; towards today. American
capitalism is for the short term. Here real life is so real that it
doesn't exist. I feel in the air a great hunger for error, for the
useless, for the vagabond. At any time now the hippies will
be reborn, I bet. As you can see, I am very homesick for
Brazil. One day I'll continue this "guide." After all, as Tom
Jobim used to say: "To live overseas is nice, but it's shitty; to
live in Brazil is shitty, but it's nice."

Besides American personal coldness and excessive consumerism,
Brazilians also have problems dealing with American racism. I observed
that middle and upper-middle-class Brazilians want their children to
integrate into American society through the white-American world,
even when, in many cases, the skin color of their children makes such

an enterprise almost impossible. In general, however, after living in the United States for a while, Brazilians acquire a more acute perception of the content and consequences of both Brazilian and American racisms. The excerpts below show how this perception varies according to people's different social positions and skin color,

The first guy I had sex with was this black American from Saint Louis that I dated for 9 months. I didn't like the experience, he was very racist. My God he was racist! He was the first person who made me feel black. Because you know, we have racism in Brazil but it is a hidden racism, you mix with everybody and such and it is only from the moment you want to mix with a white family that racism shows up. This is what racism is in Brazil for me, a hidden racism, worse than the one here because here they show it: I don't like you, that's it. You're white, you're black. That's it. In Brazil it's all camouflaged, you know, that pretense? But he made me feel black because he only took me to eat black food, to black movies. Music was black only, at his house he had no music by any whites! Ah, no, I didn't like it no. Everything he owned had to be better that what the whites had. The clothes had to be better than the whites, the car was better. He was a bus driver. He owned a Corvette. At that time Corvettes were Blacks' cars. It was extremely expensive. Even today Corvettes are expensive, right? It was him, him, him and his color. So he'd never go up to my apartment because he found out my boss was white, that I worked for a white woman, can you believe it? (Telma, age 46).

In Brazil there is prejudice towards very dark skin and very light skin. If I go to Brazil with my skin the way it is now, people will bother me to no end! I'll be discriminated against. I have to go to the beach in order to catch some color! But it has to be at 6 o' clock in the morning so that no one sees my whiteness. So white skin is totally out, and a very dark one is totally out. But they are much more tolerant toward mixed colors and don't create a problem. They look more at your hair, right? Is the hair bad, is the hair good. If your hair is good and you have dark skin, you're white. And they are more tolerant in general. There's a lot of [racial] mixture. The parents and the grandparents of a person who is more or less brunette may have been black. And it's harder to be prejudiced, racist, when you have that blood coursing through your veins... I believe the Brazilian may have a bit of prejudice towards the Japanese. It's not that he thinks the Japanese is bad or good, but it's more in terms of sexual attractiveness. Japanese women do not have a body like Brazilian women; they don't have those hips, those legs. But this story that we're better doesn't exist. To the contrary, Japanese do well, they are the ones who go to college. In the beginning I was very bothered by the separation between things here. The separation of Latinos, of Koreans, of Blacks. Everyone here is segregated in relation to everyone else. For example, in Brazil I had various Jewish friends and I never even knew they were Jews. I only know today they are Jews because I am here now and I see their last name and I put things together. When I was in Brazil I didn't know, and this didn't make the slightest amount of difference to me. In the beginning I didn't like it [here], I didn't feel comfortable. I wanted to take part, for example, in black culture because I think that the black Americans are the closest thing we have here to Brazilian culture, they are the most emotional, they have more intense physical contact. I had more access to black culture here because the daughter of my Brazilian baby sitter came to visit me for a month, and she is black, adolescent, paid more attention to things, flirted. But I am bothered by this segregation, just like I am bothered in Brazil by its veiled racism. There is racism, no one says it openly, but they continue making little jokes... Well, here you can't tell any jokes. And here they can survive it better because they have their own group, their own culture. A niece of mine is the only black girl in a school of 500 students in Brazil. She's completely isolated, though she's from the middle class. So I want to bring her here, have her stay six months, know black culture, learn to be assertive, to be aggressive and to protect herself and to have self esteem. To like herself as she is. In

Brazil blacks are motivated to say they are not blacks, to deny it. Because there is this continuum of races, they tend to go toward the whiter side, to marry whites, to whiten themselves. Not here, they don't want to whiten. They want to remain black (Paola, age 35).

What bothers me about racism here is this, and once I even had this discussion at a community meeting in the neighborhood where there was a black man, pure breed, combative. He wanted to argue. That began to irritate me because we started talking in terms of Latinos, Americans. Here they call me a Latina. I am considered a Latina. And here comes this gentleman who does nothing else in life except study his roots and complain, you know? He brought out that story about how he suffered with slavery, his family suffered... Because they have a lot of that here in books, movies, everything! I said: why don't you find a job, why don't you study and earn a diploma and affirm yourself? And forget your black ancestors that suffered so much. Girl, I left afraid he was going to grab me on the street corner and beat me up... But I feel that here there is this thing, this endless debate over racism. Although deep down I think there is a certain amount of business interest regarding this. They want to stand out, of course, they're human beings. But they should stand out in a positive way, not by bringing out this subject all the time and calling everyone racists. What happens is that there are so many protections here for them, in laws, that if you look at it they are doing very well, not really that badly, but now they want more. Now, in Brazil things are different, we call each other "neguinho," we have affection, they do not hate us. The difference here is that there is no integration. You can see, the groups here are all separate, Latinos, Blacks, Whites. And the Asians; here there are even only Asian neighborhoods. So it's a society in which you get together with your own culture. Now everyone goes to Brazil and becomes a Brazilian. There's none of this silliness of African-American, Japanese-American, this nonsense. By the way, they're beginning to throw this racism thing around in Brazil, which I think is a pity, because it's so nice not to have this, right? In Brazil there are none of these stories of pure races, it's very difficult, no one is. I am descended from Indians and Portuguese. But I am proud of this, I believe that by being mixed we become stronger. I am mixed-race, a typical Brazilian, well mixed and I love Brazil. And I don't like this thing here (Nilce, age 47).

There's a side of America that is very fascist. I have the distinct impression that if America had not been allied to the Allies in the Second World War, they could have been allied to the Nazis because there is a very strong reactionary side, a conservative and fascist side in American culture. This boldness to admit that one is from the right, that one is racist, without any shame at all, sickens me. And demonstrations of this capacity for totalitarianism are present throughout different moments in American history. McCarthyism is an example of this. In America there is this hidden capacity for harshness, this capacity for judging others. This Puritan thing of pointing one's finger, of owning the truth, understand? This frightens me about America. Because even with all of its defects in Brazil, we are a country in which even the right is ashamed of being the right. This is a blessing! A racist is ashamed of being racist, in this aspect Brazil is blessed. Here people are proud of being racists, and I think this is something very dangerous (Ivan, age 44).

Despite the pointed differences and ways of facing them, Brazilians become used to life in the United States and many of them cannot even think of living in Brazil ever again. Some of these Brazilians picture Brazil as Dante Alighieri's Hell. Thinking of Brazil as decadent, poor, and violent helps them feel better about their choice and overlook some shortcomings of life in the United States. However, there are other Brazilians who, being able to distinguish what is good or bad about living in the United States and Brazil, still prefer to live in the United States. These cases are generally those of people who have lived here longer and somehow feel they already belong.

It's funny because I've been living here for ten years and to this day I get confused with dates and with the time. Maybe that's because I work mostly as a free-lancer, I don't know, but I have to have lots of calendars around or I feel totally lost. And I need clocks. This thing about it being 8pm and the sun being out leaves me totally confused. In Brazil I don't even need a watch, I know the time merely from the light of day. When I want to know the time I only need to look out the window. Another thing that makes no sense is the months. There is no February without Carnival, understand? I don't know, sometimes I have the feeling that everything is a collage. The moon doesn't have the same meaning, the beach doesn't have the same meaning. The majority of Brazilians here want to live by the beach because they believe they can reproduce the beach culture that exists in Brazil here. But it is nothing like it, it's completely different . Here the water has another temperature and the people have a totally different way of dealing with the body [...] On the other hand, I've built up a very great intimacy with the streets on which I walk and with the places where I go. I notice every change that takes place in my neighborhood. And there are so many other things that tie me to Los Angeles (Annie, age 36).

Beyond any romanticism, life in the United States is easier for those whose lives would be easy in Brazil. Those who would like to return to Brazil are the ones who have not integrated as they expected or are going through problematic situations connected to jobs, marriage, children and so forth. In this case, Brazil is seen as an escape. They believe that they can find in Brazil everything that they cannot find here. However, after living here for a couple of years, no matter how much they complain about the United States or how much they idealize life in Brazil, only a few Brazilians actually take the chance to return to Brazil.

Conclusion

There are many conclusions to which this study leads, and some of them have already been presented throughout the chapters. Here, I want to discuss two issues. The first is the connection between globalization, national borders and immigration. One of my arguments to explain the flow of Brazilian immigrants to the United States, especially to Los Angeles, is the extent of the American economic and cultural expansion in Brazil. American imperialism, now also called globalization, has spread American culture and values all over the world.[55] While the consequences of this are not always predictable, one of them is certain: a great percentage of people from all over the world is raised dreaming of living an American life where it seems to make the most sense, in the United States. Many of them will have or will create the conditions to effectively realize this dream because many of them are, in their hearts, "true" Americans already. Considering the political and bureaucratic reality of the national borders, the expansion of American culture to the benefit of capitalist accumulation is perverse because it creates the illusion that all people in the world can be American, whereas the reality is that only those who happen to be born in American territory are granted that privilege. In this perspective, but also in the perspective of human rights, a more liberated, and ideally completely free, movement of people is desirable. As in the case of the capitalist expansion, the contingent economic or cultural effects of migration should not become an argument to restrain the movement of people. Yet human rights are not considered, and the regulation of the flow of people through the establishment of borders and other devices effectively creates a situation of "apartheid" from which only a few groups benefit.[56] Although apparently faceless, the expansion of capitalism changes spaces, peoples, and creates relationships that do not necessarily follow the general rules of devaluation and exploitation that work between countries or groups located in different positions in the international division of labor. Thus, it is tremendously complicated to justify the maintenance of national borders in a world whose dominant ideologies have affected individuals across the globe. The only reason to create the institution of "illegal aliens" is to maintain certain levels of exploitation by regulating prices in the labor market. Ironically, the United States, the prime example of Western democracy, lives well with the belief that the immigrants that it produces through its imperialist expansion across the globe are simply "illegal aliens" who should receive the same attention that the Greek and Roman ancient societies gave to their slaves.

Considering these facts, and considering also that migration is a clear outcome of economic and cultural disorders produced by capitalism, I want to agree with Bob Sutcliffe (1997:333) and say that my utopia is "that the obligation to move from one's place of residence in order to survive or prosper should be reduced to the minimum possible, and all people should have the right to voluntary migration."

Thus, if it is true that Brazilians migrate to the United States attracted by American labor and consumer markets, what would happen if Brazil also had a market as competitive and dynamic as the American? What would happen if the world were not divided between North and South or between First and Third Worlds?

North and South and First and Third Worlds are also expressions of a more basic division: the division of society into classes. The capitalist system survives at the expense of the inequality produced to justify the exploitation of a social class or group by another. It is this way that capital and power are produced, accumulated and concentrated. In this case, I would dream of an apparently impossible world: one with no social classes, no exploitation and no inequality. A world with thousands of economic and cultural centers and not only those consecrated by the historical needs of the capitalist concentration. Once the fundamental barriers built to exploit and opress were put down, all others would follow. In this case, barriers built around color, gender, nationality would become needless. Consequently, the control of people moving from one nation to another would also become unnecessary. The "ilegal alien" category would go forever to the realm of scientific fiction, and all men would be citizens in any country they were at.

In a world with such characteristics, Fortaleza, capital of the Brazilian state of Ceará, for example, would be as central as Los Angeles and could (why not?) have its own movie industry. Perhaps in the world that I am dreaming of, the role of Fortaleza, Salvador or Rio de Janeiro would be to teach the world the art of amusement and joy. In my world the current fable of the ant and the cicada would be rewritten, since it would be established that the work of the cicada is as important as the ant's. In my world, instead of a unique narrative, we would have multiple ones. Not multiple narratives submitted to the same fashion industry like we already have now; we would have multiple narratives, multiple fashions and multiple fashion industries. In a global world where the exchange between people was not based on the dollar, individuals would continue to move from a place to another for innumerable motives, but mainly out of curiosity to learn new and different possibilities of living. Unlike now, the migrant populations would not only go to economic centers, and all places in the world would pottentially attract visitors and immigrants. Many Brazilians would continue migrating to the Unites States but, unlike today, many Americans would also migrate to Brazil. Instead of being treated as "aliens," immigrants would be seen as important reservoirs of knowledge about other worlds and possibilities of living. Instead of feeling threatened by the presence of immigrants, the hosting society would feel proud of having been chosen. They would feel truly honored, knowing that, among so many alternatives, that person or that family chose their street, their city, their country. Thus the hostesses would be more patient about teaching their guests the new language and all codes connected to the new life style. They would be also anxious to find out about the world from which the immigrant is coming. Both would equally benefit from the encounter since the beginning.

In my utopia, instead of a result of the needs of a system of production that first uproots people and later dehumanizes them by transforming them into "cheap labor," immigration would be produced by the need that individuals have of becoming more human through the contact with other expressions of humanity.

Even though utopias also work as guides to political action, the reader might be expecting some more practical wisdom from an anthropological work. In this case, my second issue is addressed to those Brazilians (or other immigrants) who might wonder about, or try to extract from this book, some clues about their own possibilities of "success" in the United States. I would generally say that coming to the United States is as much of a worthwhile experience as going to any different country or culture is in terms of the changes that such a movement entails. But it might be helpful to reiterate here a point I have presented throughout this study. In principle, your chances of "success" depend basically on four factors: the feasibility of your dream, your social background in your country of birth, the connections that you may have already established in the United States, and the specific skills valued in the labor market that you might possess. Depending on how these factors are articulated you may or may not achieve your intended goals. Chances of success are generally greater for those who have a good understanding of their purposes and have developed concrete ways to achieve them. Thus, the more one knows about the dynamics of American society and one's own position in it the better. This knowledge, however, does not come only from books or movies but also from experience, and the ideal situation is to create practical strategies that will combine one's knowledge with one's desires. In any case, one must remember that things usually take longer than expected and also require a level of patience that many of us were never intended to develop.

Notes

1. Sá's *Cultural Adaptation and Barriers among Brazilian Graduate Students in the United States* (1980:49) affirms, "the single biggest obstacle facing Brazilian graduate students in the United States is language. From new arrivals to people nearing the completion of advanced degree programs, the problem of speaking and writing a second language takes priority over nearly all other problems. Adapting to new foods, to new concepts of time, to new sorts of interpersonal relations, to the limitations of money, to the shock of moving itself, and to the lack of an extended family are all secondary to acquiring the skills of communication." Specifically regarding the TOEFL, he says, "the skills one needs to pass the TOEFL examination are not the same skills that are needed to function as a graduate student in the United States" (ibid: 55).

2. Many Brazilian social scientists have dedicated some attention to understanding the different outcomes of the Anglo-Saxon and Latin-Iberian worlds in the American continent. See, for instance, Moog (1954); Freire (1975), and Ribeiro (1971 and 1999).

3. The analysts clash about the purpose and outcomes of what became known as the Monroe Doctrine. Dexter Perkins (cited in Rappaport 1964:11) proposes that the famous December 2, 1823 declaration had a dual origin and a dual purpose. "On the one hand, it was the result of the advance of Russia on the northwest coast of America, and was designed to serve as a protest against this advance and to establish a general principle against Russian expansion. On the other hand, the message was provoked by the fear of European intervention in South America to restore to Spain her revolted colonies, and was intended to give warning of the hostility of the United States to any such intervention." Edward H. Tatum, Jr. (ibid: 22-23) proposes "that England was the key power in the formation of American foreign policy." Arthur P. Whitaker (ibid: 34-35), however, disagrees with

him by proposing instead "further evidence that the Monroe Doctrine was not directed primarily against British designs on Cuba or on Latin America at large is furnished by Monroe's own statement that it was directed primarily against France." In relation to the outcomes of the Monroe Doctrine policies for the hemisphere, Luis Quintanilha (ibid: 99-100) proposes that "at the time of its enunciation, the Monroe Doctrine was intended to be, essentially, a policy toward Europe; not a policy for the Hemisphere. [...] It is only by virtue of later interpretations – rather misinterpretations – that the momentous Message was gradually fashioned into a Machiavellian policy for intra-Hemisphere consumption. From a candid but commendable United States gesture against European interference, the Doctrine was turned into a ruthless axiom, utilized by Washington administrations to suite the interest of what is known as *"Yankee Imperialism."* Because the Doctrine – certainly through no fault of its victims – was perverted to the point of being invoked as a justification for attacks against the sovereignty of the nations which it claimed to protect, it bulks large today as a stumbling block in the way of inter-American relations. "Paramount interests," "Manifest Destiny," "Big-Stick Policy," "Watchful Waiting," "Dollar Diplomacy," "Paternalism," "Protectionism" – in short, "Yankee Imperialism" – are slogans that have become irrevocably connected, in the minds of Latin Americans, with the words, "Monroe Doctrine."

4. Gustavo Ribeiro, a Brazilian anthropologist who studied Brazilians in San Francisco, also felt uneasy about the reduction of Brazil to three or four images. He says (1997a:7): "It is a little anti-climatic for an anthropologist doing research abroad on people from his country to find that in the end national identity is reduced to its most stereotypical expressions: carnival, feijoada [the Brazilian national food], capoeira [a mixture of martial art and dance], samba, soccer, and not the least g-string bikinis (also known as dental floss bikinis)." Brazilians in general, even the ones who could be closer the national image, feel uneasy about its limits and political consequences. For an insightful interpretation of Brazilian national identity in relation to the elements that are included or excluded in its composition, done from the perspective of a Brazilian born in Rio Grande do Sul, a state that does not fit the tropical stereotype, see Oliven (1996). For a brief appraisal of the negotiation of Brazilian identity among Brazilians see also Ribeiro (1997a) and Beserra (1998).

5. There is a considerable body of work produced by Brazilians about or based on their experiences in the United States. Among the personal testimonies and novels I had access to are the following: Veríssimo (1944); Lima (1955); Novaes (1985); Henfil (1985); Delazeri (1987); Bicalho (1989); Scotto (1993); Bahiana (1994), Motta (1997), and Vilas Boas (1997). For scholarly literature about similar issues, see Freyre (1936), Lima (1985), DaMatta (1991), and Ramos (1990).

6. Before the 1950s, Brazilians coming to the United States "were temporary residents, predominantly from the upper class, traveling for leisure, or in some cases to study in one of the prestigious academic institutions in the United States" (Davis 1998:4).

7. The increase of the migratory movements towards Europe and the United States on the 1980s is not only a Brazilian phenomenon. It is connected with general rearrangements in the world economy from the 1980s onwards. See, among others, Sassen (1988); Portes (1995), and Pelegrino (2002).

8. For more information and discussion about the demography of Brazilian population in the United States, see Davis (1997); Goza (1994); Margolis (1994; 1995a; 1995b); Martes (1999); Riedinger (1997) and Sales (1999).

9. The sharp difference between males (35 percent) and females (65 percent) in my sample has to do with the fact that one of the associations that I researched is for females only. It certainly does not reflect the reality of the Brazilian immigrant population in Los Angeles as a whole.

10. Besides other bibliographic references cited throughout this book, see also Assis (1995; 1996); Bogus (1995); Carnesi (1996); Cortêz (1988) Goza (1993; 1995; 1998); Messias (1997); Sasaki (1995; 1998); Sá (1998); Sprandel (1992), and Zaborowski (1999).

11. For more detailed analysis of the 1980s crisis that motivated Brazilian emigration, see De Biaggi (2002); Goza (1992); Margolis (1994); Martes (1999), and Sales (1999).

12. An epistemology of the academic production related to issues connected to the late capitalist expansion, such as development and modernization, is very recent. It has only begun in the last ten years. See Escobar (1995).

13. Such a process has, on one hand, displaced people from colonized or peripheral territories and, on the other hand, created a labor market,

especially for cheap immigrant labor, in the central capitalist countries or regions within central or peripheral territories. See, for instance, Piore (1979), and Portes (1981).

14. A large amount of literature has been produced concerning the issues of post-colonialism and globalization. See, for instance, Fanon (1963; 1967); Memmi (1991); Said (1992; 1994); Balibar and Wallerstein (1991); Stolcke (1995); Larrain (1994); Hall (1978; 1981; 1983, 1988, 1993), and Wolf (1982).

15. I am aware of other possibilities of developing anthropological studies in socially differentiated immigrant populations. Di Leonardo (1984), for instance, develops her study of Italian-Americans in California by studying families, which is also a very productive way of understanding different patterns of immigrant integration and getting over old myths about immigrant integration and immigrant ethnic communities in the United States.

16. In order to ensure my informants' privacy, I have altered all names, although I have retained the Portuguese, American, or other ethnic character of all given names and surnames. All quotes from interviews as well as other quotes from books originally in Portuguese were translated by Paulo Simões.

17. That first visit was the only time that my children accompanied me on my fieldwork "trips". Sergio, my husband, went one or two more times, but I basically decided to assume my work as mine, not as a family business.

18. Between November of 1997 and December of 1999, I participated in about thirty Saturday services, fourteen potlucks, a camping day at Cedar Falls (San Bernardino Mountains), two wedding parties, two Christmas celebrations, three farewell parties and several birthday parties.

19. City of Hope is a non-profit medical and research center, ranked by U.S. News and World Report among the top ten healthcare charities in the United States. Volunteer work and donations support City of Hope (see http:// www.buildinghope.com,/).

20. Brazilian surfers may annoy American and other international surfers competing for waves and awards, but the last thing I would propose is that they have anything to do with any bad reputation that Brazilians might have in Southern California. It is rather the opposite: many Brazilian surfers have received international awards, and, at least, among their peers, they have a good reputation.

21. There is a vast body of scholarship on American imperialism in Latin America. See, for instance, Ianni (1976); Cardoso (1972 and 1977); Cardoso and Faleto (1969); Dos Santos (1970; 1971 and 1972), and Dorfman and Mattelart (1972).

22. Antonio Carlos Jobim, Sergio Mendes, João and Astrud Gilberto are also well known among American intellectuals and jazz lovers in general. But they do not seem to have reached a public as broad as Carmen Miranda's. More recently, Gisele Bündchen, a Brazilian top model hired by Victoria's Secret, is also becoming popular in American and Global medias. But it is a different situation because the way she presents herself does not reinforce the usual stereotypes of Brazilian women.

23. Bourdieu and Wacquant's "On the Cunning of Imperialist Reason" is a very interesting article about American studies of race as a tool of U.S. cultural imperialism. They call attention to the recent transnational scholarly dialogue regarding race in Brazil and denounce the imposition of an American tradition, model, and dichotomy of race on Brazil (Bourdieu and Wacquant 1999). For a deeper understanding of race in Brazil, from the perspective of both Americans and Brazilians, see also Fernandes (1955; 1969); French (2000); Freyre (1946); Hasenbalg (1988); Harris (1964); Hess and Da Matta (1995); Nascimento (1979); Skidmore (1993); Wagley (1952).

24. The Seventh Day Adventist Church is one of the fastest-growing Christian churches in the world today, adding one new member by baptism every 44 seconds, and organizing five new congregations daily. The total number of churches is 43,270 (Dec. 31, 1997). Updated 18 September 1998 by Jonathan Gallagher (Data available at www.adventist.org).

25. Adventists speak in at least 725 languages and another 1,000 dialects, leading to the establishment of 56 Church-owned printing plants and editorial offices, including the newest in Russia and Bulgaria. The first denominational publishing house at Battle Creek, Michigan, began operating in 1855 and was duly incorporated in 1861 under the name of Seventh-day Adventist Publishing Association. The Health Reform Institute, later known as the Battle Creek Sanitarium, opened its doors in 1866, and missionary society work was organized on a statewide basis in 1870. The first of the Church's worldwide network of schools was established in 1872, and 1877 saw the formation of statewide Sabbath school associations. In 1903, the denominational headquarters were moved

from Battle Creek, Michigan, to Washington, D.C., and in 1989 to Silver
Spring, Maryland, where it continues to form the nerve center of ever-
expanding work.

26. My estimate is based on the number of Adventist families affiliated
with the churches of Chino and Glendale. I also included families attending
American Adventist churches who had been mentioned by my interviewees.
I have not included single people.

27. The University of California - Extension charges 1,950 dollars for
a ten-week (20 hours/week) course of English. The cost for room and board
is estimated at 2,000 dollars. Thus the approximate cost for a quarter-long
English course at UCR is 4,500 dollars.

28. Other scholars studying Brazilians in the United States have also
observed that they generally explain their *Latinidade* in a way that seeks to
detach them from the mainstream image of Latinos. However, no effort has
been made towards understanding what is behind Brazilians' refusal to
identify with Latinos. See, for instance, Ribeiro 1997a and Margolis 1994.

29. Brazilians are not the only Latinos who seek to detach themselves
from the Latino label. Gilda Ochoa's "Mexican Americans' Attitudes and
Interactions Towards Mexican Immigrants: A Qualitative Analysis of
Conflict and Cooperation" shows that similar attitudes are also observed
among Mexican Americans. See also Oboler (1992); Gomez (1992), and
Gimenez (1988; 1992).

30. The relationship between colonizer and colonized has been studied
in different contexts by many authors from both sides of this relationship.
Memmi (1965); Fanon (1967); Said (1992 and 1994), and Stolke (1993) are
just a few among many others that have discussed the issue and connected
ideological and moral aspects with economic ones.

31. For more information about Palmer Harder's missionary work in
Brazil see Harder (1995).

32. Unfortunately, I was unable to interview Pastor Edilson to
understand his period from his own perspective and be able to offer a more
impartial version of it.

33. This is relatively common among middle class immigrants
working in jobs intended for lower classes. Castro (1985) observes that
Colombian women in New York do not consider their identities there but
survive by maintaining their home identities. Margolis agrees with that in
the case of Brazilians in New York. She says (1994:231): "Although they

are now blue collar or service workers...[they] still see themselves as members of the middle class. Their ideological references are based on this idealized class position."

34. See, for instance, Brodkin (1988) on Jewish immigrants in the United States.

35. The number 200 refers to the number of women listed on the Brazilian Women's Group mailing list. If one considers the monthly meetings, this number falls to about 40, which is the media of women who generally attend the reunions. But not all women who attend are active members; that is, not even 40 women pay their monthly fee.

36. The absence of a group where Portuguese can be spoken daily prevents not only Brazilians married to Americans from teaching Portuguese to their children, but also Brazilians married to Brazilians. In the case of the latter the children always learn some Portuguese because their parents speak Portuguese at home. The case of Brazilians married to Americans is much more complicated. In this case, teaching Portuguese to the children requires a very strong determination to do so, and, most importantly, time to do so. Thus, it is a very difficult task, perhaps impossible, in the case of working mothers (I owe this observation to Ruth Walsh).

37. The mailing list that I used to produce the map of the Brazilian Women's Group members' geographical distribution was last updated in January of 1998 and it contains 140 names. The most recent list (Dec 1999) contains 200 names.

38. The women who live in San Bernardino County are connected to the group through friends from LA whose husbands also work for Odebrecht, a Brazilian multinational construction company that it is building a dam in the Santa Ana basin. Odebrecht operates internationally and it is listed among the 500 hundred largest international companies (Forbes, 1999:172).

39. The reputation of *Paraibanas* as tough women was spread countrywide through "Paraíba," a song composed by Luiz Gonzaga, a well-known northeastern singer and composer. In this song he refers to *Paraibanas* as follows: "Today I send you a hug, little one/masculine Paraíba/Macho woman, yes sir." The idea is that *Paraibanas* have to be serious, brave and tough in order to meet the needs of their hard lives (droughts and political uprisings).

40. I would say that connecting the image of Brazilian women with prostitution is only one among other by-products of the Brazilian carnival. By interviewing Americans and other non-Brazilians at the 1999 Hollywood Palladium Carnival in Los Angeles, I was led to relativize the idea of sexuality connected to the Brazilian carnival. One of the interviewees, a white-American male, about 40 years old, said that he associates carnival with music, dance, festivities, and sexuality. Joy of sexuality. He said, "You know, for me the whole thing is very sexual, but sexual in a very special way. It is like the celebration of the body with music, joy. It is a very positive way of bringing out sexuality to the public scene. The whole thing; music, freedom, costumes... all lead to a very special way of celebrating the body." He proposed much more than the easy connection of carnival with sex, including in his perception all the magic and poetry connected with the general idea of carnival. This notion was the most common among the people I interviewed.

41. Latino population in Los Angeles comprises 4,697,509 out of a total 14,595,427 population. Sabagh & Bozorgmehr (1996:102) refer to projections prepared by the California Department of Finance which estimate that this population will increase substantially from slightly under 15 million in 1990 to nearly 24 million in the year 2020. They add, "this increase is likely to result from the expansion of the Latino population from nearly 5 million in 1990 to 12 million in 2020."

42. Even though the space reserved for Latinos in the United States is generally that of "second class", there are specific regions or cities where certain Latino groups have changed such a reputation, Miami, for instance. In New York, where Latinos have mostly meant poor Puerto Ricans, the reputation is similar to that of Los Angeles, where the stereotype was built to refer to immigrant Mexican peasants (Portes 1993; Stack 1992).

43. When discussing similarities between Caribbean writers and Southern novelists in the United States, Garcia Marquez (1999:A17) suggests that "it makes more sense to think of the Caribbean not as a geographical region surrounded by its sea but as a much wider historical and cultural belt stretching from the north of Brazil to the Mississipi basin. Mark Twain, William Faulkner, John Steinbeck and so many others would then be just as Caribbean as Jorge Amado and Derek Walcott."

44. I want to call attention to the fact that particular trajectories lead Brazilians to relate and become friends and/or dates of different "ethnics."

For example, whereas in Raquel's experience Arabs do not have a place, I met several other Brazilian women who not only relate and date Arabs but also prefer them to others. The ones I have talked to stressed Arabs' cultural resemblance to Brazilians, especially in terms of sensuality.

45. Mercedes Foster was the first organizer of the event.

46. The Brazilians who I interviewed at the Hollywood Palladium Carnival generally complained about one or another aspect of it. However, most of them ended up saying thinks like "You know, we are so isolated in LA, so needy of Brazilian culture, that an event like this comes as a blessing."

47. Giménez (1992:15) states that "it is among the ranks of the poor and the lower strata of the working classes that rejection of the Hispanic label might become more pronounced and a coalition under the Latino label or a combination of Latino and national-origin identities might be formed."

48. Several black Brazilians that I interviewed referred to the difficulties of relating to black Americans. They usually say that the black world in the United States is too limited (segregated) when compared to the black world in Brazil. This is even truer in the cases of the mulatos (morenos) whose color is not an issue in Brazil and becomes an issue here. The different ways Brazilians have of dealing with the color issue in Los Angeles will be discussed in chapter seven.

49. For analyses of racial relations and nationalism in the United States and Brazil see among others: Becker (1957); Fernandes (1955; 1969); Freyre (1946); George (1963); Gunnar (1962); Hasenbalg (1988); Horsman (1981); Harris (1964); Hess and Da Matta (1995); Nascimento (1979); Omi and Winant (1994); Skidmore (1993); Wagley (1952); West (1993).

50. Although the samba-school parade is the most internationalized expression, there are also other expressions of Carnival in Rio de Janeiro. See Da Matta (1991). For other expressions of Carnival in Brazil see Queiroz

51. Savigliano (1995:9) proposes "the 'exoticism' maneuver is not unlike the civilization-progress' maneuver, but it is more persuasive and pervasive. Civilization and progress can be reached through 'development,' the colonized are told. But 'exoticism' is always there to remind us of the difference between the old, really 'civilized' peoples and the ones only

recently, incompletely brought into civilization - the colonized who can never fully overcome the fact of carrying 'primitiveness' in their blood."

52. Here I'm accepting Raymond Williams' requirements for a Marxist analysis of cultural facts; "see together the means of production and the conditions of the means of production. For the condition of the means of production are quite crucial to any understanding of the means of production themselves... the latter involves not just techniques but whole social relationships" (1979:304-306).

53. Ivo Pitanguy is an internationally famous Brazilian plastic surgeon who is well-known among Hollywood actors. He lives in Rio de Janeiro.

54. This is not always true; it depends on how much Brazilian currency costs in relation to the dollar. In general, in similar circumstances, the wages are much lower in Brazil and this, after all, justifies, in many cases, the immigration to the United States.

55. "Globalization... is not a serious idea. We, the Americans, invented it as a means for concealing our policy of economic penetration into other nations." (J. K. Galbraith, interview, Folha de São Paulo, October 2, 1997). See also Vilas (2002).

56. See, for instance, Sklair (2000) and Amin (2000).

Bibliography

Amin, Samir. *Accumulation on a World Scale.* Sussex: Harvester, 1974.

Amin, Samir. Capitalism, Imperialism, and Globalization. In *The Political Economy of Imperialism: Critical Appraisals*, edited by Ronald Chilcote. Boulder: Rowman & Littlefield, 157-168, 2000.

Anderson, Benedict. *Imagined Communities.* New York: Verso, 1994.

Assis, Gláucia de O. Estar Aqui, Estar lá... O Retorno dos EmigrantesValadarenses ou a Construção de uma Identidade Transnacional? *Travessia* 8(22): 8-14, 1995.

Balibar, Etienne and Immanuel Wallerstein. *Race, Nation, Class – Ambiguous Identities.* London/New York: Verso, 1991.

Barth, F. (ed). *Ethnic Groups and Boundaries.* Boston: Little, Brownand Company, 1969.

Bahiana, Ana M. *América de A a Z.* Rio de Janeiro: Editora Objetiva, 1994.

Becker, G. *The Economics of Discrimination.* Chicago: University of Chicago Press, 1957.

Beltran, Gonzalo A. *El Processo de Aculturacion.* Mexico City: Universidad Nacional Autonoma de Mexico, 1958.

Beserra, Bernadete. Keeping the Flame: Brazilian Gauchos in Los Angeles. *Brazzil* 10(156): 26-27, 1998.

Beserra, Bernadete. Move your Body! Brazilian Carnival Takes over the World. *Brazzil* 10(158):19-24, 1999.

Beserra, Bernadete. Brazilians in Los Angeles: Imperialism,
    Immigration, and Social Class. Ph.D. Dissertation, University of
    California, Riverside, 2000.
Beserra, Bernadete. Quem Pode Representar Quem? Notas sobre
    Sentimentos e Relações de Poder numa Pesquisa de Campo. Paper
    presented at the X Encontro de Ciências Sociais do Norte e
    Nordeste, Salvador, 2001.
Beserra, Bernadete. Migrações Internacionais e Imperialismo: O Caso
    dos Brasileiros Adventistas em Los Angeles. In *Demografia e
    Transições Migratórias Recentes*, edited by Adelita Carleial.
    Fortaleza: IPLANCE, 2002.
Bicalho, José V. *Yes Eu Sou Brazuca*. Governador Valadares, Minas
    Gerais: FUNSEC, 1989.
Bogus, Lucia M.M. Brasileiros em Portugal: Novos Movimentos
    Migratórios ou Volta às Origens? *Travessia* 8(22): 16-19, 1995.
Bohning, W. R. *Studies in International Labour Migration*. London:
    Macmillan, 1984.
Bonacich, Edna. A Theory of Ethnic Antagonism: The Split Labor
    Market. *American Sociological Review* 37 (October): 547-559,
    1972.
Bonacich, Edna. Asian and Latino Immigrants in the Los Angeles
    Garment Industry: An Exploration of the Relationship between
    Capitalism and Racial Oppression. Working Papers in the Social
    Sciences, vol. 5, n. 13. Los Angeles: Institute for Social Science
    Research, UCLA, 1990.
Bonacich, Edna. Latino Immigrant Workers in the Los Angeles Apparel
    Industry. In *Latino Social Movements - Historical and Theoretical
    Perspectives*, edited by Rodolfo D. Torres and George Katsiaficas.
    New York and London: Routledge, 141-163, 1999.
Bottomore, Tom (ed.) *A Dictionary of Marxist Thought*. Oxford:
    Blackwell, 1991.
Bourdieu, Pierre. *Distinction: A Social Critique of the Judgment of
    Taste*. Cambridge, Massachusetts: Harvard University Press,
    1984.
Bourdieu, Pierre. The Forms of Capital. In *Handbook of Theory and
    Research for the Sociology of Education*. New York: Greenwood
    Press, 241-258, 1986.

Bourdieu, Pierre. What Makes a Social Class. *Berkeley Journal of Sociology: A Critical Review* 32: 1-17, 1987.

Bourdieu, Pierre. Social Space and Symbolic Power. In *Other Words: Essays towards a Reflexive Sociology.* Palo Alto: Stanford University Press, 123-139, 1990.

Bourdieu, Pierre. *Language and Symbolic Power.* Cambridge, Massachusetts: Harvard University Press, 1990.

Bourdieu, Pierre. Structures, Habitus, Power: Basis for a Theory of Symbolic Power. In *Culture/Power/History: A Reader in Contemporary Social Theory,* edited by Nicholas B. Dirks, Geoff Eley, and Sherry B. Ortner, 155-199, 1994.

Bourdieu, P and Loic J. D. Wacquant. *An Invitation to Reflexive Sociology.* Chicago: University of Chicago Press, 1992.

Bourdieu, P and Loic J. D. Wacquant. On the Cunning of Imperialist Reason. *Theory, Culture and Society* 16(1): 41-58, 1999.

Brazilian Embassy [Roa Lynn]. Brazil and the USA: What Do We Have in Common? Washington, DC: Brazilian Embassy Cultural Section, 1999.

Brewer, Anthony. *Marxist Theories of Imperialism.* London and New York: Routledge & Kegan Paul, 1987.

Brodkin, Karen. *How Jews Became White Folks and What That Says about Race in America.* New Brunswick, N.J.: Rutgers University Press, 1988.

Cardoso, F. H. Dependency and Development in Latin America. *New Left Review* 74: 83-95, 1972.

Cardoso, F. H. The Consumption of Dependency Theory in the United States. *Latin American Research Review* 12(3): 7-24, 1977.

Cardoso, F.H. and Enzo Faletto. *Dependency and Development in Latin America.* Berkeley: University of California Press, 1969.

Carnesi, Mark. An Investigation of Gender Differences in the Occurrence of Adjustment Problems and Utilization of Help Sources among Brazilian Undergraduate Students in American Colleges and Universities. Bowling Green: Bowling Green State University, 1996.

Castles, Stephen. The Process of Integration of Migrant Communities. In *Population Distribution and Migration,* New York: United Nations, 1998.

Castles, Stephen and Godula Kosack. *Immigrant Workers and Class Struggle in Western Europe*. London: Oxford University Press, 1972.

Castles and Miller. *The Age of Migration: International Population Movements in the Modern World*. London: MacMillan Press, 1990.

Castro, Mary G. Work versus Life: Colombian Women in New York. In *Women and Change in Latin America*, edited by June Nash and Helen Safa. South Hadley, Mass.: Bergin & Garvey, 231-259, 1985.

Castro, Mary G. Latinos nos EUA - Unindo Américas, Fazendo a América de Lá, ou Perdendo a Nossa América? *Travessia* 4(21): 14-20, 1991.

Chavez, Leo R. Settlers and Sojourners: The Case of Mexicans in the United States. *Human Organization* 47(2): 95-107, 1987.

Chilcote, R. H. A Critical Synthesis of the Dependency Literature. *Latin American Perspectives* 1(4): 4-29, 1973.

Chilcote, R. H. and Edelstein, J. C. *Latin America: Capitalist and Socialist Perspectives of Development and Underdevelopment*, Boulder, Westview Press, 1986.

Chomsky, Noam. From Cold War to Gulf War. *Living Marxism*, 29, 1991.

Collins, Patricia Hill. *Black Feminist Thought*. Boston: Unwin Hyman, 1990.

Cortêz, Cácia. *Os Brasiguaios*. Brasil: Agora, 1994.

Davis, Darien. The Brazilian-Americans: Demography and Identity of An Emerging Latino Minority. *The Latino Review of Books* 3(1-2): 8-15, 1997a.

Davis, Darien. To Be or Not to Be Brazilian: Carmen Miranda's Quest for Fame and 'Authenticity' in the United States. Paper presented at the IV Meeting of the Brazilian Studies Association, Washington, DC, 1997b.

Davis, Mike. *City of Quartz*. New York: Vintage Books, 1992.

Davis, T. M. (ed.) *Open Doors 1993/94: Report on International Educational Exchange*. New York: Institute of International Education, 1994.

DaMatta, Roberto. *Relativizando: Uma Introdução à Antropologia Social*. Petrópolis: Vozes, 1981.

DaMatta, Roberto. *Carnival, Rogues, and Heroes*. Notre Dame/London: University of Notre Dame Press, 1991.

DeBiaggi, Sílvia. *Changing Gender Roles - Brazilian Immigrant Families in the U.S.* New York: LFB Scholarly, 2002.

Delazeri, Jatir. *Um Ítalo-Gaúcho em Los Angeles*. Porto Alegre: EST, Escola Superior de Teologia São Lourenço de Brindes, 1987.

Dias, Antônio Gonçalves. *Poesias completas*. Rio de Janeiro: Edições de Ouro, 1968.

Di Leonardo, Micaela. *The Varieties of Ethnic Experience*. Ithaca and London: Cornell University Press, 1984.

Dorfman, Ariel and Armand Mattelart. *Para Leer el Pato Donald (Comunicacion de masa y colonialismo)*, Mexico: Siglo Veintiuno Editores, 1972.

Dos Santos, Theotonio. The Structure of Dependency. *American Economic Review* 60(May): 231-236, 1970.

Dos Santos, Theotonio. The Crisis of Development Theory and the Problem of Dependence in Latin America. In *Underdevelopment and Development: The Third World Today*, edited by H. Bernstein. Harmondsworth: Penguin Books, 1970.

Escobar, Arturo. *Encountering Development – The Making and Unmaking of the Third World*. Princeton, New Jersey: Princeton University Press, 1995.

Fanon, Franz. *The Wretched of the Earth*. New York: Grove Press, 1963.

Fanon, Franz. *Black Skin White Masks*. New York: Grove Press, 1967.

Fernandes, Florestan. *The Negro in Brazilian Society*. New York: Columbia University Press, 1967.

Fernandes, Florestan, and Roger Bastide. *Relações Raciais entre Negros e Brancos em São Paulo*. São Paulo: Editora Anhembi, 1955.

Foner, Nancy. *Jamaica's Migrants: A Comparative Analysis of the New York and London Experience*. New York: Center for Latin American and Caribbean Studies, New York University, 1983.

Foner, Nancy (ed). *New Immigrants in New York City*. New York: Columbia University Press, 1987.

Frank, Andre Gunder. The Development of Underdevelopment. *Monthly Review* 18(9): 17-31, 1966.

French, John D. The Missteps of Anti-Imperialist Reason: Bourdieu, Wacquant, and Hanchard's Orpheus and Power. *Theory, Culture, and Society* 17(1): 107-128, 2000.

Freyre, Gilberto. *Sobrados e Mocambos.* São Paulo: Companhia Editora Nacional, 1936.

Freyre, Gilberto. *The Masters and the Slaves.* Berkeley: University of California Press, 1946.

Freyre, Gilberto. *O Brasileiro entre Outros Hispanos: Afinidades, Contrastes e Possiveis Futuros nas suas Inter-Relações.* Rio de Janeiro/Brasilia: Livraria Jose Olympio Editora/MEC, 1972.

Garcia Marquez, Gabriel. Cutting Clinton Down to Less than His Size. *The Press Enterprise*, Sunday, February 7. A-17, 1999.

Gardezi, Hassan N. *The Political Economy of International Labour Migration.* New York: Black Rose Books, 1994.

George, H. *American Race Relations Theory: A Review of Four Models.* Lanham: University Press of America, 1984.

Georges, Eugenia. *The Making of a Transnational Community: Migration, Development and Culture Change in the Dominican Republic.* New York: Columbia University Press, 1990.

Georges, Eugenia. Gender, Class and Migration in the Dominican Republic: Women's Experiences in a Transnational Community. In *Towards a Transnational Perspective on Migration: Race, Class, Ethnicity and Nationalism Reconsidered,* edited by Nina Glick-Schiller, Linda Basch, and Cristina Blanc-Szanton. Annals of the New York Academy of Sciences 645:81-99, 1992.

Gimenez, Martha. Minorities and the World-System: Theoretical and Political Implications of the Internationalization of Minorities. In *Racism, Sexism, and the World-System,* edited by Joan Smith et al. Westport: Greenwood Press, 39-56, 1988.

Gimenez, Martha. U.S. Ethnic Politics: Implications for Latin Americans. *Latin American Perspectives* 19(4): 39-56, 1992.

Gimenez, Martha et al. Introduction to The Politics of Ethnic Construction: Hispanic, Chicano, Latino…? *Latin American Perspectives* 19(4): 3-6, 1992.

Gomez, Laura. The Birth of the 'Hispanic' Generation: Attitudes of

Mexican-American Political Elites toward the Hispanic Label. *Latin American Perspectives* 19(4): 45-58, 1994.

Goza, Franklin. Samba Arrives to Canada, or, Brazilian Immigration to Ontario. Bowling Green, Ohio: Canadian Studies Center, Bowling Green State University, 1993.

Goza, Franklin. Brazilian Immigration to North America. *International Migration Review* 28: 136-152, 1994.

Goza, Franklin. An Examination of Remittance Activity among Brazilian Immigrants in the U.S. and Canada. Bowling Green, Ohio: Canadian Studies Center, Bowling Green State University, 1998.

Haberly, David T. *Three Sad Races: Racial Identity and National Consciousness in Brazilian Literature.* Cambridge-New York: Cambridge University Press, 1983.

Hall, Stuart. Cultural Studies: Two Paradigms. In *Culture, Ideology and Social Process*, edited by T. Bennett et al. London: Batsford Academic, 1981.

Hall, Stuart. The Problem of Ideology – Marxism without Guarantees. In *Marx, A Hundred Year On*, edited by B. Mattews. London: Lawrence and Wishart, 57-85, 1983.

Hall, Stuart. *Marxism and the Interpretation of Culture.* London: Macmillan, 1988.

Hall, Stuart. The Local and the Global: Globalization and Ethnicity. In *Culture, Globalization and the World-System: Contemporary Conditions for the Representation of Identity*, edited by A. D. King. Binghamton: State University New York Press, 1993.

Harder, Palmer. *62 Anos Missionário no Brasil.* Engenheiro Coelho, SP, Brasil: Imprensa Universitária Adventista, 1995.

Harris, Marvin. *Patterns of Race in the Americas.* New York: Walker and Co., 1964.

Harris, Richard. Globalization and Globalism in Latin America: Contending Perspectives. *Latin American Perspectives* 29(6): 5-23, 2002.

Hayes-Bautista and J. Chapa. Latino Terminology: Conceptual Bases for Standardized Terminology. *American Journal of Public Health* 77(1): 61-68, 1987.

Henderson, J. and Castells, M. *Global Restructuring and Territorial Development*. London: Sage Publications, 1987.

Henfil. *Diário de um Cucaracha*. Rio de Janeiro: Editora Record.1985.

Hess, J. and DaMatta (eds.) *The Brazilian Puzzle: Culture on the Borderlands of the Western World*. New York: Columbia University Press, 1995.

Holt, Lauren. MILA Samba School: The Construction of Samba in Los Angeles. Paper for Portuguese 199, University of California, Los Angele, 1995.

Horsman, R. *Race and Manifest Destiny: The Origins of American Racial Anglo-Saxonism*. Cambridge, Mass.: Harvard University Press, 1981.

Ianni, Octavio. *Imperialismo e Cultura*. Petropolis: Vozes, 1976.

Ianni, Octávio and Marcos Kaplan. *América Latina y Estados Unidos; Relaciones Políticas Internacionales y Dependencia*. Lima: Instituto de Estudios Peruanos, 1973.

Kay, Cristobal. *Latin American Theories of Development and Underdevelopment*. London: Routledge, 1993.

Kearney, Michael. From the Invisible Hand to Visible Feet: Anthropological Studies of Migration and Development. *Annual Review of Anthropology* 15:331-61, 1986.

Kearney, Michael. The Local and the Global: The Anthropology of Globalization and Transnationalism. *Annual Review of Anthropology* 24:547-65, 1995.

Kearney, Michael. [Im]migrants National Origins and Transnational Ties: Mexicans in the United States: The Shaping of Research and Policy Debates. Prepared for European University Institute Forum: "Reflections on Migration Research." Florence, 1999.

Kearney, Michael. Struggle and Difference: The Jiujitsu of Transnational Indigenous Resistance and Domination. In *History in Person: Enduring Struggles and Identities in Practice*, edited by D. Holland and J. Lave. Santa Fé, NM: School of American Research Press, 247-280, 2001.

Kristeva, Julia. *Strangers to Ourselves*. New York: Columbia University Press, 1991.

Klintowitz, Jaime. Nossa Gente Lá Fora. Primeiro Censo da Emigração Encontra Diáspora de 1,5 Milhão de Brasileiros e Mostra que as

Colônias Criaram Raízes no Exterior. *Veja* 29 (14): 26-29, 1997.

Laclau, Ernesto. Feudalism and Capitalism in Latin America. *New Left Review* 67(3): 19-38, 1971.

Lamphere, Louise (ed.) *Structuring Diversity - Ethnographic Perspectives on the New Immigration.* Chicago and London: University of Chicago Press, 1991.

Larrain, Jorge. *Theories of Development.* Cambridge: Polity; Cambridge, Mass.: Basil Blackwell, 1988.

Larrain, Jorge. *Ideology and Cultural Identity - Modernity and the Third World Presence.* Cambridge: Polity Press, 1994.

Lima, Alceu Amoroso. *A Realidade Americana.* Rio de Janeiro: AGIR, 1955.

Lima, Roberto K. *A Antropologia da Academia: Quando os Índios Somos Nós.* Petrópolis/Niterói: Vozes/Universidade Federal Fluminense, 1985.

Marcus, George. Ethnography In/Of the World System: The emergence of Multi-Sited Ethnography. *Annual Review of Anthropology* 24:95-117, 1995.

Margolis, Maxine. *Little Brazil - An Ethnography of Brazilian Immigrants in New York City.* Princeton, NJ: Princeton University Press, 1994.

Margolis, Maxine. A Minoria Invisível: Imigrantes brasileiros em Nova York. *Travessia.* Janeiro-Abril, 1995.

Margolis, Maxine. Brazilians and the 1990 United States Census: Immigrants, Ethnicity, and the Undercount. *Human Organization* 54(1):52-59, 1995b.

Martes, Ana C B. *Brasileiros nos Estados Unidos: Um estudo sobre imigrantes em Massachusetts.* São Paulo: Paz e Terra, 1999.

Martes, Ana C B. Emigração Brasileira: Formação de Mercados de Consumo de Produtos Brasileiros no Exterior. *Revista RAE* 41(1), 2001.

Massey, D.S. The New Immigration and Ethnicity in the United States. *Population Development Review* 21:631-652, 1995.

Massey, D.S. et al. Theories of International Migration: A Review and Appraisal. *Population Development Review* 19:431-466, 1992.

Memmi, Albert. *The Colonizer and the Colonized.* Boston: Beacon Press, 1991.

Messias, DeAnne. Narratives of Transnational Migration, Work, and Health: the Lived Experiences of Brazilian Women in the United States. Master's Thesis, San Francisco University, 1997.

Ministério das Relações Exteriores. Brasileiros Residentes no Exterior - Tabelas. Retrieved on January 8, 2003, www. mre.gov.br, 2001.

Mintz, Sidney. A Note on the Definition of Peasantries. *Journal of Peasant Studies* 1:91-106, 1973.

Mintz, Sidney. *Sweetness and Power: The Place of Sugar in Modern History*. New York, N.Y.: Viking, 1985.

Moog, C Vianna. *Bandeirantes e Pioneiros*. Rio de Janeiro/Porto Alegre: Editora Globo, 1954.

Morawska, Ewa. The Sociology and Historiography of Migration. In *Immigration Reconsidered: History, Sociology and Politics*, edited by Virginia Yans McLaughlin. New York: Oxford University Press, 1993.

Morse, Richard M. *O Espelho de Próspero*. São Paulo: Companhia das Letras, 2000.

Motta, Nelson. *Nova York é Aqui - Manhattan de Cabo a Rabo*. Rio de Janeiro: Objetiva, 1997.

Muñoz, Carlos Jr. *Youth, Identity, Power: The Chicano Movement*. London: Verso, 1990.

Nascimento, Abdias do. *Brazil: Mixture or Massacre: Essays on the Genocide of a Black People*. Dover, MA: Majority Press, 1979.

Newell, C. *Methods and Models in Demography*. New York: Guilford Press, 1988.

Novaes, Carlos E. *A Travessia Americana*. São Paulo. Editora Ática, 1986.

Oboler, Suzanne. The Politics of Labeling: Latino/a Cultural Identities of Self and Others. *Latin American Perspectives* 19(4): 18-36, 1992.

Ochoa, Gilda L. Mexican Americans' Attitudes toward and Intercations with Mexican Immigrants: A Qualitative Analysis of Conflict and Cooperation. *Social Science Quarterly* 81(1): 84-105, 2000.

Omi, M. and Howard Winant. *Racial Formation in the United States: From the 1960s to the 1990s*. New York: Routledge, 1994.

Petras, Elizabeth M. The Global Labor Market in the Modern World Economy. In *Global Trends in Migration: Theory and Research on*

International Population Movements, edited by Marx M. Kritz, Charles B. Keeley, and Silvano M. Tomasi. Staten Island, N.Y.: Center for Migration Studies, 44-63, 1981.

Petras, James. The Myth of the Third Scientific-Technological Revolution in the Era of Neo-Mercantilist Empires. *Latin American Perspectives* 29(6): 44-58, 2002.

Piore, Michael J. *Birds of Passage: Migrant Labor and Industrial Societies*. NewYork: Cambridge University Press, 1979.

Porte, Alejandro. *The Economic Sociology of Immigration: Essays on Networks, Ethnicity, and Entrepreneurship*. New York: Russel and Sage Foundation, 1995.

Portes, Alejandro and Alex Stepick. *City on the Edge: The Transformation of Miami*. Berkeley: University of California Press, 1993.

Portes, Alejandro and John Walton. *Labor, Class, and the International System*. New York: Academic Press, 1981.

Portes, Alejandro and Rubén G. Rumbaut. *Immigrant America: A Portrait*. Los Angeles: University of California Press, 1990.

Poulantzas, Nicos. *Classes in Contemporary Capitalism*, London: Verso, 1974.

Poulantzas, Nicos. *State, Power, Socialism*, London: Verso, 1978.

Ramos, Alcida R. Ethnology Brazilian Style. *Cultural Anthropology* 5(4): 452-472, 1990.

Rappaport, Armin (ed.) *The Monroe Doctrine*. New York: Holt, Rinehart and Winston, 1964.

Redfield, Robert. The Folk Society and Culture. In *Eleven Twenty-Six*, edited by Louis Wirth. Chicago: University of Chicago Press, 1940.

Redfield, Robert. The Folk Society. *The American Journal of Sociology* 52:293-308, 1947.

Redfield, Robert. *The Little Community: Viewpoints for the Study of A Human Whole*. Chicago: University of Chicago Press, 1955.

Rex J. and Mason D. (eds). *Theories of Race and Ethnic Relations*. Cambridge: Cambridge University Press, 1987.

Ribeiro, Darcy. A Aculturação Indígena no Brasil. In *Minorities in the New World*, edited by Charles Wagley and Marvin Harris. New York: Columbia University Press, 1958.

Ribeiro, Darcy. *The Civilizational Process*. Washington, DC: Smithsonian Institution Press, 1968.

Ribeiro, Darcy. *The Americans and Civilization*. New York: E.P.Dutton & Co., 1971.

Ribeiro, Darcy. *O Povo Brasileiro: A Formação e o Sentido do Brasil*. São Paulo: Companhia das Letras, 1999.

Ribeiro, Gustavo. Street Samba: Carnaval and Transnational Identities in San Francisco. Paper presented at the IV Conference of Brazilian Studies Association, Washington, DC, 1997a.

Ribeiro, Gustavo. Vulnerabilidade e Ambiguidade: Cidadania na Situação de Emigrante em São Francisco, Califórnia. Paper presented at the I Conferência sobre Imigrantes Brasileiros no Contexto das Novas Migrações Internacionais. Lisboa, 1997b.

Ribeiro, Gustavo. O que faz o Brasil Brazil: Jogos Identitários em São Francisco. In *Cenas do Brasil Migrante*, editeb by R. R. Reis and Teresa Sales. São Paulo: Boitempo, 1999.

Riedinger, E. Brazilian Americans, An Emerging Hispanic Group in the United States. Paper presented at the IV Conference of Brazilian Studies Association, Washington, DC, 1997.

Romero, M; P. Hondagneu-Sotelo, and Vilma Ortiz. *Challenging Fronteras - Structuring Latina and Latino lives in the U.S*. New York & London: Routledge, 1997.

Roseberry, William. *Anthropologies and Histories – Essays in Culture, History, and Political Economy*. New Brunswick and London: Rutgers University Press, 1989.

Rushdie, Salman. *The Satanic Verses*. New York: Viking Penguin Inc., 1989.

Sá, João Menezes de. Attachment to Childhood Places in Adult Memory and Brazilian Immigrant's Sense of Well-Being in the USA. Ph.D. Dissertation, University of Massachusetts, Amherst, 1998.

Sá, Samuel M. A. Cultural Adaptation and Barriers among Brazilian Graduate Students in the United States. Ph.D. Dissertation, University of Florida, Gainesville, 1980.

Sales, Teresa. Imigrantes Estrangeiros, Imigrantes Brasileiros: uma Revisão Bibliográfica e Algumas Questões para Pesquisa. *Revista Brasileira de Estudos de População* 9(1):50-64, 1994.

Sales, Teresa. O Brasil no Contexto das Migrações Internacionais. *Travessia* 8(21):5-8, 1995.

Sales, Teresa. *Brasileiros Longe de Casa*. São Paulo: Cortez Editora, 1999.

Sales, Teresa and Maria do Rosário Sales (eds.) *Políticas Migratórias: América Latina, Brasil e Brasileiros no Exterior*. São Carlos: Editora da Universidade Federal de São Carlos, 2002.

Said, Edward. *Orientalism*. New York: Vintage Books, 1979.

Said, Edward. *Culture and Imperialism*. New York: Vintage Books, 1994.

Sarramea, Adriana. Imperialism, Women, and the Third World: The Mothers of Plaza de Mayo. Master's Thesis, San Francisco State University, 1992.

Sasaki, Elisa M. Dekasseguis - Trabalhadores Nipo-Brasileiros no Japão." *Travessia* 8(21): 20-22, 1995.

Sasaki, Elisa M. O Jogo da Diferença: a Experiência Identitária no Movimento Dekassegui. Master's Thesis, Universidade de Campinas, 1998.

Sassen, Saskia. *The Mobility of Labor and Capital. A Study in International Investment and Labor Flow*. Cambridge: Cambridge University Press, 1988.

Sassen, Saskia. *The Global City: New York, London, Tokyo*. Princeton: Princeton University Press, 1991.

Savigliano, Marta. *Tango and the Political Economy of Passion*. Boulder: Westview Press, 1995.

Scotto, Luiz A. *46th Street : O Caminho Americano*. São Paulo: Editora Brasiliense, 1993.

Silverman, Sydel. The Peasant Concept in Anthropology. *Journal of Peasant Studies*. 7(1):49-69, 1980.

Sinha, Mrinalini. *Colonial Masculinity: The 'Manly Englishman' and the Effeminate Bengali' in the Late Nineteenth Century*. Manchester and New York: Manchester University Press, 1995.

Skidmore, Thomas E. *Black into White - Race and Nationality in Brazilian Thought*. Durham and London: Duke University Press, 1993.

Sklair, Leslie. The Transnational Capitalist Class and the Discourse of Globalization. Retrieved on June 10, 2002, http//www.

Bibliography

globaldimensions.net/articles/Sklair/Lsklair.html

Sprandel, Márcia Anita. Brasiguaios: Conflito e Identidade em Fronteiras Internacionais. Master's Thesis, Museu National, Universidade Federal do Rio de Janeiro, 1992.

Stack, John and Christopher Warren. Ethnicity and Politics in Miami. In *Miami Now! Immigration, Ethnicity, and Social Change,* edited by Guilhermo Grenier and Alex Stepick. Gainesville: University of Florida Press, 1992.

Steward, Julian H. et al. *The People of Puerto Rico.* Urbana: University of Illinois Press, 1955.

Stolcke, Verena. New Boundaries, New Rhetorics of Exclusion in Europe. *Current Anthropology* 36(1): 1-24, 1995.

Stolcke, Verena. Is Sex to Gender as Race is to Ethnicity? In *Gendered Anthropology,* edited by Teresa del Valle. London: Routledge, 17-37, 1993.

Sutcliffe, Bob. Freedom to Move in the Age of Globalization. In *Globalization and Progressive Economic Policy,* edited by Dean Baker, Gerald Epstein and Robert Pollin. Massachusetts-Amherst: Cambridge University Press, 1997.

Taussig, Michael. *Colonialism, Shamanism and the Wild Man,* Chicago: University of Chicago Press, 1987.

Torresan, Angela. Quem Parte, Quem Fica: uma Etnografia sobre migrantes Brasileiros em Londres. Master's Thesis, Museu National, Universidade Federal do Rio de Janeiro, 1994.

Torresan, Angela. Ser Brasileiro em Londres. *Travessia* 8(23), 1996.

Thomas, W. I and Florian Znanieck. *The Polish Peasant in Europe and America.* Urbana and Chicago: University of Illinois Press, 1996.

Veríssimo, Érico. *Gato Preto em Campo de Neve.* Porto Alegre: Globo. 1944.

Vilas, Carlos M. Globalization as Imperialism. *Latin American Perspectives* 29(6): 70-79, 2002.

Vilas Boas, Sérgio. *Os Estrangeiros do Trem 'N.'* Rio de Janeiro: Rocco, 1994.

Wagley, Charles. *Race and Class in Rural Brazil.* New York: UNESCO/Columbia University Press, 1963.

Waldinger, Roger and Mehdi Bozorgmehr (eds). *Ethnic Los Angeles. New York:* Russel Sage Foundation, 1995.

Wallerstein, Immanuel. *The Modern World System: Capitalist
   Agriculture and the Origins of the European World Economy in
   the Sixteenth Century.* New York: Academic Press, 1974.
West, Cornel. *Race Matters.* Boston: Beacon Press, 1993.
William, Raymond. *Politics and Letters.* London: New Left, 1979.
Wolf, Eric. Types of Latin American Peasantry: A Preliminary
   Definition. *American Anthropologist* 57:452-471, 1955.
Wolf, Eric. Closed Corporate Peasant Communities in Mesoamerica
   and Central Java. *Southwestern Journal of Anthropology* 13:1-18,
   1957.
Wolf, Eric. *Peasants.* Englewood Cliffs, NJ: Prentice-Hall, 1966.
Wolf, Eric. The Vicissitudes of the Closed Corporate Peasant
   Community. *American Ethnologist* 13(2): 325-329, 1986.
Wolf, Eric. *Europe and the People without History.* Berkeley:
   University of California Press, 1982.
Zaborowski, Denise. The Migratory Process of Brazilians Living in
   Los Angeles: An Analysis of Subjective Experiences. Ph.D.
   Dissertation, University of California, Berkeley, 1999.

Index

Printed in the United States
60517LVS00002B/445-468